Powering
THE

In fond memory of
my parents,
Peggy and Ed Koppel

Powering
THE
Future

The Ballard Fuel Cell and
the Race to Change the World

TOM KOPPEL

WILEY

John Wiley & Sons Canada, Ltd
Toronto • New York • Chichester • Weinheim • Brisbane • Singapore

John Wiley & Sons Canada Ltd
22 Worcester Road
Etobicoke, Ontario
M9W 1L1

Canadian Cataloguing in Publication Data

Koppel, Tom
   Powering the future : the Ballard fuel cell and the race to change the world

Includes index.
ISBN 0-471-64421-8

1. Fuel cell industry – British Columbia – North Vancouver. 2. Ballard Power Systems Inc. I. Title.

HD9697.B324B34 1999   338.7'621312429'0971133   C99-931896-9

Production Credits
Cover & text design: Interrobang Graphic Design Inc.
Printer: Tri-Graphic Printing
Author Photo: David Borrowman

Ballard® is a registered trademark of Ballard Power Systems Inc.
Nafion® is a registered trademark of Dupont.

Printed in Canada
10 9 8 7 6 5 4 3 2 1

CONTENTS

ACKNOWLEDGEMENTS

I would like to thank Mary S. Aikins, Western Canada editor of *Reader's Digest*, for working with me on the magazine assignment that led to this book, and to the BC Arts Council for the grant that helped support me while writing it. I am also in debt to my agent, Jennifer Barclay of Westwood Creative Artists, to editors Karen Milner and Ron Edwards for their guidance and suggestions, and to my wife Annie for bearing with my late night "Ballard attacks."

I want to express my gratitude to Geoffrey Ballard and his partners, Keith Prater and Paul Howard, who gave me very extensive interview time for this book and for the article that preceded it. I am also grateful for personal communications and interviews (some in person, some over the phone, in 1989 and 1997/98) with: Shelagh Ballard, Mike Brown, Ken Dircks, Danny Epp, Chris Gardner, Martin Hammerli, John Horton, James Huff, Bill Kelly, David McLeod, Firoz Rasul, David Scott, Daniel Sperling, Fred Steck, and Mossadiq Umedaly.

For help in obtaining published materials, I would like to thank John Perry, Jr. of Energy Partners, George Wise of General Electric, Lynn Delgaty at the National Research Council library, and the Daimler-Benz public information office.

I enjoyed the cooperation of Ballard Power Systems while writing the *Reader's Digest* article, but regrettably that changed after the company became aware that I was working on a book. As CEO Firoz Rasul wrote to me in 1998, "you will not receive support or cooperation from Ballard." And indeed, once my plans were known, no one working for Ballard or its allied companies replied favourably to my requests for further information. This book is, therefore, entirely unauthorized by Ballard Power Systems.

Preface

I t is a grey and wet November morning as I pay my fare and board the Number 158 BC Transit bus that runs from New Westminster to Port Coquitlam on the outskirts of Vancouver, British Columbia. We pull out of the holding area near the elevated Skytrain station and speed off into steady rush-hour traffic. Other than the slapping of the windshield wipers and occasional hiss of the air brakes, it is extremely quiet inside, especially at the front, where I first take a seat near the driver. Then I move briefly to the rear seats and notice a high-pitched whine coming from the engine area. Unlike ordinary engine noises, though, the sound hardly changes in tone or intensity as we accelerate. This bus is different.

This bus is powered not by a noisy and dirty diesel engine but by Ballard fuel cells. These electrochemical devices take hydrogen and air and convert them directly to electricity, which in turn runs an electric motor. As with a battery, the core of the fuel cell has no moving parts, and thus nothing to wear out. And like batteries, there is no combustion or nasty by-products of high-temperature chemical reactions. Unlike batteries, though, there is no need for slow recharging. The bus is quickly refuelled with compressed hydrogen back at the garage. And the only emission is water so pure you can drink it. When I get off the fuel cell bus, it pulls away almost silently, leaving a plume of water vapour in the air.

The Ballard fuel cell promises nothing less than to solve some of the world's worst air pollution problems. Yet, it all began with a handful of people working on shoestring budgets for a tiny Canadian company, Ballard Power Systems, in the little-known city of North Vancouver.

A quiet, pollution-free bus plying the streets of the Pacific Northwest may seem like a modest beginning, and in some ways it is. This is one of only three fuel cell buses in a test fleet based in Greater Vancouver. In Chicago another three Ballard buses are also carrying paying passengers. But these buses are just the tip of the fuel cell iceberg, the first rays of dawn in the coming age of clean, renewable hydrogen power.

Two of the world's largest automobile companies, Daimler-Benz (now DaimlerChrysler) and Ford, have bought large stakes in Ballard Power and thrown their financial, technological and marketing muscle behind its fuel cell. Daimler-Benz already has a spiffy little compact prototype car, powered by Ballard fuel cells, on the road in Germany, and has announced its intention to put fuel cell cars on the market by 2004. Toyota and General Motors are also committed to putting fuel cell cars on the road around 2004 or very shortly thereafter. Nearly every other auto manufacturer in the world expects to do so by 2010. And Shell, Texaco and ARCO, three giant oil companies, are tackling the problems of the necessary fuel infrastructure. The race is on.

I first visited the Ballard company in 1989 to see the fuel cell for an article for *Financial Post Moneywise* magazine.[1] In the lab, which was very modest at the time, technician Ken Dircks flipped a switch and dazzled me with the full power of six aircraft landing lights. As I began to sweat, I walked over to the lab bench and put my hand on the fuel cell, which was the size of a large car battery. It was only slightly warm. There was no noise, vibrations or fumes, and the only emission was a trickle of distilled water into a beaker. Yet it was kicking out 4000 watts of power, as much as a sizeable gasoline generator. Who could doubt that this thing had the potential to sweep the world?

Impressed, I followed the development of the Ballard cell as it was drastically improved and commercialized. In 1996, Daimler-Benz put a Ballard-powered prototype mini-van on the road and the world at large really began to take notice. In 1997, *Reader's Digest* gave me an assignment to write about Geoffrey Ballard and how his small company had brought the world a technology that the major corporations had known about but neglected for decades.[2] Because Ballard was a neighbour on Salt Spring Island in British Columbia and was retired from the company that bears his name, it was easy for me to drop in on him. In leisurely fashion, I could talk with him in the living room of his lovely seaside home, or in the kitchen, sharing coffee with him and his wife Shelagh. At first he concentrated on explaining the technology itself and the impressive rise of the company he had founded. Soon, though, he loosened up and regaled me with candid stories about himself, his dreams and his intriguing career.

Listening to Ballard's tale, I began to realize that this was much more than just the story of an environmentally friendly technology that promises to improve our world quite dramatically within the next few decades. In many ways, it was the classic story of David and Goliath. Against stiff odds, the feisty little company from the back streets of BC, led by an unabashed zealot, had prevailed against the doubts and barely concealed obstructionism of the giants of modern industry. Then, as icing on the cake, Ballard Power had become a runaway stock market success, its share price surging more than tenfold in only three years.

It was also a scientific, engineering and business achievement with many lessons to teach us: about the value of personal fortitude and the pay-off for hard work and trusting one's vision and intuition; about how ethically based choices in business, made by people with true commitment, are often more likely to succeed than those that focus narrowly on the bottom line; about how a small, agile company working on a shoestring budget can sometimes achieve what a large, bureaucratic one cannot, no matter how much money it throws at a problem. It was even the exemplary case of how a very small amount of government seed money was leveraged to create an entirely new industry.

Sometimes a gritty tone of determination crept into Ballard's voice as he talked about the battles he had fought. Some of the struggles were against the government, especially the US government, for whom he had worked for years. Some pitted him against the big oil and automobile companies. Others brought him into conflict with sceptics and more cautious types even within his own company. It had been a long road, a journey that had led him to financial reward and widespread recognition only in the last few years.

As he opened up, Ballard became remarkably candid about the deep frustrations he had experienced. He loathed smugness and excessive prudence. He was willing to take risks and anxious to get on with the task at hand. He was convinced that he and his company had the solution to one of the world's most urgent problems, yet for years hardly anyone seemed willing to listen. Even at Ballard Power there were recriminations over his style and personal rivalries that quietly festered.

I realized that Ballard was a driven man who was still trying to prove things to himself, even still acting out and replaying battles from his childhood. It may take such a person to push the world forward against the inevitable inertia and resistance. But this made him anything but an easy person to work with. He knew exactly what he wanted, and it was not, first and foremost, money. He operated, though, in a government, science and business milieu that was peopled largely by more conservative and bottom-line-oriented minds. Utterly certain that he was right, he was ready to make enemies and offend people to prove it.

Then I got to meet Ballard's key partners, Keith Prater and Paul Howard, and saw how well the three of them complemented each other. Prater was the knowledgeable chemist, Howard the practical engineer. Together with Ballard they formed a remarkably effective team. They also shared a common moral bent and fundamental decency. This instilled within their company a culture of loyalty, teamwork and dedication that could not have been bought at any price.

I met Mike Brown, the Vancouver venture capitalist who was the first outsider to recognize the business potential of the Ballard fuel cell. Brown became the financial brains behind the company's expansion and its daring decision to leapfrog beyond the small, safe and tempting niche markets for fuel cells. Instead, Ballard Power went for broke and tackled the much larger markets of stationary power generation and transportation. I met and interviewed technical and science people, like Danny Epp and Fred Steck, who had done much of the hands-on work that put the Ballard fuel cell into a class of its own.

And I met the next generation of executives, Firoz Rasul and Mossadiq Umedaly. I had briefly interviewed Rasul during my 1989 visit. Eight years later, he and Umedaly outlined to me the carefully thought out and well-balanced program of corporate expansion and financing that they were pursuing. They had taken the fuel cell to ever higher levels of technical capability and marketed it successfully to such key partners as Daimler-Benz and Ford.

What Ballard Power has achieved was by no means inevitable. There was a neglected technology waiting for someone to embrace and perfect it. There were wise government funding decisions. There were the founding partners, who inspired and attracted a core of dedicated and talented people to their company. There were the business brains who took the startling technological advances and marketed them. And there was the urgent and increasingly obvious need for cleaner power. Without all these factors, the current state of fuel cell development and commercialization might not have been reached for decades.

Ballard Power is still a relatively small company, but it will not be for much longer. Already, it is thirty-five per cent owned by DaimlerChrysler and Ford, and their representatives sit on its board of directors. Already, manufacturing and production specialists are assuming more important roles within the company, while the professional scientists, design engineers and marketing types see their roles reduced. Already, Ballard is expanding beyond its base in British Columbia with facilities in California and Germany. Increasingly, crucial decisions about the Ballard fuel cell will be taken elsewhere, notably in the boardrooms at DaimlerChrysler, Ford and other allied corporations. And many of the key players at Ballard have recently left the company. So this is an ideal time to look back and see how it all came about. How a tiny company, for the first few years little more than "three guys and a prayer," brought such a revolutionary and beneficial technology to the world.

Miracle
VALLEY

The long road to a new and better energy technology began in southern Arizona cactus country, a half kilometre from the Mexican border. In 1975 Geoffrey Ballard, trim and athletically built, with jet-black hair, poked his way through a small cement block motel and held his nose. The dozen or so ground floor units were strewn with broken glass, piles of garbage and soiled mattresses. The stench of urine and excrement made him gag. For years illegal immigrants had hidden there briefly after crossing the border into the US.

Ballard, a forty-three year old Canadian scientist and engineer, was looking for an affordable building to turn into a laboratory, and the motel was just about perfect. It was a twenty-minute drive from his home. There was plenty of room for storage upstairs. The internal walls could be knocked out to create large open areas. Best of all, the price was right: only $2000. It was owned by a religious cult that had used it to house temporary visitors to its commune. In recent years, though, the cult had become embroiled in scandal and had fallen on hard times. The motel had long stood empty. Now the group's leader, who still lived across the road, needed cash. He called the place "Miracle Valley."

Geoffrey Ballard wasn't expecting miracles, though, just many years, decades even, of hard work. He bought the motel and got his kids to help him haul out the junk and burn it in big piles. But the building still stank. So he phoned up the local fire department and persuaded them to bring in a pumper truck and use the place for a training exercise. Their high-pressure hoses blasted the paint right off the walls, cleaning out every last cobweb and mouse turd. As he stood back, watching them work, Ballard planned out the work tables, the ventilation systems, the machine shop, and the rest area. And he thought about his goal: to develop a viable technology that could power an electric car and reduce the world's dependence on fossil fuels.

He realized that it was bound to be a long haul. In the early stages, in fact, the entire focus was to be on developing an improved battery. It would be eight years before this work led to the fuel cell itself, but Ballard had never been one to quit when faced with set-backs. He had a deeply ingrained stubborn streak that gave him the personal fortitude needed to meet difficulties in life with a sense of stoicism. Nor did he readily accept it when told that something could not be done. This just spurred him on to prove himself by overcoming the obstacles. This resolute drive and need to do things his own way appeared quite early in life, largely as a reaction to an unhappy childhood that left him with a bruised ego and a need to compensate for it.

Ballard was born in 1932 in Niagara Falls, Ontario. His mother, Jessie Marguerite Mildred, traced her origins to a wealthy and socially prominent British Quaker family, the Rowntrees, who ran Rowntree chocolates in York, in northern England. Like the Wedgwoods and the Cadburys, the Rowntrees were Victorian-era Liberals, a paternalistic dynasty that believed in instilling strong company loyalty by providing model factories and housing for their employees. Jessie Mildred was largely raised by her uncle, Seebohm Rowntree, who was dedicated to political and social reform and had written books with such titles as "Poverty, a Study of Town Life," and "Betting and Gambling, a National Evil." Ballard's mother passed on to him a sense of moral and social rectitude that would show itself in his commitment to alternative energy and in the corporate culture of the company he founded.

His father, Archibald Hall Ballard, was born in Staten Island, New York, when the ship his parents were taking from Britain to Canada was diverted to New York harbour because of winter weather and ice on the St. Lawrence River. This unplanned circumstance was to give Geoffrey a claim to dual US-Canadian citizenship, which simplified his status when he went to work for the US Army. Archibald Ballard studied electrochemical engineering at the University of Toronto and then specialized in the area of radiation.

Soon after the Second World War broke out, the laboratory director at the company where Archibald Ballard worked in Ontario fell overboard from a boat during a cocktail party and was swept over Niagara Falls to his death. Through this quirk, Ballard was promoted to the post of lab director at an unusually early age. When the German Blitz hit Britain, the Ballards took in a dozen British schoolchildren, who were evacuated to safety in Canada for the duration of the war. Because of his engineering specialty, Archibald Ballard was away most of the time in Oak Ridge, Tennessee, working on the atomic bomb. With his father away, and the house full of other kids, young Geoffrey never had the love and attention that he craved during these formative years.

For grade eight, he was sent off to a private school. Feeling himself "shunted aside" by his family, the young boy was lonely, miserable and hurt. This initiated a lifelong tug-of-war with his father—"a real personal competition" he calls it—in a desperate attempt to win the elder Ballard's approval. "The only way I would ever get my father's attention," he thought as he got older, "was to be successful in the field of science and science management. I wanted to do *better* than he had." When Geoffrey's own science career began to take shape, he resolved to reach the position of laboratory director at an even earlier age than his father. And in the end he did, at thirty-six. (His father was in his late forties before he reached a comparable position.)

At thirteen, Geoffrey wanted to set up an ice cream stand, but he needed a licence. The aldermen in Niagara Falls were absolutely amazed when, at their meeting, the young Ballard stood up and introduced himself as the person who had submitted the application. They mumbled that he had to be at least eighteen and turned him down. It galled him to be rejected for failing to meet such an arbitrary standard.

In high school Ballard showed more aptitude for sports than he did for math or science, getting no better than Cs in most subjects. Yet, in conflicts with some of his teachers, he admits, he displayed more than a touch of arrogance. Through his mother, he had acquired a strong grounding in the literary classics, "and I didn't think my teachers had even a smattering of understanding of the great poets or writers."

This personal hubris and impatience with the shortcomings of others carried through to later life. "My wife has known him for over twenty years," says one long-time colleague, "but she still finds him intimidating. Just because of his approach to people. He does not suffer fools at all. I think this may come from his own version of self-doubt." Another colleague thinks that Ballard's problem has always been that "he's just too damned bright to deal with normal people."

When Ballard went out for football in high school, the coach treated him initially as something of a mama's boy and left him mainly on the bench. Then, one game, with injuries mounting, the coach put him into the line at centre. The opposing team immediately mowed him down, breaking his nose. Blood poured down his jersey, but he ignored it and insisted on playing out the game. Afterwards, the coach said, "I had no idea that you were so single-minded. You've earned yourself a spot on this team." Throughout my life, Ballard says, "I've always viewed the setbacks as just something that had to be endured" on the road to achievement.

From high school, Ballard went off to Queen's University in Kingston, Ontario, where he met his wife, Shelagh. He married her and graduated in the same year, 1956, with a degree in geological engineering. This equipped him for a career in oil exploration, working first in Alberta for Shell. It was the tail-end of the era in which horses were still used. Ballard enjoyed riding and camping out in the Rocky Mountains with a crew and string of twenty horses. The year he left Shell, they switched to helicopters. Next he was off to the Mediterranean and Turkey as a drill-site geologist for Mobil.

At one location in Turkish Kurdestan, he studied the stratigraphy—the layers of geological deposits. Mobil wanted to drill into a sand shale sequence, which was typical of the Persian Gulf. But Ballard thought this was wrong. "We're on the edge of a basin," he told them, "We should be looking at a reef." Because he was young and without a Ph.D., they brushed him aside, drilled, found nothing, and soon allowed their lease there to lapse. A few years later, Shell acquired a lease in the same area, drilled into an ancient reef and struck oil on the first try. The find eventually became a producing oil field. The experience reinforced Ballard's growing scepticism about conventional wisdom and the validity of expert credentials.

This was typical, he says, still capable of fuming over it decades later, of the way he was treated in the Oil Patch. "When I had an idea, I was always told that I wasn't hired to do those sorts of things, that Doctor so-and-so," invariably a geologist with full academic credentials, "would decide what the exploration program would be. That's one reason why I went back and got a Ph.D.," earning a doctorate in geophysics at Washington University in St. Louis, Missouri.

His father (who did not have a Ph.D. himself) was extremely critical of this move, telling his son in no uncertain terms that it was irresponsible for a man with a wife and family and secure job to go back to graduate school. "To walk away from that, just to satisfy my ego was, in his eyes, the height of stupidity."

With the doctorate to give him standing, Ballard signed on as a civilian scientist with the US Army and spent ten years involved in an extremely broad range of scientific research. Not all of it was geophysics. In fact, he was also given advanced training in management methods and became a generalist overseeing research specialists in a diversity of scientific disciplines. The Pentagon selected him as one of a small group of young "comers" to participate in a series of defence-related science seminars. He was flown all over the country, visiting military installations and high-level research centres, and got to know people of influence throughout America's military-industrial establishment.

Most of the research in the labs where he was posted, in New Hampshire, New Jersey, and Arizona, had little or no immediate connection to weapons development. But it did make him privy to sensitive information. His security clearance was so high that by the early 1970s, when terrorism became a major concern, he was forbidden to fly on civilian airliners lest he be hijacked.

By 1973 Ballard was working at Fort Huachuca, Arizona, at the army's laboratory for advanced telecommunications. He and Shelagh had bought a house in nearby Sierra Vista. They had three school-age sons and an active social life that centred on the local tennis club. Then the first OPEC oil crisis struck. In the winter of 1973-74, Americans were forced to line up at gas stations, many for the first time in their lives. The US government responded by establishing a new office of energy conservation and went looking for a scientist to head its research department. Because of Ballard's track record in science management and experience in the energy sector, the Army seconded him to Washington as director of research. The initial appointment was for six months. Shelagh and the boys remained in Arizona.

Ballard rented a small furnished apartment and threw himself into the new assignment, working long hours and drinking a bit too much in his free time. His task was to create a research plan with the long-term goal of achieving energy self-sufficiency for the United States. Under his supervision, teams of scientists studied such alternative energy sources and technologies as oil shales, solar energy, tidal, geothermal and wind power, and battery-powered vehicles. Based on their recommendations, he formulated plans suggesting how and where further research and development should be conducted and funded.

He plunged into the new job assuming that he would be doing something truly worthwhile. Before long, though, disillusionment set in. He gave briefings to politicians, and the plans were submitted to the congressional bureaucracy, but Ballard quickly saw that very little was going to be implemented. "Energy systems are notorious for their long gestation periods, often twenty years or longer," he says. But in the US research and development funding system, he learned to his chagrin, "there had to be a pay-off in a product within five to seven years in order to justify the public money being put in." Mainly this reflected the short-term vision of US electoral politics. "There are political cycles involving re-election, so the politicians didn't want to put money into systems that were going to come to fruition in some other generation. You sent out the plans, and they hacked and cut at them."

Another problem was Washington's traditional pork barrel system of divvying up funding money by state or congressional district. "Pieces of the plan were farmed out to research centres or laboratories or universities in states where political favours were due. Some state, say Tennessee, might have priority for the next dose of research money," whether this made scientific sense or not. "In the US, this gets overridden in times of war, but this was a time of peace."

A final irritant was that many mornings, when Ballard arrived at his office, he found a thick stack of mail on his desk. These were letters written by citizens to the federal government or to members of Congress making suggestions on energy issues. Most of the ideas were ill-informed, unoriginal or worse, says Ballard, but they had to be answered. "So the first half of my day was totally wasted responding to inane questions from congressional constituents." It drove him up the wall.

Ballard began to ponder his future. He soon decided that the US was just not going to tackle the energy conservation problem seriously, and he had no intention of sticking around and going through the motions. He was earning a very handsome salary, just one notch below that of a member of Congress. Already in his forties, though, Ballard wasn't interested in wasting his life. "If you studied a problem and were blocked by politics, you found another way. I wasn't willing to be bought off—in a sense—to receive a good salary and hold a prestigious job, but not do what I thought needed to be done." Nor did he want to spend his life fighting city hall. If you try to do that, he says, "you become an angry sort of person."

Beyond his on-the-job frustration, Ballard gradually came to the conclusion that the entire focus on conservation as such was ill-conceived and bound to fail. Coming from the oil industry and the military, he had entered the job without particularly strong views on either conservation or alternative energy. But when he saw that the US was not going to pursue the solutions he had suggested, he began to look at the nature of the problem more deeply.

On the one hand, it was true that the world's industrialized countries could not continue to consume the lion's share of the world's energy resources, much of it in inefficient vehicles burning non-renewable fuels. In 1974, the transportation sector, which was almost entirely dependent on petroleum, used fifty-three per cent of all the crude oil consumed in the US. This increased by 1987 to sixty-four per cent, which was eight per cent *more* than the entire US production of petroleum. By the 1980s, transportation was responsible for about half of all pollutants that form smog in American cities, more than half of the toxic air pollutants and up to ninety per cent of the carbon monoxide. So, cutting down on fossil fuel consumption was clearly a worthwhile goal.

But when he looked beyond the developed world, the long-term picture came into clearer focus. "The real disaster that's coming at us," he realized, is that countries like China and India are inevitably going to attempt to reach Western standards of living. But because of this drive towards higher living standards, the solution had to go far beyond simple conservation.

In fact, he became convinced that energy conservation, per se, was neither the real issue nor the main solution to the world's energy problems. Looking at US energy sources in the light of his Washington research, he saw that there was no imminent shortage of energy itself; it just needed to be harnessed by technology in new and better ways. Plenty of energy was available from the sun, wind, tides, and hydroelectric power. "We have huge tides in some of the bays in the United States, for example." Moreover, at that time, before the Three-Mile Island reactor scare and the Chernobyl disaster, nuclear energy from uranium still seemed like a viable source of future energy for the United States. (It has remained a leading source in some countries, notably France.) And there was the long-term promise of clean energy from nuclear fusion.

While still in Washington, Ballard began to see the increasing emphasis on energy conservation, "training people to use less," as just another example of erroneous conventional wisdom, and he still thinks he was right. "It won't work," he insists. "You just cannot train China and India to conserve energy, because they want the same standard of living that we enjoy. And that is based largely on energy consumption per capita. Yes, energy conservation can play a minor role in the transition stages" to a new energy economy, one based largely on hydrogen. But to see energy conservation as a means or mechanism by which we solve the world's problems, he argues, is "just putting your head in the sand."

The real challenge, Ballard thought, was to find a better energy conversion system or device, a convenient and economical way of taking energy from an abundant source and converting it to a usable, and preferably portable, form, especially for transportation and communications. This would not require the Third World to forego rising per capita energy use. And only such a technological magic bullet held out the promise of drastically reducing the world's dependence on fossil fuels.

"I was able to see this very clearly," he says, "because I was hired into that slot, which had its focus on conservation. So it was easy for me to see the fallacy of that approach. What I was concerned with was the conversion device and the techniques of conversion. And it was the fact that America was not going to reach for a technical solution," but instead was taking the conservationist approach, and not even pursuing it effectively, "that led me to believe there was no future for me in that place."

If the government is not going to search for a better energy technology, he resolved, *then I will*. On a visit home in spring 1974, he told Shelagh that he wanted to walk away from the Washington job and his army career to pursue energy alternatives as a private consultant and entrepreneur. It was not an easy personal decision. Once again, his father severely criticized him for turning his back on a secure job and striking out on his own. "Why am I always the one out in left field?" he agonized to Shelagh, knowing that their financial future would be uncertain. "You just see things differently," she reassured him. "You've been right before, so why doubt yourself. Go for it. We'll always put food on the table. I'll help."

By then, Ballard already had a concrete vision. From his work at the army communications command in Arizona, he had seen that the miniaturization of communications technology, from radios to computers to video cameras, was fast outpacing the development of the portable power sources that make them useful. "Solid state electronics were being revolutionized, but the energy sources were not changing" to keep pace. People were carrying around lightweight, hand-held video cameras, but being dragged down by heavy battery packs that required long recharging times. "To improve portable power sources and reduce them in weight—that was the challenge." The market for a more compact, high-powered energy source, he thought, was guaranteed.

And beyond communications there loomed the much larger energy needs of transportation. One of the studies his teams had done in Washington was on electric vehicles powered by storage batteries. "Electric cars were quite common at the turn of the century," he says. In fact, in 1900 in the US there were an equal number of battery-powered cars, gasoline buggies, and steam cars—about 2,000 each. By 1915, the number of battery-powered vehicles in the US had grown to almost 40,000, but by then with the arrival of the Model-T Ford (1908) a much larger number were gasoline powered. Of the battery vehicles, most were light trucks and delivery vans. Among the vans, in fact, where the limited range and need to recharge were not such a handicap, battery-powered vehicles outnumbered gasoline types by four to one. Nearly all had lead-acid batteries, which were relatively inexpensive.

With cheap oil and mass-produced internal combustion engines, though, both steam and electric cars soon disappeared from the roads. There was nothing inherently wrong with electricity to power cars. In principle, it is a far more efficient use of energy than the internal combustion engine.* The only problem was with the batteries—they didn't go very far and took many hours to recharge.

Ballard looked at electric cars and saw that there hadn't been enough work done on batteries to eliminate them as an alternative. A few companies and universities had financed small pilot projects, but most of these used conventional lead-acid storage batteries (the kind used to start our cars and trucks) where no real technological breakthroughs had been made.+ Little more than sleek-looking golf

---

* All heat engines, including internal combustion ones, are limited by the laws of thermodynamics, as shown by French physicist Nicolas Carnot in 1824.
+ Even in 1996 and 1997, General Motors's highly touted EV-1, which was leased to a few hundred customers in the American Southwest, used lead-acid batteries that had hardly changed in decades. Its range was only around 130 km (eighty miles) before recharging. A more recent EV-1 has improved batteries with about twice the range, but still much less than an average car goes on a tank of gasoline, and recharging is still slow.

carts, these experimental vehicles were based on the strategy of cutting the weight of the rest of the vehicle and improving the aerodynamics. All suffered from the handicaps of short operating range and long battery recharging times. None of the projects had been well financed. In Ballard's view, they represented little more than just "puttering around."

Ballard wanted to look at battery chemistries with much higher energy densities, or, in other words, much lighter weight for a given power output. One of the main problems with conventional batteries for transportation is the weight of the lead. (Another is the long—usually overnight—recharging time.) Even twenty-five years after Ballard's first efforts, when auto manufacturers have finally put battery-powered cars into production, road tests show that the weight of the batteries drastically reduces performance on uphill climbs. (In fact, many of today's battery-powered vehicles are so-called hybrids, with a modest gasoline engine to keep the battery charged and help with hill climbing and acceleration.) Battery weight also causes poor road handling, especially on turns, where the heavy load can cause the vehicle to lean excessively or fishtail.

But what if a much lighter metal than lead could be used and higher power density achieved?

Back in Arizona, Ballard had a tennis pal, Ralph Schwartz. They trusted each other and had already toyed with going in on at least one financial venture together, a private tennis club in Sierra Vista. Schwartz, a burly, grey-haired man, about fifteen years older than Ballard, was an engineer and quirky self-employed inventor. He owned a small ranch and had made and lost several fortunes on his inventions. Probably the biggest winner was the disposable plastic syringe. But he was always willing to risk what he had on the next big opportunity and was forever scouting around for a new and interesting challenge.

Ballard mentioned that he was planning to leave the army and wanted to work on alternative power and propulsion systems. Schwartz told him about a battery chemistry he knew of based on lithium, the lightest of all metals, and sulfur dioxide. "Primary," or single-use, non-rechargeable batteries using this combination were just being developed on the East Coast, Schwartz said. Could the chemical process be reversed to make the batteries rechargeable? Schwartz wondered. He had even tinkered a bit with the chemistry himself and with promising results. "Can you put together a team of scientists and engineers?" Schwartz asked Ballard, who had excellent contacts throughout the US energy and high-tech research community. "Let's see if lithium batteries can be made rechargeable." Ballard agreed and took a minor financial stake in the company Schwartz set up for this venture, American Energizer.

For starters, they needed a good electrochemist. Ballard had a friend in the chemistry department at the University of Texas at El Paso, who recommended that they speak to a thirty-one year old colleague, Keith Prater. Even as a child, Prater had always loved science. In high school he had gone one summer to a "science camp" at the University of Kansas, where he did so well he was selected to return and spend a second summer doing serious research in geology.

Schwartz and Ballard hopped into Schwartz's Cadillac, drove through the mountains and marched in on the skinny young professor to make their pitch. Prater chuckles when he recalls their first meeting. "They had a certain swagger to them. Ralph was wearing a silk neckerchief, fancy boots and a cowboy hat. He always dressed like a successful rancher. And here I was, a young university professor in my sneakers and jeans. For his part, Geoff is extremely intelligent. He exudes confidence when it's necessary. By then, he had quite a track record with the army and working with the Secretary of Energy." Prater was a bit overawed.

The professor was frank, admitting that he had no significant experience with batteries. "That's fine," said Ballard, "I don't want someone who knows about batteries. They know what won't work. I want someone who is bright and creative and willing to try things that others might not try. That's where breakthroughs come from." Intrigued by the challenge and somewhat flattered by their trust in him, Prater signed on to help part-time as a consultant, while continuing with his academic research and teaching.

Until then, Schwartz and Ballard had little more than a concept. "Ralph only knew enough chemistry to get into trouble," says Prater. "But in an Edisonian way, he had mixed some things together. He threw in an eye of newt and a bit of bat's wing and heated it up and stuffed it in, and it sort of worked." In the single-use battery, Prater knew, lithium from an electrode reacted chemically with sulfur dioxide to produce electricity and a lithium salt as a discharge product. To reverse the process, a current had to be put through the battery to break down the salt and deposit metallic lithium once again on the electrode. This allows the entire reaction to be repeated.

"What Keith Prater brought forth immediately," Ballard says, "was that we didn't know what was produced when lithium and sulfur dioxide react, and that nobody seemed to know. It wasn't in the literature, and until we knew it, we couldn't turn around and reverse the reaction. So that had to be the first question."

Prater's challenge was to identify the lithium/sulfur dioxide discharge product and isolate (or synthesize) a sample of it. Schwartz had had the contents of a discharged primary lithium battery analyzed, and the analysis had come out with something Prater knew could not be right. Prater made an educated guess that the discharge product should be lithium dithionite.

It was not a regularly available chemical. In fact, his search of the literature came up blank. Since he couldn't just phone up a chemical supply house and order some, he set out to make it in his university lab. First he bought a closely related sodium salt, and changed it to the desired lithium salt in a vertical glass tube, full of the salt and resin beads, called an ion exchange column. To do this, Prater explains, "You pour through lots and lots of a solution containing lithium ions, and what goes on the bead is the lithium. Then you pour through a solution of the sodium salt. The sodium goes on the resin and the lithium comes off, and what comes out at the bottom of the column is what you want, the magic ingredient."

"Geoff, I've got it," Prater announced proudly over the phone, when he had made his first sample of lithium dithionite. "It wasn't rocket science," he admits. "But the chemical was pretty reactive and had to be quickly dried in order to be stable. That's probably why the analysis Ralph Schwartz had commissioned had not found the chemical." To Prater's knowledge, nobody had ever isolated the stuff before.

Soon they were getting help from some colleagues of Prater's at the University of California at Berkeley, where they had access to expensive specialized equipment. Schwartz bought a construction-site trailer for $400 and gutted it to use as a laboratory. Ballard had begun doing geophysical consulting work for industrialist John Horton, who was refitting a submarine in North Vancouver, BC, for oil exploration. Horton also owned a freeze-dried food plant in San Leandro, California, and allowed them to park the trailer against a loading bay and tap in for power. In between other projects, Ballard and Schwartz spent week-long stints at their makeshift California lab, while Prater flew in for quick consultations.

The eureka experience came when Prater arrived with the first sample of lithium dithionite. They mixed it in a beaker with solvents, but it did not dissolve as expected. It just formed a sort of slurry. Nevertheless, they put in two electrodes, one a mesh of copper, the other a stainless steel mesh, and charged it up by running an electric current through it. If they could get electricity back out of it, they knew, they had a battery of sorts. Hovering anxiously, they hooked up a tiny flashlight bulb and—lo and behold—it glowed. "Son of a gun," said Prater. They repeated the process again and again, and the little desktop cell gave a stable output of about three volts. These were three dedicated, hard-nosed guys. Instead of breaking out the champagne, they just kept discharging and recharging their crude device. "That's the stage," says Ballard, "where you do an endurance check and watch it for days." The tiny single cell was a breakthrough, but a practical battery, they knew, would take real money to develop.

Enter John Horton, the industrialist with the submarine in British Columbia, who became their financial godfather. The Horton family's keystone firm was the huge Chicago Bridge and Iron Company. Ballard had met Horton in the mid-1960s at a management workshop in New York, when Ballard was with the Army. One exercise assigned at the workshop was to simulate decisions using computers, which were still a novelty to most business types. Horton was the only other engineer in sight, so he teamed up with Ballard. They figured out how the program worked, modified it to their advantage and swept away the competition. They also talked geophysics and hit it off personally.

By 1974, when Ballard and Schwartz began their battery project, Horton had bought the *Auguste Piccard*, a twenty-eight metre (ninety foot) long submarine. One of the world's largest non-military submersibles, it was originally built to carry tourists to the bottom of Lake Geneva during a world exposition, and was sold at auction a few years later. Horton needed a package of geophysical instruments designed to do detailed seismic survey work for oil exploration. He remembered Ballard, tracked him down and hired him as a part-time consultant.

When the lithium cell in San Leandro got to the point where it could be discharged and recharged twelve or fourteen times, it began to look like a potentially valuable technology. Ballard convinced Horton that a large lithium battery might be a viable power source for his submarine, and Horton agreed to finance the battery's development to the tune of several thousand dollars a month.

Meanwhile, in Arizona, with his only paid employment being part-time consulting work for Horton, Ballard and his wife were forced to find ways to make ends meet. They drew on some accessible Army pension money that Ballard had accumulated and made a down payment on a slightly funky old restaurant for Shelagh to run. Called the "Outback," it was an isolated place, located coincidentally at the foot of Ballard Mountain along the desert highway between Wyatt Earp's home town of Tombstone and the world's largest open-pit copper mine. There was a leaky roof, hippie waitresses, and rattlesnakes in the parking lot. The menu ran mainly to steaks and seafood. On weekends, a country and western band played. Working together, Geoffrey and Shelagh fixed the place up and added a deck with a spectacular view of the mountains.

When need be, the whole family pitched in. On busy days, the three boys would bus tables and Geoffrey Ballard mixed drinks behind the bar. One time, when he was away, Shelagh turned the tap in the kitchen and nothing happened. No water. The pump had burned out. But customers had to be served. Frantic, she phoned home. "Don't worry, Mom," said Curtis, the oldest son, who had just received his driver's licence. "We'll bring you water." The boys filled every jug, bottle, and plastic container in the house, raced twenty-five miles out to the restaurant and saved the day. The training evidently took. Today, alongside their other careers, the three Ballard sons run a popular bar and restaurant in Vancouver.

With the battery funding in place, Ballard and Schwartz bought the fleabag motel on the Mexican border. They knocked out many of the interior walls to create open working space, installed fume hoods to vent chemical vapours and built in shelves and workbenches. One area became a machine shop, with a drill press, lathe and a heat press for making battery electrodes. Another area had racks of chemical glassware and a small still for purifying and separating chemicals. They equipped an office with old desks and chairs, and a rest area with a coffee pot and patio furniture. They furnished one unit properly and hired a Vietnamese couple as caretakers. Recent immigrants to the United States, they were hard workers who also pitched in as lab assistants.

In addition to the battery work, Ralph Schwartz used the motel to develop a gizmo he called a brake equalizer. An early form of anti-lock braking system, it was a small device that fit into the hydraulic lines of an automobile and pulsed the brakes so they did not suddenly lock up. Schwartz and Ballard, with major help from Keith Prater, were also developing a novel system of storing whole human blood for transfusions, but most of that work was being done in California and Texas. Ballard had a minor financial stake in both of these technologies through Schwartz's Southern Arizona Manufacturing Company, or SAMCO, and through SBR Labs Inc., which stood for Schwartz-Ballard-Research.

To work on the battery, Ballard and Schwartz commuted to the motel from nearby Sierra Vista. Periodically, a handful of cronies would join them for intensive weekends running experiments. There was a retired chemist from California named Bramson, who was in his 80s but still quite perky. And there was Lynn Marcoux, an electro-chemist; he was a friend of Prater's from their undergraduate days together at the University of Kansas and then in Texas. Some years later, Marcoux would be chief scientist of the Ballard company's battery divisions in British Columbia. John Horton's cousin, Horace Koessler, had an interest in the technology; he sometimes pitched in at the motel and later invested in the battery.

Keith Prater was the other key member of the team. He had an old, two-seat Piper airplane, which allowed him to fly in regularly from El Paso, landing the plane in a field adjacent to the motel. It was full of cattle that kept getting in the way, forcing him to chase them off the runway prior to take-off. Because of the proximity to the Mexican border, Prater jokes, he was always nervous about carrying his little samples of white powder and kept expecting to be pounced on and questioned by federal agents.

The motel lab was an informal place, strictly jeans and sweat-shirts, rather than white coats. The marathon sessions, when a push was on, were stimulating and fun. When the men got hungry, they either went out for a bite or brought in pizza and beer. Working until exhausted, they would grab quick naps on chaise longues and get back to their chemistry or stints in the machine shop. But basically, they worked right through the weekend. If they began to fade, there was a coffee-maker to give them a lift. Ballard drove himself so hard the others called him "the bulldozer."

It was an exciting time. The entire team knew that their vision and goal were extremely ambitious. Success, in the form of a light-weight but powerful rechargeable battery, might lead to nothing less than a revolution in energy use. It would probably make them all rich as well.

Not that they had any illusions. When they talked about the potential of a battery-powered electric car, they were aware of its likely limitations. The problem, says Keith Prater, is that "one of the fundamentals of electrochemistry tells you that the faster you recharge a battery, the shorter the life of that battery is going to be." This makes it impossible "to cram into a battery the amount of energy you put into a gas tank in two or three minutes." Which is one reason why the fuel cell is a preferable technology. "But at that time, the fuel cell did not exist in anybody's mind as an option." It had performed well in space, but the types suitable for use on earth were plagued with problems and astronomically expensive. "So the best thing was a better battery. And if you extended the range of a battery-powered electric vehicle from thirty miles to 150 or 200 miles, then you can imagine that there would be a very substantial change in the market potential for electric vehicles."

The fact that the battery they were developing was intended for a submarine did not distract them from this larger vision. "We looked at the sub as a test bed," says Ballard. If you could perfect the rechargeable battery, "you could then apply it to a car." In fact, for test purposes the submarine had advantages. "Being able to experiment with these batteries and having a strong pressure hull between you and this thing was a nice idea. Having it under water also made it a lot safer. We expected failures." And failure could be dangerous.

They were careful, but mishaps occurred. Ballard unlocked the lab one morning to find solvents and chemical beads splattered all over, and shards of glass embedded in the ceiling. A large ion exchange column, the glass apparatus used to manufacture batches of lithium dithionite, had exploded during the night. Fortunately, nobody was around. A similar thing happened another time. The amounts of dithionite involved on these occasions were relatively small, so the damage was minor but unsettling none the less.

The actual battery for Horton's submarine, however, was a different story. Each unit was a spool-shaped device about the size of a large hatbox. Designed to be ganged together and fit into a cylindrical pod attached outside the pressure hull, it held two kilograms of lithium dithionite, which, as Prater had already found out, was an extremely unstable substance. And, in chemical jargon, "unstable" is often a euphemism for explosive. "We thought we'd got it pretty well under control," says Ballard. "We had it in acetyl nitryl. We didn't think it was dangerous. But it turns out, in hindsight, that we didn't know that much about it. In fact, we had created quite a dodgy situation. A high-powered battery is basically just a controlled bomb. Whenever you put chemical compounds together that create electricity, you've essentially got an explosive situation." He shakes his head and laughs. "If it had decided to detonate, there would have been another Crater Lake down there in Arizona. And no more motel, I'll tell you! We were very, very lucky."

Ballard, Schwartz, Prater and their colleagues beavered away for about two years in their motel lab and made steady progress. By 1977, though, Ballard was spending a lot of his time away from home, especially in North Vancouver, working on the instrument package for Horton's submarine. He missed his wife and family. And he found that being based in a "backwater town" in southern Arizona was not good for his career. "I wasn't publishing papers. I wasn't going to scientific meetings. I was in danger of being forgotten," says Ballard. He had begun with a dense network of useful contacts, but these might not last. "Pretty soon I'll be 'Geoff who?'" he worried to himself. A major urban centre would be a much better base of operations.

He and Shelagh also felt the pull of home. They'd had a long-term plan to return eventually to Canada, and wanted their children to have at least some experience of Canadian schools and life during their formative years.

Keith Prater, too, had been shuttling back and forth between El Paso and Vancouver. He had taken a leave of absence from his academic job to put in time on both the battery and the blood storage work. As he took his seat on a flight to Vancouver in January 1978, he saw an attractive woman coming up the aisle. He hoped she would choose the empty seat next to him, and she did. Her name was Mei Lin Yeoell. She was English, but had been raised in Malaya, hence the Oriental name. She lived in Vancouver and was returning from a business trip to Rio de Janeiro. They were both involved with other people at the time, but they exchanged addresses and found a pretext to meet again. After two years of commuting, Prater resigned his tenured university position and relocated to British Columbia. Mei Lin and Keith were married.

Although the rechargeable lithium battery showed promise, Ralph Schwartz decided to focus on his other projects. Geoffrey Ballard was committed to alternative energy. With their bank manager as witness, they shook hands and paid each other one dollar. Ballard transferred all his interest in the blood work and brake equalizer to Schwartz. Schwartz, in turn, handed over his interest in the battery technology to Ballard, who became president and CEO of the new Vancouver-based company, Ultra Energy.

Engine *of the* Future

When he relocated to North Vancouver, Geoffrey Ballard set up his Ultra Energy operation in a corner of the large shed-like building that was dominated by John Horton's submarine. North Van, as locals know it, was a bustling industrial and commercial city with a population of around 30,000 in 1977. Situated at the base of a steep mountain, and so close to the bush that bears and cougars sometimes wander into town, it lies just across Burrard Inlet from downtown Vancouver. Horton's building, and the later headquarters of the Ballard company, were down near the waterfront a few blocks from the railway tracks that carry open cars of sulphur, wood pulp and other raw materials to the piers for export, mainly to Asia. The Ballards bought themselves a house a short drive away in affluent West Vancouver, a seaside bedroom community well removed from industry.

At its peak, work on the submarine involved a staff of twenty to twenty-five people. The chief engineer and operations manager was a big, good-natured mechanical engineer named Paul Howard who was to play a leading, day-to-day role directing the fuel cell work as well. Born in 1943, making him the same age as Keith Prater, Howard had earned his degree from the University of Toronto, worked for six years in Ottawa and then come out to BC in 1971 to "look around."

By the mid-1970s, work on the sub was essentially complete, says Howard, so he switched to working with Ballard and Prater on the rechargeable battery. One of the reasons Horton was refitting the submarine in BC was the possible availability of Canadian government money to subsidize its research and development. Much of Howard's effort was also focused on trying to hustle up government money for the battery.

The large, spool-shaped battery being developed for the submarine worked, but not well enough. Each time it was recharged, the power output was a bit lower, like the spring of a watch running down. Ballard and Prater still thought it had great potential, but Horton eventually ran into money problems with the entire submarine project. Meanwhile, the sub's refit (minus the lithium battery) was complete, so Horton pulled the financial plug on the battery and leased out the vessel, which was shipped to Colombia to explore for sunken Spanish treasure galleons.

Fortunately for Ballard, there was an alternative funding source. Horton's cousin, Horace Koessler, was a non-practicing physician who had inherited money and owned a large lumber company in Montana. He had long taken an interest in the battery and had pitched in on some of the marathon weekends at the Arizona motel. Nicknamed "Shorty" because he was about six-foot five, Koessler owned a small floatplane and was looking for someone to join him on a month-long flying jaunt around the Arctic.

There was just one hitch. Koessler had such poor eyesight that he wore glasses as thick as pop bottles and still could barely see. The only reason he had been able to get a pilot's licence was that, as a physician, he could sign his own medical release. He also had gimpy legs and was generally a physical wreck. "Not at all a person you would want to trust your life to," says Ballard.

Koessler made Ballard an offer he couldn't refuse. Come with me on the Arctic trip, he said. "You'll have a whole month to persuade me to invest in the battery." Desperate for financing, Ballard swallowed his qualms and agreed. But in preparation, he enrolled in a quickie emergency flying survival course. It was designed for people who fly a lot together, such as husbands and wives, so that if the husband, for example, has a heart attack the wife can land the plane. Ballard was shown how to use a plane's radio to communicate with the tower, but the key skill was learning how to bring the plane to within about a metre of the runway and "come down with a thump."

The trip was a near disaster. When they stopped at Inuvik, near the mouth of the Mackenzie River, they had to go into the office to file a flight plan. Ballard, with his better eyesight, filled out the form, while Koessler hobbled around the room, squinting at things. When Ballard handed the paper to Koessler and said "sign there," the tower manager, who happened to be there, exploded. "Good God," he said to Ballard, "you're not going to let him fly the plane, are you?" Ballard replied, "Sure, he's the pilot." The official was horrified and stared at them in disbelief.

Later, they were flying over mountainous terrain heading for Yellowknife more than 600 kilometres (400 miles) away. The ground was rising, while the cloud cover got ever lower, a tricky situation. Suddenly Koessler turned to Ballard and said, "This damned carburetor is stuck. The throttle's stuck. I can't change the engine speed." The only choice was between leaving the engine on or switching it off.

They were over an area full of little muskeg ponds. Being forced lower by the cloud ceiling, Koessler chose to put the plane down on one of the ponds while there was still enough visibility. Swooping in fast, he killed the engine and let the plane drift to a stop. They found themselves floating in about half a metre of water on top of almost bottomless muck. Trying to paddle, they couldn't get the plane anywhere near the shore. The muck was so viscous they weren't able to force the pontoons through it. So they tied up to a small floating muskeg island in the middle of the pond.

Then it started to rain—hard. Soon it was coming down in solid sheets; there was little choice but to sit it out. For three days they watched it pour. They made mayday calls on their radio, but nothing happened. They were equipped with survival gear, including a tent and Primus stove, so there was little immediate danger. "But winter was approaching," says Ballard, and they were hundreds of miles from nowhere. Finally, they rigged a tarp over the engine and got the cowling off. Ballard studied the engine, located the problem and straightened out a carburetor linkage. This allowed them to take off from the pond and make it home safely. Koessler put $300,000 into the battery, which kept work going for about five months.

This reprieve gave Ballard time to find a new source of money, a Chicago company called Firenetics that manufactured smoke detectors. Many run on batteries that are good for only a year or two. Firenetics wanted Ultra Energy to develop a single use lithium smoke detector battery with extremely long life, up to ten years. As an incentive Firenetics was also willing to fund work on the rechargeable battery. This looked like solid, long-term financing, and Ballard was delighted. Firenetics put in around $2 million over several years and acquired about eighty per cent ownership in Ultra Energy. By then, 1978, Ultra Energy, no longer tied to the submarine project, had moved into its own premises.

After about a year of development, Ultra Energy had succeeded in developing a practical smoke detector battery. Firenetics moved to commercialization, having Ultra Energy's staff help oversee construction of a battery plant in Hong Kong that would turn out 180,000 of the little batteries a day. With this project under way, the future of Ultra Energy looked secure. So secure that in early 1979 Keith Prater and Mei Lin got married. Two weeks later, though, the roof caved in.

Paul Howard took a phone call one Friday afternoon advising him that Ultra Energy's bank accounts were frozen. Firenetics, he learned, had filed for voluntary bankruptcy in Chicago. The cause was a dispute and resulting lawsuit between Firenetics and General Electric. Because of Firenetics's overwhelming ownership stake in Ultra Energy, the bankruptcy dragged down the Canadian company as well. A million-dollar cheque from Firenetics to Ultra Energy, Howard heard to his dismay, was not going to be honoured.

Alone in the office at the time, Howard was stunned. He called the company's two dozen employees together and said, "I don't know what's going to happen, but I'll tell you right now, we don't have any money, as of today, to pay your salaries. We'll keep you posted."

That weekend, Ballard, Prater and Howard met at Ballard's house in an attempt to pick up the pieces and to map out a strategy. They quickly decided to start a new company of their own. The idea was to capture the knowledge of batteries and electrochemistry that they had acquired, and to keep as much of their technical team together as they could.

Ballard was eleven years older, with a name that carried considerable weight, much greater business experience, and an extensive network of contacts, especially in the energy sector. Prater and Howard had been very minor shareholders in Ultra Energy and would have gladly accepted minor shares in the new firm. "I know I would have been perfectly happy with ten per cent," says Howard, "because Geoff was much more senior and we were still a little wet behind the ears. I was a good engineer and Keith was a good electrochemist. We were good at what we did, but we had no pretensions."

Ballard, though, proposed that ownership be divided equally, one-third each. "I want you to be equal partners," he told them, "because I want you to take it as seriously as I do and work as hard as I intend to. And there's lots of work and responsibility to go around." If we succeed, he added, "there will be plenty of money for all of us."

"Geoff was generous and probably wise," says Prater, looking back at this turning point in his personal and professional life. "It motivated Paul and me in a way that being an employee, or even a minor owner, would not have." Howard agrees: "In retrospect, I believe it was one of the far-sighted things that Geoff did, because I don't think we understood the significance of ownership." It made Howard realize that he had to make an even greater effort than before. "We grew from that. Eventually, I felt that I probably was equal. But it took us maybe ten years to get to that point. In the meantime, I think, we each pulled our weight a lot more than if it had been just Geoff in charge. I credit Geoff with having vision. I wouldn't have made us equals. We're all very wealthy today because he made us one-third owners. But it met his mandate. He's got the wealth that he wants. He doesn't mind if we have it too."

At the time, though, financial security was far in the future, and the three of them were scrambling. Howard and his wife, for example, were right in the midst of building themselves a new house. Fortunately, Darlene Howard had a decent executive position with the phone company, so there was at least one steady income. And Paul Howard could spend his spare time putting siding on the house. But they also had two kids to support.

A small upstairs office, just opposite the Ultra Energy building, was available for rent. The new partners took it, moved across the street and hung out their new shingle as Ballard Research. Shelagh Ballard pitched in as unpaid secretary for the first half year or so, typing letters, handling the phone, keeping the books. In fact, legally, she was an equal owner with her husband in his one-third of the company.

The Ballard partners complemented each other well. Paul Howard remembers people saying, "three people together, it'll never work." But it did, "because we never competed. Geoff didn't want to do what I did. I didn't want to do what Keith did; I couldn't have done it anyhow." Howard describes himself as a "details guy." "I'm the kind of guy who builds things. I look after the books. Keith and Geoff had no interest in that kind of thing. Keith was a great scientist. He understood electrochemistry. Geoff had the contacts and would counsel us, advise us, teach us. He had the experience." Prater agrees. "Geoff was clearly the leader. He was the executive. Paul was the chief engineer. I was the chief scientist."

The division of labour in the first months of the new company called for Howard to hold the fort by staying in the old building and doing what he could to maintain the battery team and capability. Meanwhile, Prater and Ballard would search for new business and try to find ways of paying the bills. Under court order, tags were put on all the company's equipment, and Howard was responsible for seeing that it didn't disappear out the back door. "Technically," he says, "we were not in receivership in Canada although they were in Chicago. And if we were put into receivership, we wouldn't be able to do some of the things we wanted to do to raise money."

Howard was able to negotiate a deal with the landlord and other creditors that kept them out of formal receivership and allowed the building to remain unlocked. This was crucial. It meant that any companies interested in investing in the battery technology could be taken through the premises and shown what had been accomplished.

Similarly, he had to keep their many suppliers on side and patient. He went to them and said, "We'll do the best we can to pay you off. We can't make promises, but please try to stick with us." In all, they owed between $150,000 and $200,000.

To the employees, he said, "Our only value is our knowledge, what's in our heads. If any of you are in a situation financially where you can stay with us, we'll do what we can to rebuild the business. We have no money, but if we get any, we'll pay you as soon as we can."

Ballard and Prater, meanwhile, pulled out all stops to find new work and create a new profile as a contract R & D company. Prater, who knew Spanish, even did some translating of information from Nicaragua and Costa Rica, because there were some possible consulting contracts there.

Some of the employees could not afford to wait to be paid and drifted off to other work. But about ten of them were willing to stick around without any guarantees. Whenever a bit of money did dribble in, it was doled out in thousand-dollar instalments to keep these loyal employees afloat. In the first few months the Ballard partners got some money from their "Chinese connection," the Hong Kong plant that was being set up to manufacture the smoke detector batteries. It was close to production, so Ballard Research was paid to send some of its people over to help set up equipment that had already been shipped prior to the Firenetics bankruptcy. That paid the bills for a brief spell.

Meanwhile, Geoffrey Ballard got on the phone and scoured his contacts in the oil industry. Were any of them interested, he asked, in picking up the asset value of the rechargeable battery from the court in Chicago? Many oil companies at the time were trying to diversify and become more broadly based energy firms. Portable energy sources like batteries seemed to fit the bill. The first to express interest was Ballard's old employer Shell Oil. He told Shell that he needed a relatively small amount of money to keep his team together. Why don't you pay us $10,000 up front, he suggested, to prepare and make a formal presentation, a "show and tell." Shell agreed.

"So we were able to give everyone $1000," says Howard. "That kept our people going for a bit and kind of got Shell on the hook." After that, "they gave us about $15,000 every two weeks to keep things going, so we could at least pay the rent and give everyone a little money—an equal amount. We did that for five or six months."

Shell became interested enough in the rechargeable battery, in fact, that they made an offer to buy out what was left of Ultra Energy—the company, its equipment and its technology. "And we were actually to the point where it looked like this was going to happen," Keith Prater recalls. "They had made offers for all the minority shareholders' stock—in addition to paying off all the creditors, so the bankruptcy thing would go away. My wife and I actually went on a holiday, a sort of honeymoon to Tahiti. It looked like this thing was really going to happen. And we came back to find that one of the minority shareholders had held out for a slightly sweeter deal, and Shell had walked away."

Next the Ballard partners approached Amoco and made a similar pitch: pay us to make a presentation and help keep us going. Once again, it worked. Within a few days, a vice-president from Amoco was on a plane to Vancouver carrying a cheque for $10,000. For another six to eight months, says Howard, Ballard Research remained in limbo, its research program largely stymied. "It was almost a comedy. We did a little bit of work. Once we got a little money for materials we could buy a bit with cash. But it was mainly a holding pattern; we weren't advancing the technology, but we were keeping our team of people together."

By mid-1981, though, Amoco finally decided to commit itself to a long-term contract that got Ballard Research out of the hole.

"Amoco's focus was on the rechargeable battery," says Prater, "to the extent that when they signed on they specifically said they were not interested in the non-rechargeable version, and that was left on the table, a scrap that was thrown to us."

The Amoco funding removed the biggest threat that had been hanging over the Ballard partners and their reputation. Part of the Amoco deal was to provide some extra money—about $150,000—to pay off the Vancouver area creditors. "We work in Greater Vancouver," Howard told them. "You're big Amoco. We've got creditors here that we think should be paid. And technically it's not your responsibility, but this is our backyard." Amoco agreed.

Howard recalls with relief how they wrote out the cheques and he went around personally to a few of the bigger creditors and paid off the debts. After one and one-half years of babying along the creditors, "we were able to pay them all off, one hundred cents on the dollar. With no interest. But almost all of them had written it off. They didn't expect to see any of the money. And I tell you, we built up a real loyalty. Every supplier was paid off. This was for the chemicals, the metals, the gases." It gave the new Ballard Research company great credibility.

The Amoco contract obligated Ballard Research to work exclusively on the rechargeable battery for two years. The Ballard team could not make further progress on the single-use version or diversify into any new areas. "But it became relatively profitable," says Howard. Operating on a cost-plus basis, "we were making money. We had no ownership in the technology, but the funding was at a good level after 1981." Ballard's later marketing manager David McLeod goes further: "It was 'fat city,' a beautiful contract that paid everyone ninety days in advance." Amoco pumped in around $3 million a year for the next half-dozen years.

Ballard Research made halting progress on the rechargeable battery, but it never became a practical technology. "It kept getting more and more complex," says Ballard. "Every time you did something to it, it needed more and more refinements and complexities in trying to overcome the difficulties. And that's usually the sign of a technology that's not going to become commercial." By 1987, Amoco bailed out, taking its ownership in the rechargeable battery with it.

But as early as 1983, as the end of the two-year moratorium on other research approached, the Ballard partners began looking for other consulting work and other technologies in which they might be able to develop a stake. The problem, says Howard, was that "we didn't own anything. We were just hired guys, only as good as the next job we got. You can never leverage a consulting company to make any real money. And Geoff was ten years older and getting grey hair. Not that he was ready to retire yet, but he asked himself, 'What am I going to do? What is the future when you hire yourself out?' That's when we began to look at other opportunities."

They took a shotgun approach. They had a big carbon dioxide laser, which had been used to weld the caps onto batteries, and considered using it to engrave an assortment of giftware products. They looked at taking computer software and combining it with suitable hardware to produce a line of computer-assisted design and manufacturing equipment. They looked into specialized polymers and even formed a separate company for this work, which still exists semi-independently under the larger Ballard corporate umbrella.

Already during this period, they began to develop the tightly knit, family-like corporate culture that came to characterize the company. Giving everyone involved a stake in the company and its success was the basic principle. At the top, the founders were equal shareholders. During the struggle to keep the team together in the early days of Ballard Research, they divided whatever funds were available equally among the loyal employees. When the company began to make a profit, they considered offering employees stock bonuses but decided that their stock, at the time, was essentially worthless. Instead, they instituted a plan under which forty per cent of the profits was shared equally among all the employees.

During the search for new business opportunities, Paul Howard was delegated to look for potential sources of government money. One day, reading a Canadian government bulletin, he came across something that would take the company in an entirely new direction. It was an RFP, or request for proposals, from the Department of National Defense, with major involvement by the National Research Council. It called for bids to produce a low-cost solid polymer fuel cell, the type that had first been developed by General Electric to fly in the Gemini space program. It later came to be better known as the proton exchange membrane (PEM) fuel cell.

Howard had never even heard of fuel cells, but he took the item to his next meeting with Ballard and Prater. "Look at this," he said. "What's a fuel cell? Is this anything for us?" "A fuel cell is electrochemistry," said Prater. "It's right up our alley." Although no electrochemist, Geoffrey Ballard also knew a bit about fuel cells. A few researchers at the US Army lab he directed in Fort Monmouth, New Jersey, had worked on one type of fuel cell. It turned out not to be one that made it into the first rank of fuel cells that are considered viable technologies today, but it gave Ballard his first exposure to the area.

Ballard immediately saw the tie-in to alternative energy that had been his dream for years. He welcomed the opportunity to work on such a technology at government expense and was intrigued by its potential for the huge transportation market. The fuel cells that had been developed to that time, mainly in the US space program, had incorporated large quantities of extremely expensive materials, especially platinum, niobium, and gold. "Wow," said Ballard, "if we could just substitute ordinary materials and bring down the costs, you have the engine of the future."

CHAPTER THREE

A Notable
SURFACE
of ACTION

In August 1965 the Gemini V spacecraft, carrying astronauts Gordon Cooper and Pete Conrad and boosted by a Titan II rocket, blasted off from the Kennedy Space Center into low earth orbit. The Gemini program, which was the bridge between the one-man Mercury flights and the three-man Apollo moon flights, had already put astronauts into space. But this launch was different. The flight plan called for staying in space for eight days, which would surpass the efforts of the Soviet Union and set a new record for duration. It was also different in another way. It was the first manned space flight to rely on fuel cells as a source of electrical power. And they were PEM cells, the same basic type that would be developed and refined to become the Ballard fuel cell.

In 1965 fuel cells as such were nothing new. In fact, they had been around for well over a century, and electrochemistry itself (the generation of an electric current through chemical reactions) had been known even longer. In fact, it predates the generation of electricity by mechanical means, which was first achieved by Michael Faraday in 1831, when he rotated a copper disk between the poles of a horseshoe magnet.

Ancient Greek and Roman physicians used a type of electric fish, the torpedo ray (akin to the better-known electric eel) to treat migraine headaches, epilepsy, and gout through a kind of electric shock therapy. This practice became popular again in Europe after the Renaissance. Around 1800 the Italian physicist, Count Alessandro Volta, who had studied electric fish, invented the first electrochemical battery, the voltaic pile. He called it an "artificial torpedo" because of its resemblance to the electric organ of the torpedo ray.

The fuel cell was the next big advance in electrochemistry. It was pioneered by Sir William Grove, a Welsh-born, Oxford-educated professor of physics who also trained for the bar, practiced patent law and served as a justice in Britain's Court of Common Pleas. It was Grove who first formulated the principle of conservation of energy, which he stated in 1846, a year earlier than the German scientist Hermann von Helmholtz, who is often given the credit.

Grove also showed that when steam came into contact with a heated platinum wire, it decomposed into hydrogen and oxygen. And he experimented with the electrolysis of water. Electrolysis is familiar to most people from the high school science demonstration in which gaseous hydrogen and oxygen are produced when an electric current is passed through water. One day, Grove disconnected such an electrolytic cell in his lab and observed a reverse flow of current. He realized that, just as he could use electricity to split water into hydrogen and oxygen, it should be possible to generate electricity by combining these two gases.

Grove demonstrated his first working fuel cell in 1839 during a talk he gave at the Royal Institution in London. It generated only enough electricity to deflect the needle of a galvanometer. By 1842, though, he had constructed a bank of fifty such cells, which he called a gaseous voltaic battery. Today this would be called a fuel cell stack.*

Grove's device consisted of a long row of glass tubes with the upper ends closed and the lower ends open but immersed in diluted sulfuric acid as an electrolyte. The sealed upper parts of the tubes contained, alternately, gaseous hydrogen and oxygen. Each tube also had a strip of platinum foil in it, positioned so that it was in contact with both the gas and the electrolyte. These were the electrodes, which he wired in series to add their voltages together. (Fuel cells typically operate in a range between 0.5 and 0.9 volts, which is much too low for most practical uses.) The platinum acted as a catalyst in the process. The set-up generated enough current that Grove could use it, in turn, to decompose water in an adjacent electrolytic apparatus. As one history of the fuel cell notes, he was "quick to realize the beautiful symmetry inherent in the 'decomposition of water by means of its composition.'"[3]

Grove's invention did not deliver enough power, though, to compete with conventional galvanic cells or storage batteries. He recognized that this was because the reaction generating electricity was only taking place in the tiny region of the triple contact between the gas, electrolyte, and electrode. What was needed, he said, was to increase this to create a "notable surface of action." Grove himself did not pursue the technology further, but his achievements in electrochemistry and the law earned him a knighthood.+

---

* In electrochemistry, a single unit containing an anode, cathode, and some sort of electrolyte (to conduct ions) is generally called a cell. A combination of such units is a battery, by analogy to a battery of cannons. Similarly, a number of fuel cells grouped together could be called a fuel cell "battery," but to distinguish it from common storage batteries, they are usually called a "stack."

+ In a Grove-type fuel cell, neither the platinum nor the sulfuric acid are part of the chemical reaction. Hydrogen ions (or protons, which are simply hydrogen atoms stripped of their electrons) are produced at the anode (positive electrode). These ions are transported to the cathode (or negative electrode) through the electrolyte, while the electrons reach the cathode via the external circuit. At the cathode, oxygen molecules combine with the hydrogen ions, while gaining the electrons from the external circuit, producing water.

The basic principle of a modern PEM fuel cell—like Ballard's—is the same as the Grove cell, except that the electrolyte is a solid polymer (an ion exchange or "proton exchange membrane," or PEM, through which hydrogen ions can pass) rather than a solution of sulfuric acid.* Notice that the platinum is not part of the reaction. This is the very definition of a catalyst. It makes the reaction possible but is not consumed or depleted.

Grove's invention largely languished until 1889, when Ludwig Mond and Charles Langer, also working in England, attempted to turn it into a practical device. They were also the first to call it a "fuel cell." Replacing the oxygen with air and the pure hydrogen with an impure industrial gas obtained from coal, they tried to solve the problem of the limited triple contact area by using an electrolyte in a quasi-solid form, that is, soaked up by a porous material like asbestos or plaster of Paris. Their device generated 1.5 watts, but they decided it had little commercial potential, largely because of the high cost of platinum. That problem—the cost of platinum—would plague PEM cells right up to the 1990s.

Electrolysis can decompose many more chemical compounds than just water. In fact, it is used to produce various chemicals in a wide assortment of industrial processes. By the same token, not all fuel cells, which are essentially the reverse of electrolytic cells, involve simple reactions of hydrogen and oxygen. Throughout the first half of the twentieth century, attempts were made to build fuel cells that could convert coal or carbon directly to electricity. In 1921 a high-temperature (1000°C) cell was developed using a molten carbonate salt. It had a carbon anode and an iron oxide cathode, but it floundered on corrosion and materials problems. Today, though,

---

* Other types of fuel cells employ somewhat different chemical reactions, and in some cases more complex ions, but all have in common that ions are transported through an electrolyte and electrons through an external circuit.

molten carbonate cells are one of the five leading fuel cell technologies that are being developed, especially for stationary power generation.*

British scientists continued to dominate fuel cell development. In 1932, Francis T. Bacon, an engineer at Cambridge University in England (and a descendant of the seventeenth-century philosopher Francis Bacon) tried to get around the problem of the high cost of platinum as a catalyst. Platinum and other noble metals, including palladium, ruthenium, and gold, are favoured as catalysts because they can resist the corrosive effects of strong acid electrolytes. But they are not the only possible catalysts. Bacon built a hydrogen/oxygen cell that had an alkaline electrolyte, which allowed him to use relatively inexpensive nickel as the catalyst. He also raised the operating temperature and pressure within the cell to increase the rate of the chemical reaction. At around 200°C and forty-five times atmospheric pressure, he got the best results. Together with various co-workers, Bacon spent nearly three decades, interrupted by the Second World War, refining his cell.

In 1959 Bacon demonstrated a stack of forty cells. Each was about twenty-five centimetres (ten inches) in diameter and consisted of two porous nickel plates with a concentrated solution of potassium hydroxide sealed under pressure in between. The stack cranked out five kilowatts, enough to power a welding machine, a circular saw, even a small, two-ton fork lift. In fact, its power density (wattage for a given surface area, weight or volume) compares well with much more recent fuel cells.

But the Bacon cell had significant drawbacks. It had to be preheated to at least 150°C before it generated top power. To keep from "poisoning" the electrolyte, Bacon could not use fuels containing

---

* Besides PEM and molten carbonate, the other types, named according to their electrolytes, are the phosphoric acid, alkaline, and solid oxide fuel cells.

traces of carbon compounds, or air containing even minute amounts of carbon dioxide. Instead, pure hydrogen and oxygen were required, and even today, this remains a drawback for alkaline fuel cells; the hydrogen must be pure and the air "scrubbed" to remove carbon dioxide.

In 1959, the same year that Bacon showed off his first really successful cell, the Allis-Chalmers farm equipment firm of Milwaukee, Wisconsin called out the press for a novel demonstration. As reporters watched, a company engineer ploughed a field with a fuel cell-powered tractor. Like Bacon's, it was an alkaline cell, but it operated at a much lower temperature and had a noble metal catalyst coated onto nickel electrode plates. The stack consisted of 1008 cells and generated around fifteen kilowatts, enough to run a twenty-horsepower electric motor. It ran so quietly that the driver could enjoy listening to a radio while he worked.

But this one also had drawbacks. Like the Bacon and other alkaline fuel cells, it required pure hydrogen and would only work on air that had been scrubbed to remove traces of carbon dioxide. It never was commercialized, and the prototype was eventually put on display at the Smithsonian Institution in Washington, DC.

By the time the Allis-Chalmers tractor was ploughing the rich soil of Wisconsin, a new heavyweight corporate contender, General Electric, had entered the competition to develop a practical fuel cell. GE first got involved in 1953 because a coal company in Pennsylvania had shown interest in fuel cells for stationary power generation. GE sent two chemists to Pittsburgh to look at the work there, which was based on previous research by a Russian scientist named Davytan. GE was not particularly impressed, but to protect its interests in the power field, the company established a very modest program at its research laboratory in Schenectady, New York, under the head of physical chemistry, Herman A. Liefhafsky.

The second man assigned to the project was Willard Thomas Grubb, who had studied chemistry at Harvard. Known at GE as Tom Grubb, he had a serious demeanour but also a dry sense of humour and love for music. At lunchtime he often slipped away to play a baby grand piano that was kept backstage in the laboratory's auditorium.

Grubb got an inspiration from an unlikely source, the common water softener. As an unpublished GE report on Grubb's work states: "The heart of a water softener is a polymer called an ion-exchange resin or ion-exchange membrane, depending on whether it's in the form of resin balls or a plastic sheet." In such a system, positive ions are "hooked to polymer chains in a loose enough way that they can move around easily. In water softening, they can get out into the water, changing places with the calcium ions that made the water hard. The calcium trapped in the ion-exchange material can be taken away with the resin or membrane."

Grubb proposed to build a fuel cell using a sulfonated polystyrene resin as the electrolyte. Hydrogen ions, he reckoned, would migrate through the membrane and combine with oxygen ions on the cathode side. He tried it, and the principle worked. By the end of 1954 he had a crude but working cell, and in 1955 he applied for a patent. This first PEM cell seemed to have very limited utility, though. It only worked on nearly pure hydrogen and oxygen. GE was interested in large-scale power generation using ordinary air and a cheap fuel, so Grubb's work languished for a few years.

Then came Sputnik and the space race, and with it revived interest in fuel cells for extraterrestrial applications, where pure oxygen and hydrogen were being carried on board in any case and cost was hardly an issue. In 1958 GE assigned another Harvard-trained chemist, Leonard W. Niedrach, to work with Grubb. Niedrach hit on a better way of making the cell's electrodes by depositing the platinum catalyst on a fine metal mesh and bonding this directly to the polymer membrane. (Today, in a Ballard cell, the catalyst is coated onto carbon paper or cloth, which is then bonded to the membrane; the combination is called the membrane electrode assembly.)

Niedrach's improvement turned the PEM cell into a practical device, although only a tiny one at first. GE had a cute demonstration model that was mounted on a wooden board. The cell itself was disk shaped and looked a lot like a small hockey puck. It was fuelled by a balloon filled with hydrogen. It put out only two one-hundredths of a watt, but that was enough to spin a toy propeller.

Grubb received the patent for his membrane, but Niedrach also considered himself the inventor of the GE cell. To settle the budding dispute, Liefhafsky got the two men together. "Listen, Tom," he said, "if you hadn't gotten the idea of using the ion exchange membrane there would never have been an invention. And, Len, if you hadn't figured out how to make the electrode it never would have gone anywhere. So from now on, it's the Grubb-Niedrach fuel cell."

In 1959—the US was still putting up its first small space satellites and Geoffrey Ballard was just a young field geologist exploring for oil—GE put several more scientists onto the PEM project and began funding it in part with contracts from the US Army. In two years, the research laboratory spent a total of $1.1 million. Soon GE had its first contract with the newly formed NASA, which led to the rapid expansion of the program and eventually to the decision to use GE's PEM fuel cell on the Gemini spacecraft. The actual Gemini work was done by GE's newly created Direct Energy Conversion division in West Lynn, Massachusetts.

Back at the research centre in Schenectady, though, GE made no further effort to develop the PEM cell. Its need for pure gases and its use of expensive platinum were a show-stopper for terrestrial use. GE put all its pure research money and expertise into trying to develop other types of fuel cells, ones that might be able to run on cheap fuels. Grubb, Niedrach, and five colleagues spent five years and $8.5 million in a futile effort to develop a more commercial fuel cell. As the GE retrospective states, "This is where nature refused to cooperate. The GE team never found a substitute for platinum, or a way to cut down enough on its use… and the hoped for commercial markets never opened up." The PEM cell was simply too expensive. "The fuel cell in a car, or in major military applications, or for any consumer or industrial uses at all was as far away as ever."

In Massachusetts, though, GE's engineers took the PEM cell and turned it into an effective, albeit costly, space technology. NASA chose the GE cell as one of the fuel cell types with the greatest potential. In fact, it was a small GE test cell that became the first fuel cell of any kind to go into space on an unmanned sub-orbital flight in October 1960. By early 1962 a prototype being tested in Massachusetts had completed fifty hours delivering its rated output of twenty-five watts.

But the GE cell was not the only one in contention. Francis Bacon had continued working on his alkaline cell in England. Then, in the early 1960s he transferred the concept to the Pratt and Whitney Division of United Aircraft Corporation in Connecticut. (Subsequently the company became United Technologies Corporation—UTC—and its fuel cell division, today called International Fuel Cells, is one of the leading fuel cell manufacturers in the world.)

To reduce the cell's weight for space flight, Pratt and Whitney greatly reduced its operating pressure while increasing its temperature. The modified cell produced much less power than before, but it was still the best available in the mid-1960s. Thus it was the Pratt and Whitney alkaline fuel cell that was ultimately chosen to provide on-board power for the Apollo moon missions, which required considerable electrical power for up to two weeks. In improved form, it still powers the space shuttle.

But GE's PEM cell appeared to be adequate for shorter orbital flights. It was also further advanced than the alkaline one when the race to the moon was officially launched by President Kennedy in

May 1961 and was expected to be ready sooner. Besides, NASA did not want to put all its fuel cell eggs in a single basket. GE was chosen to develop its cell for the two-man Gemini orbital flights of the mid-1960s. (The very short, one-man Mercury orbital missions used only batteries.)

At the heart of the Gemini fuel cell was the ion-exchange membrane that Tom Grubb had developed. The porous electrodes consisted of fine metallic wire screens (made of titanium on which the platinum catalyst had been deposited) bonded to either side of the membrane. Abutting each electrode were current collectors made of niobium metal. (Ballard would call them flow field plates and make them out of much cheaper graphite.) There were tiny channels for the flow of gases and tubes containing a coolant to draw off excess heat. On the oxygen side of the cell, the current collectors also held wicks to absorb the water produced in the reaction and draw it off by capillary action.

The Gemini system consisted of six fuel cell stacks. Each could be operated as an individual 350-watt unit, but groups of three were connected in parallel and built into a pair of cylindrical pressurized tanks about 0.6 metres long and 0.3 metres in diameter (two feet by one foot). Each of these combined units weighed about thirty-two kilograms (seventy pounds) and produced a maximum of one kilowatt of power plus half a litre (one pint) of water for each kilowatt hour of operation. These were hand-crafted devices that cost literally hundreds of thousands of dollars per kilowatt.

The GE fuel cells were troublesome beasts. Astronaut Michael Collins compared them to Arctic huskies. "Unlike batteries," he said, "they had character," and "like sled dogs, some were stronger and pulled more than their share of the electrical load; others were malingerers and had to be coddled and rested periodically."[4] Before each launch "the crew was handed a piece of paper listing the latest state of health of each cell."[5] This showed "how many volts it was then capable of producing at light and heavy loads. In flight, actual volt-meter readings were compared with predicted output, to warn of impending failure."[6] In addition, the cell stacks had to be cleansed or "purged" periodically by "force-feeding" them with bursts of extra hydrogen and oxygen.

The cells were also expected to provide much of the crew's drinking water. "Unfortunately," said Collins, "the water produced by them turned out to be the color of strong coffee."[7] It was contaminated by organic particles the astronauts called "furries" and was undrinkable.

However temperamental, the GE cells did their job, but not without giving NASA many a serious fright. The first relatively short Gemini flights in early 1965 relied on battery power not fuel cells. Then came Gemini V, an ambitious eight-day flight that carried the GE fuel cells for the first time. Almost as soon as Gemini V was in orbit, following a perfect launch, the problems began.

After only two orbits, Pete Conrad checked his instruments and noticed that the fuel cells' oxygen pressure gauge was falling steadily. Eventually it sank to less than one-tenth its expected value. Under orders from the ground, the astronauts had to shut the fuel cells down and cut their use of electricity drastically. Back on Earth, NASA went into emergency mode in case the flight had to be cut short. The fleet of twenty ships and one hundred planes spread around the world was alerted that it might have to be ready to recover them as early as the next afternoon. (Gemini V had back-up batteries to provide limited power in the meantime.) This meant scrapping some of the planned activities.

The problem was eventually traced to a heater that had failed to warm the supply of liquid oxygen enough to turn it into a gas. Partial fuel cell power was restored the next day, and the flight continued at a reduced rate of power consumption. But this meant insufficient power to keep the craft in a stable orientation. It was allowed to drift, and the crew had to endure days of tumbling motion. They landed safely, and NASA officials bravely deflected suggestions from the press that the spacecraft was a lemon. Such was the less-than-auspicious debut of the PEM fuel cell in space.

There was more trouble ahead. In December 1965 both Gemini VI and Gemini VII were launched. The Gemini VI capsule, which used batteries, was launched only after Gemini VII had been in orbit for over a week, and it stayed up only twenty-five hours. During this flight it performed the delicate but important task of practising rendezvous techniques with Gemini VII.

Gemini VII stayed in orbit for fourteen days, which gave its fuel cells a challenging test. Problems showed up early in the flight. First, fuel cell warning lights flashed intermittently, although the cells seemed to be working correctly. Then one cell became flooded with excess water. The astronauts were able to correct the problem but expected it to reoccur. Again, they were ordered to cut back on fuel use and told to monitor the troublesome cell carefully.

After the safe Gemini VII splashdown, NASA and GE scrambled to modify the system in time for the next flight. The main changes were a simplified method of removing water and the addition of sensing instruments that could better pinpoint the source of any malfunctions. "The fuel cell itself," noted *The New York Times*, "has been all but exonerated."[8] But the system malfunctioned again on the Gemini XII flight in November 1966. Some sections had to be turned off. Then the GE cell became a historic curiosity as the Apollo program went ahead, powered by the Pratt and Whitney alkaline fuel cell system.

After the Gemini program, GE continued work on its PEM fuel cell for a few years. The greatest improvement was the adaptation for fuel cell use of a new membrane. Under the trade name Nafion®, this had been developed by the Dupont corporation for the industrial-scale "chlor-alkali" method of producing chlorine gas by electrolysis.

It was also considered promising for use on board submarines to produce oxygen for breathing by means of the electrolysis of sea water.

With this improved membrane, the GE cell attained drastically longer operating life and a considerably higher power density. The company announced hopefully that it expected these improved fuel cells to go into widespread commercial use and saw them as especially suitable for powering remote television cameras and other communications equipment. GE would not even discount their eventual use to power automobiles, although the company conceded that size and cost would have to be brought down dramatically.

That never happened. GE put very limited resources into PEM and eventually sold its fuel cell division. And so it was that by 1983, when the Ballard partners received the Canadian government's request to develop a PEM fuel cell, nobody else was backing it. Most of the GE patents had either expired, or would expire by the time commercialization made the patents issue relevant.

Most government and industry money for fuel cell development in the US, Japan, and Europe was going into other types of cells, especially the phosphoric acid fuel cell. The only place where significant research was being done on PEM cells was at Los Alamos National Laboratory, where the first atomic bomb was built. Even there, work was funded at a very modest level and was mainly limited to computer modelling and the testing of components supplied by private corporations.

Nobody was really sponsoring PEM. As Geoffrey Ballard has said, for his company it just sort of fell onto the table.

CHAPTER FOUR

An **Opportunity** *for* CANADA

T o Geoffrey Ballard the fuel cell request for proposal (RFP) may have seemed like a fortuitous surprise. But a half-million-dollar contract does not come out of nowhere, least of all in Canada, where research money for high technology has always been tight. In fact, the contract only came about after a small group of scientists in academia, government, and the military had been watching fuel cell development for some years. In retrospect, it represents the all-too-rare case of clear and timely technical and economic thinking in government and shows how a small amount of government seed money can go a long way and lead to the establishment of a successful new industry.

There were three main centres in Canada where people were interested in fuel cells. One was the University of Toronto. Another was the Canadian military's main research lab in Ottawa. The third was Canada's National Research Council. All eventually coordinated their fuel cell efforts.

At the University of Toronto the spark plug was an engineering professor named David Sanborn Scott, who has been called "an environmentalist, energy analyst, and visionary."[9] (Today Scott is at the University of Victoria, where he runs a lab that designs and builds PEM fuel cells and until recently headed the Institute for Integrated Energy Studies.)

Scott is a big, robust man who likes to wear hiking shoes and vests and has a photo of his sailboat hanging on his office wall. With his broad smile and bare dome, he reminds you of the Mr. Clean commercials. After studying at Queen's University (like Geoffrey Ballard, who many years later became a close personal friend) he got his Ph.D. at Northwestern University in Illinois, specializing in deep-space electric rocket propulsion. He began teaching at the University of Toronto (U of T) and in 1976 became the chairman of the department of mechanical engineering, where he chose to focus his research on energy systems and became fascinated by hydrogen. Later he served on Canada's Hydrogen Technology Advisory Group. Other members of Scott's group at the U of T included Ronald Venter, Charles Ward, and Derek McCammond, who have been active in hydrogen and fuel cell development since that time.

The more Scott learned about hydrogen, the more he thought it was a clean, attractive fuel. But his epiphany came in the late 1970s when he attended a conference in Stuttgart, Germany, dealing with hydrogen-powered airplanes. A prominent Italian scientist, Cesar Marchetti, gave a talk and presented diagrams showing how, over the course of human history, a succession of energy sources have dominated. Coal largely replaced wood, for example, and then oil replaced coal. An arrow-like time line pointed into the future, which would be dominated by such sources as uranium and sunlight.

The diagram also presented the ways those sources were converted into useful forms or energy "carriers." Both oil and coal could be burned, for example, and turned into an energy carrier called electricity. Off in the future was hydrogen, which was the most flex-ible energy carrier of all, since it could be derived from almost any hydrocarbon or from water using virtually any energy source. It could then be used to run an internal combustion engine, power a jet plane or rocket, or it could be converted directly to electricity by fuel cells. "I looked at that," says Scott, "and thought, my God, this whole thing is not just important or attractive, it's inevitable." Scott was an overnight convert to Marchetti's vision of the energy future and came home a passionate advocate for a hydrogen-based econ-omy, including fuel cells.

He soon coined a useful new term, "energy currency," which was eventually picked up by many people, including Geoffrey Ballard. Unlike the related concepts of energy carrier, energy vector or sec-ondary energy source, energy "currency" nicely captures the idea that hydrogen is like money in the bank. It can be generated from many energy sources and then converted into many useful applications. It can be saved up at times when production is convenient and cheap and expended when needed.

Scott emphasizes the difference between energy sources and energy currencies. "Gasoline, heating oil, and natural gas are energy sources," he told the *Winnipeg Free Press* in 1980, "because we take them from the ground. They are also energy currencies because we can carry them around in our cars or pump them into our homes. Nuclear, tidal, solar, and wind are also energy sources. But they're not functional as energy currencies because you can't put a windmill on your car or a reactor in your home. We convert those sources to make a currency—electricity."[10]

So far so good. Electricity can be sent through the power grid to our homes and provide us with heat, light, refrigeration. But it can't do everything. "The trouble with electricity as a currency to replace gasoline and heating oil," Scott adds, "is that it can't be stored very well, and it isn't very practical: electricity can't power a jet airplane. But we can use electricity to make another currency, hydrogen, which can be stored and carried around much like the conventional energy currencies we use today."* It can even be distributed through pipelines. He pauses, then adds vehemently, "hydrogen is the only alternative to hydrocarbon fuels."[11]

With messianic zeal, Scott set out to promote hydrogen as an energy currency, and with it, fuel cells. He began by talking up hydrogen to key people in government. He wrote articles and technical papers. He gave interviews. He and colleagues in Toronto built fuel cells and experimented with them. He got a particular kick out of using one to run a little, brightly coloured table-top merry-go-round, which he still has at his institute in Victoria. Scott jokes that these were probably the first painted ponies and zoo animals in the world to prance to the power of fuel cells.

In the early 1980s Scott's efforts were focused on alkaline fuel cells, similar to those that had flown on Apollo and that today power the space shuttle. Not only was alkaline the most powerful type of cell at the time, it was also a relatively mature and proven technology. And it had an additional advantage, especially for the province of Ontario.

"One reason for my interest in alkaline," he says, "was that it uses pure hydrogen, while the other fuel cells were developed to use low-purity hydrogen." And pure hydrogen is what comes from electrolysis, which Scott thought gave Ontario a potential economic edge. He looked around Toronto and saw the headquarters of the

---

* It is important to note that while hydrogen is an excellent energy currency, it is not itself an energy source. It is the most abundant element in the universe and is plentiful on Earth in the form of water. But because hydrogen combines so readily with other elements, it does not naturally occur on Earth in its free (gaseous) form. It is not, therefore, an available energy source on its own. Energy from another source is needed to create free hydrogen. That is why hydrogen is a currency, a way of taking energy from one source and converting it to another use. Of course, hydrocarbon fuels *are* sources of hydrogen—most industrial hydrogen is made from natural gas, for example, rather than from water by means of electrolysis—but most are non-renewable, and when used to make hydrogen they release carbon dioxide, a greenhouse gas, into the atmosphere.

Electrolyser Corporation, one of the world's largest producers of electrolysis plants. He looked north and saw that Ontario had enormous potential for hydroelectric power. Out to the east along Lake Ontario was the giant Pickering nuclear power plant with its CANDU reactors. These had vast excess capacity in off-peak hours.

"You can't store electricity," says Scott. But you build hydroelectric and nuclear power plants for peak capacity, so that they will be able to satisfy power demands "at the absolute peak moment of the whole bloody year. And by definition, any other time is below that peak, and you have that capacity to generate electricity which is just sitting there." Many generating stations are actually shut down at night or on weekends. Why not keep them going? he asks rhetorically. For both hydroelectric and nuclear power, "your marginal cost," the cost of generating an extra kilowatt hour of electricity, "becomes trivial." The infrastructure is already in place. The off-peak capacity could be used to make hydrogen, which can be stored, as natural gas is now, and used when needed. So with electrolytic hydrogen and fuel cells "you really could create an economic advantage."

One early use for hydrogen that Scott hit upon was fuel cell locomotives. "I was looking for a nice platform for fuel cells, an application where you had minimal infrastructure requirements, and everything kind of went click." He thought about Toronto's commuter rail system, with its double-decker GO (for government of Ontario) trains. Operating them on fuel cells, he thought, would be an ideal first step to entering the transportation market.

Although Scott's proposal was never put into effect by Ontario, he still thinks the idea was "extraordinarily sweet," because it would have made a significant dent in the Toronto region's air pollution yet it required hardly any additional resources. "The GO trains are running back and forth, burning diesel. And they're noisy. They run from Burlington to Pickering. And what else do you have at Pickering? You have this nuclear power plant," where electrolytic hydrogen could be made in off-peak hours. "It would be just so damned simple," he muses. "You could scrape off the excess power and make hydrogen, and have clean and quiet trains with minimal infrastructure and cost." At the time, fuel cells were still too bulky to fit into cars or even buses, but locomotives were large enough to accommodate them. And the relative bulkiness of compressed hydrogen would also be a minor issue, because the runs are short, trains are large anyhow, and they could be refuelled each evening.

Scott began to spread the good word about hydrogen and sought funding for his research at the U of T. He went and talked to Ontario's then-energy minister, Robert Welch. This led to a series of regional initiatives, such as the establishment of an Ontario Hydrogen Energy Task Force and interest in a hydrogen-based industrial strategy by the provincial power company, Ontario Hydro. Scott and his group were to conduct a number of formal studies and reports for Ontario institutions over the next few years, which raised the profile of hydrogen and fuel cells immeasurably. He also went to Ottawa and learned that the Canadian military's main lab, the Defense Research Establishment Ottawa, had considerable expertise in fuel cells.

Fuel cells had long been of interest to the military in both the US and Canada. As early as the 1950s an experimental fuel cell built by Union Carbide was powering a portable radar set for the US Army Signal Corps. As *Reader's Digest* pointed out at the time, "Such a power plant is of particular interest to the [military] services because its lack of noise, exhaust, and telltale heat emanations make it hard for an enemy to spot."[12]

In the 1960s and 1970s the US Department of Defense funded a wide range of fuel cells to be used as mobile power generators for airfield lighting and communications. Others were to power satellites, submersibles, and buoys. There were small PEM systems as well as much larger phosphoric acid ones. Many of those for terrestrial use were designed to run on methanol as the fuel and air as the oxidant.

By the time Keith Prater went off to Los Alamos to look into PEM fuel cells, the Canadian military, too, had been thinking about fuel cells for years. At a series of defense seminars in the mid-to-late 1960s, planners discussed a wide variety of potential fuel cell applications. The land forces were interested in fuel cells for portable communications, radar, and surveillance systems. The navy saw potential for powering submersibles. The air force envisaged small, transportable ground support lighting systems for runways and taxiways.

It was small, portable power packs for communications that received the greatest attention. In the 1960s, most of these used primary (single use) batteries, which normally were good for only twenty-four hours of operation. They were cheap, but did not last long, and they weighed a lot per kilowatt hour generated. For larger power systems, rechargeable storage batteries could be used. But as Canada's Defence Research Board noted, "These batteries must be recharged when their useful energy has been used. This results in the need for a two-way supply system, or the transportation of recharge equipment, which is usually an engine-generator set. This latter equipment begins to introduce… undesirable noise factors."[13] Fuel cells, by contrast, could run for weeks or months, limited only by the size of the fuel tank.

The board was impressed by the performance of fuel cells in the Gemini and Apollo space programs, which "dramatically demonstrated that reliable fuel cells have been developed."[14] It warned, however, that fuel cells are extremely expensive, projecting costs of around $15,000 to $20,000 for a small, 300-watt unit. But it suggested that costs could be reduced quite substantially and concluded, "When all factors are considered, fuel cells in the 200 watt to one kilowatt power range seem most attractive."[15]

By the late 1970s, Canada's military had not just been thinking about fuel cells. It had been exchanging information with the US military, obtaining fuel cells from the US, and commissioning studies of its own by major companies in the fuel cell field. And it eagerly sought advice on how fuel cells might fit into the larger Canadian scientific and industrial picture.

Over the next few years, the Defense Research Establishment Ottawa (DREO) commissioned David Scott and his group at the U of T to review the state-of-the-art in fuel cell development elsewhere in the world and to gauge their potential for Canada. (Other studies were done by the U of T under the aegis of Canada's Ministry of Energy, Mines and Resources and for Transport Canada. As we have seen, there were also studies and reports for the Ontario government and Ontario Hydro.)

Most of these studies recommended further work on alkaline fuel cells. As late as 1981 in the papers Scott and his group published, alkaline cells were seen as the clear leader, and PEM cells were not even mentioned as a viable option. (By 1983 PEM came to be seen as a potential "back-up" or alternative to alkaline.) In fact, Scott and his colleagues were mainly concerned to point out the disadvantages of phosphoric acid (PAFC) and other systems that could run well on fuels that were "reformed" to make low purity hydrogen. "Fuel cells are a technology uniquely suited to pure hydrogen," he wrote. "While it is relatively straightforward to substitute air for oxygen, if anything is substituted for pure hydrogen a cluster of technical difficulties are introduced, efficiencies drop, and capital costs rise."[16]

With the governments of both Ontario and Canada interested, for a few years it looked to Scott as though hydrogen-related R & D programs would be funded at a truly substantial level, possibly millions of dollars a year. Riding this temporary wave of enthusiasm, he founded a new Institute for Hydrogen Systems at the U of T.

But Scott's dreams were not to be. The encouraging moves and initial funding had come under the Liberal government of Prime Minister Pierre Trudeau with its well-funded National Energy Program. When the Conservative government of Brian Mulroney took office in 1984, it soon made cutbacks on the energy front that scuttled most of the projects Scott saw as so promising. He has never forgotten or forgiven, and even now a tone of weary disappointment creeps into his voice when he discusses those years. He still thinks Canada missed some golden opportunities. One of the few projects that did emerge from those early efforts, though, was the Ballard fuel cell.

The early U of T studies may have favoured the alkaline fuel cell, but DREO had become interested in fuel cells even earlier and quite independently. The Canadian military was less interested in clean air and the economic advantages for Ontario. It wanted to develop fuel cells that could run on readily available liquid fuels, such as methanol, which could be reformed to produce low-purity hydrogen. Alkaline cells could not run on such hydrogen, but PEM cells could.

At DREO, the man in charge of fuel cell development was Chris Gardner, a low-key, even self-effacing physical chemist with a Ph.D. from the University of British Columbia. His specialty was spectroscopy, the study of chemical elements by the light spectra they emit. It was Gardner who commissioned some of the U of T studies, and it was he who would be directly responsible for the Ballard fuel cell contracts.

In the mid-1960s a small fuel cell group was formed at DREO, and Gardner was hired along with two or three other scientists. The idea was that he could use techniques of spectroscopy to better understand the mechanisms involved in electrocatalysis. The group was not trying to design or build practical fuel cell stacks. Although they did build some very small fuel cells of their own, this was only in order to learn about the reactions that take place in them, not to advance them towards commercialization. Gardner describes the efforts as "fairly fundamental" studies aimed at understanding such things as how the electrodes work. As in the US, most of the early work focused on phosphoric acid fuel cells, not PEM.

But Gardner's DREO group, though small, was not isolated. It was part of the larger international fuel cell network and interacted with similar groups in the US, both military and civilian. "There used to be an annual power sources conference," he says, which focused largely on batteries and fuel cells. His group nearly always sent at least one person to those meetings to listen, learn, and report back. They also had an exchange arrangement with one of the US military labs that was developing fuel cells. Through this connection, DREO obtained a fuel cell that ran on hydrazine and had been developed by the US Army as a portable field generator. Gardner's group studied it, tested it, measured its performance, and tried to understand its problems and shortcomings. They also got hold of several smaller fuel cells, including one phosphoric acid type and at least one PEM.

Their interest in PEM was enhanced in the 1970s when the Canadian military paid General Electric (which had not yet sold its PEM division and technology) to conduct a feasibility study on the potential use of fuel cells for submarine propulsion. It was only a "paper study," says Gardner. "Basically the question we asked them was to give us an estimate of what sort of size and performance" could be expected from a PEM cell, and "whether the system that they had could meet this kind of application." At the same time, United Technologies (the successor to Pratt and Whitney) did a similar study for Canada on the alkaline fuel cell technology. "During those studies," says Gardner, "we had a chance to have a closer look at these technologies and to understand what the advantages and disadvantages were."

A big disadvantage with PEM was cost, especially the high price of Dupont's Nafion® membrane, which at the time was essentially the only game in town, and the exorbitant cost of the platinum catalyst. By 1983, though, Gardner could see that the price of catalysts might not be prohibitive in the long run. New techniques were being pioneered at Los Alamos and Texas A & M University that promised to reduce the amount of platinum required by a factor of ten or more.

As further evidence that PEM could be reduced in cost, by 1983 a small US company, the A.F. Sammer Corporation of New Jersey, was making and selling PEM cells about the size of a book. Company literature stated that these "will be offered for lecture and demonstration purposes and are laid out for intermittent operation." There were twelve watt, twenty-five watt, and fifty watt models, made largely of plastic, and they cost just in the range of hundreds of dollars. As Gardner describes them, they were "extremely simple and basically designed to work off ambient pressure air and some sort of hydrogen source to produce a few watts of power." But they gave an idea of what might be possible in cost reduction.

With Ontario backing alkaline fuel cells, it seemed logical to Gardner to push for parallel development of PEM. As he wrote in a 1983 memorandum just prior to issuing the fuel cell RFP, "concentration on systems that will utilize impure hydrogen ensures that there will be no competition with the substantial program that is expected to start at the Ontario Institute for Hydrogen Systems. The Ontario program will emphasize the development of fuel cells that use electrolytic grade hydrogen."

But where would the money come from? Fortunately, besides Scott's group at the U of T and Gardner's at DREO, there was a third centre with an active interest in fuel cells, the National Research Council. In the early 1980s, much of its energy research was being funded with money from the National Energy Program, which for a few years had pots of money to throw around.

Earlier, a chemist named Martin Hammerli had been working for Atomic Energy of Canada Limited, the company that designs and builds Canada's CANDU nuclear reactors. At the company's Chalk River, Ontario, research centre he had done studies on producing hydrogen, particularly by means of electrolysis and on the storage of hydrogen. Like David Scott, he was a passionate booster of hydrogen as an area of technology that Canada should be promoting.*

At Chalk River Hammerli also worked with fuel cells and had obtained a PEM lecture cell made by General Electric for classroom demonstrations. He thought the alkaline fuel cell had major drawbacks and favoured development of PEM. "Because I had personal experience with the GE system," he says, "I knew where the weaknesses were. I knew it could be improved." Hammerli had been attending the major international electrochemistry conferences and staying on top of fuel cell developments. "I was well connected everywhere," he says. "It was my business to be well connected." He knew the fuel cell group at Los Alamos and was aware that PEM was not being actively "sponsored" or well funded by the US or any other government or major company. He also knew Chris Gardner at DREO.

In 1982 Hammerli switched jobs, moving to the National Research Council (NRC) as manager for electrochemical systems. There he was in charge of commissioning work by outside contractors. He had at his disposal about $6 million per year in funding from the National Energy Program. As he recalls it, in late 1982 Chris Gardner came to him and said he would like to find some money to have a PEM system developed. "I don't know who would be out there that could do the job," Gardner told Hammerli, "I'd like to go fishing in Canada." Hammerli agreed. "Fishing," Hammerli explains, "means going through the RFP [request for proposal] route" to find a suitable contractor.

As Gardner tells it, his lab at DREO was "one of the few government labs that was doing work in batteries and fuel cells. So we were invited to submit proposals to the NRC for funding under the National

---

* In recent years Hammerli has actively promoted hydrogen technology development in Canada, serving along with David Scott and Geoffrey Ballard on the federal Hydrogen Technology Advisory Group and around the world through the International Energy Agency. Today he is research adviser at the alternative energy division of Canada's Ministry of Energy and Technology.

Energy Program." And at NRC, "basically the electrochemical side was being looked after by Hammerli." Gardner and Hammerli together worked on drafting the RFP that led to the Ballard bid.

Through this convoluted series of connections, therefore, the first Ballard contract was funded with money from the National Energy Program that the NRC passed on to Gardner at DREO to spend and administer. And although Gardner became the official "scientific authority" for the Ballard project, Hammerli was the unofficial co-authority and was also involved in reading the reports and inspecting and evaluating the work.

It is fortunate that Hammerli was the person at NRC holding the purse strings. "I was criticized," he says, "for wasting money on this white elephant," the PEM fuel cell, "which nobody wanted because, after all, everybody knew that the alkaline system was best. I've never been afraid to say that the alkaline system has problems and that each system needs to be looked at. And I felt that for several reasons this was an opportunity for Canada."

The military significance of the project should not be exaggerated. Although technically the contract came from the Canadian military, its explicit intention was to create a technology with civilian uses as well. Moreover, it was in no way tied to a particular military application. (A few years later, to justify the third Ballard contract, a military application, namely a portable field generator, was identified and specified. But by then the Ballard cell was already making waves in the private and civilian sector, and the military interest became secondary.)

And so in 1983 the RFP went out from Chris Gardner's office. Initially it was to be a contract spanning three fiscal years with funding of $170,000 per year. Because of a delay in being tendered, in the end it ran closer to two and one-half years at a total cost of $495,000. It called for a program to develop a "low cost" PEM fuel cell that could run on "impure hydrogen produced from reforming a liquid fuel such as methanol" and "capable of meeting a number of military and civilian applications." Among the latter would be "as portable generators for cottage, boat, and industrial use as well as the prime power source for hybrid electric vehicles and in other transportation applications."

Regular progress reports would be required, and at the end of the contract three prototype fuel cell stacks in the fifty to one hundred watt range and "representing the final selection of technology" would be delivered to DREO for evaluation.

Ironically, although the Ballard project started with National Energy Program money channelled through the NRC, within the first year a new federal government came in under Prime Minister Brian Mulroney. The energy program at NRC was cancelled and funding dried up. The Department of National Defense (DND) picked up the rest of the tab for the first Ballard contract and then also funded two subsequent Ballard fuel cell contracts. "So, from 1983 to 1989 the funding source was almost entirely DND," says Gardner. "But it's also true that if that NEP carrot had not been held out at the beginning, it probably never would have happened."

Small
is BEAUTIFUL

"Hey, this is something we can do," Keith Prater enthused in the summer of 1983, when he and his partners at Ballard Research saw the request from DND for bids on the fuel cell. "Let's pursue it. It might very well turn into something." Ballard was trying to diversify and was looking at all sorts of things outside their specialty, such as giftware, laser etching, and computers. And suddenly, here was a technology in their area of competence—electrochemistry— that the government was eager to fund. "Now, I'd be lying to you if I said I had a vision that it would become as big as it is," says Prater, looking back at the turning point in his professional life. "But it certainly looked like something that might have practical applications."

Of the three Ballard partners, Prater was the trained chemist and the one who was plugged into the international electrochemistry network. He had been reading the journals and going to conferences on power sources for many years. He knew many of the specialists in the field and offered to get on the phone to find out more about PEM fuel cells. One of Prater's contacts, James Huff, had become the leader of a group at Los Alamos National Laboratory doing studies of fuel cells for transportation. Earlier, Huff had headed catalyst work at Allis-Chalmers when that company built its fuel cell tractor in the late 1950s. By 1983 Huff and his colleagues at Los Alamos were probably the best informed people in the world on PEM technology.

The Los Alamos group varied between ten and twenty people with an annual budget of about one million dollars. "We did a lot of modelling and feasibility studies, and a fair amount of basic research," says Huff, who retired after a career that eventually included several years working for Ballard Power in the early 1990s. The focus at Los Alamos was not on building hardware of their own. They *did* build and test some small, individual cells, but they made no attempt to put these together into practical stacks. This would have diverted them into engineering problems that were not their primary concern. Instead, they tackled more basic challenges, such as improving the design of the electrodes and greatly reducing the amount of platinum and other noble metal catalysts used in the cells. Mainly, though, they took cells and cell stacks that came to them from private corporations such as GE and tested their power, efficiency and other characteristics. Then they plugged the information into computers to see whether such cells and stacks, if made large enough, could be used as viable sources of power for vehicles.

Prater flew down to Albuquerque, New Mexico, rented a car and drove up through desert country to Los Alamos. The government-run techno-town clings to the slopes of a series of connected mesas and includes shopping areas, restaurants, and housing where most of the employees live. At the time, it was still in transition from the old wartime laboratory, with its wooden buildings, to the diversified modern facility that it is today. Huff's lab and office were "outside the fence," the area where secret military research was conducted, so Prater needed no special security clearance for his visit.

Huff took Prater around his lab, explaining the technology and showing him the available hardware. GE had sent Huff some PEM cells as part of a contract aiming to reduce the amount of platinum in each cell and find alternatives to the costly membrane available at that time. Huff told Prater that of the many fuel cell types, he thought PEM had by far the greatest promise, especially for transportation.

The surprising thing to Huff was how little attention had been paid to PEM. "There really had not been any funding at all in that area since Gemini," he says. "We took a look and said, performance is not the problem, it's cost." In fact, the PEM cell was then not as powerful as some other types, and GE had essentially dropped it. But no great breakthroughs in electrochemistry were required. And with improved engineering, Huff thought, it probably could be made powerful enough even to run a car. (That is precisely what happened when Ballard got to work on it.) Prater was impressed by PEM's potential.

Ballard Research had many of the skilled people and specialized equipment to make a convincing bid on the fuel cell project. But Prater thought more was needed. "To make it a credible proposal we were going to have to have relationships with people who knew some of the other stuff," such as polymer membranes and noble metal catalysts. So he followed up the Los Alamos trip with visits to scientists at universities in BC and Alberta. Several agreed to be listed as consultant on the project, essentially to "beef up" the proposal and enhance Ballard's credentials.

Prater took the lead in drafting the Ballard Research proposal. But winning such a government contract could involve more than simply sending in a document. Geoffrey Ballard knew from his experience in government that you sometimes had to bolster a bid with direct personal lobbying. He dispatched his new, young marketing manager, David McLeod, to Ottawa to talk to Chris Gardner and

Martin Hammerli and put forward the company's case. McLeod followed up with countless phone calls over the months while the bid was being reviewed.

Geoffrey Ballard did not go himself, says McLeod, because in earlier dealings with the federal government he had acquired a less-than-favourable reputation among some bureaucrats. "Geoff could be very abrasive," says McLeod. "He did not suffer fools." He sometimes had a way with government types that could annoy them without even trying. Ballard himself was quite aware of this personal shortcoming. "You go off and sell it," he told McLeod.

McLeod worried about the potential political problem, due to the fact that the electrochemistry industry seemed to be concentrated in central Canada. Most previous work in this and many other high-tech fields had gone to companies and laboratories in Ontario and Quebec. And of the six companies that DND initially considered to be likely prospects with the requisite competence, four were in Ontario, one in Quebec and only Ballard was located in western Canada. Several other companies also submitted bids, but most came nowhere near to satisfying the criteria set out by DND. In fact, only Ballard and one other turned out to be genuine contenders.

Chris Gardner and Martin Hammerli reviewed the proposals and Ballard won the contract walking away. Ballard was the "clear winner," Chris Gardner recalls. "They put in a very strong proposal." Ballard Research had shown that it understood the work that was expected and had a well-thought-out plan to tackle it. It had also listed its excellent equipment. Largely due to Ballard's battery contract with Amoco, says McLeod, "we had everything that you could possibly need in an electrochemistry laboratory."

Perhaps even more important was the long list of highly trained people, many of them with Ph.D.s, that worked at Ballard. Says McLeod, "People began to realize that this was a formidable group of people. Not that they would all necessarily be working on the fuel cell," he adds, "but just that they would be there, that this was the working environment." To Chris Gardner it was important that particular people were going to be responsible for the work itself. Paul Howard and Keith Prater, for example, were specifically written into the contract as project manager and chief scientist respectively.

"So that made the document fairly easy to sell," McLeod says. "Now, what wasn't so easy to sell was the concept that putting it in western Canada was in everyone's best interest. But in the end there was the opinion that this was a very credible bid and that, if something was going to happen with the fuel cell, Ballard may have the best chance."

In late 1983 the Ballard partners learned they had hit pay dirt and lost little time in getting started. But it was hardly a lucrative contract. Half a million dollars for some twenty-eight months of work was not a lot of money to cover salaries, equipment, supplies, and travel expenses. By comparison, in the two-year period 1959 and 1960 when GE's PEM project was in its early stages (prior to the much larger Gemini program) the company spent a bit more than $1 million in the much more valuable dollars of that era. The Ballard fuel cell was to be R & D on a shoestring.

Tight money meant cramped quarters. Ballard rented space in a small industrial bay that was just across an alleyway from an auto body shop. For years, while developing a clean and quiet technology, the fuel cell team had to endure the shriek of disk grinders next door. In summer, when the doors were open, the fumes from polyester resins and other solvents wafted in.

The entire place had only the floor space of a modest family home. And fully half of that was given over to the separate lab and office of polymer specialist Alfred (Fred or Freddy) Steck. The Swiss-born scientist had been hired mainly to work on other projects, but a few years later he would help develop a new fuel cell membrane. (Today Steck is Ballard Power's vice-president for research and development, president of its subsidiary, Ballard Advanced Materials, and in effect the company's chief scientist.) The fuel cell area was divided between the lab and a small office.

This humble Ballard annex was adjacent to, but physically distinct from, the battery building. Putting it into a separate building was a calculated move. It made clear that none of the equipment or technology there was in any way owned by Amoco, which was paying the rent on the main building through its battery contract.

And there was another consideration. Like most government contracts, the one with DND gave ownership of the narrowly specified technology to the Canadian government. But the Ballard partners realized that the fuel cell had great potential, so they decided to do parallel work on certain aspects of it, which they paid for themselves. During the course of the first contract, they tried to match the government funding, more or less. It wasn't exactly a dollar-for-dollar cash match, says Paul Howard. They counted contributions in kind, including the time that Howard and others at Ballard devoted to the project. But they felt that if they put in close to fifty per cent of the expenses they would improve their bargaining position. As a result, Ballard was eventually able to negotiate a licence for the part of the early fuel cell technology that DND had funded, for which the company paid a royalty.

With the work space arranged, they went looking for the right person to head the project. Their advertisement was answered by David Watkins, a burly 29-year-old chemical engineer with a degree from the Technical University of Nova Scotia. Keith Prater praises him as a "try-it, break-it, fix-it kind of engineer." Watkins loved to ride motorcycles, owned several of them and regularly rode them to work. For a while he let his hair grow long, and in his black leathers he reminded Paul Howard of a Hell's Angel. "He could scare you in a bar, if he wanted to," says Howard, "but actually he's a teddy bear." Watkins' prior work experience had been on unrelated technologies such as turning sewage sludge into animal feed and helping to build natural gas plants.

Two even younger men were hired to join Watkins. The first was Danny Epp, an athletically built avid sailor who hopes some day to put a fuel cell into his sailboat. Epp studied mechanical design engineering at the British Columbia Institute of Technology (BCIT) and worked in pneumatic engineering before joining Paul Howard on John Horton's submarine project. When Horton leased it out for exploration work, Epp went with the sub as operations manager when it was shipped to Colombia on its futile hunt for Spanish treasure. After that search did not pan out, he returned to Vancouver. Scouting around for something new, he contacted Paul Howard at just the right time to join the fuel cell team.

Epp's forte was the day-to-day building of hardware. "David Watkins was not a mechanical guy," says Howard, "so Danny was that pair of hands. He was very meticulous, a really good, hands-on mechanical guy. The kind of guy you would like to let play with your car." For Epp, as for the others, fuel cells were a totally new thing. "It's the first I'd heard of them," he says. And he had no idea what to expect. Little did he realize that it would change his life, and that he would still be employed at Ballard fifteen years later. (In fact, because a generous block of Ballard shares was eventually given to each member of the original fuel cell team, it made him quite well off.) "All I saw at that time was a design challenge, just another short-term project."

Unlike Watkins, Epp had specialized experience that made him ideal for tweaking a system that worked under pressure, even if at first it was not very high pressure. "Remember, I came from the submarine design world. So I was used to designing things that had O-rings in them, and pressure housings, and phlanges. I'd made similar equipment for the battery company. We were using similar materials."

Next to be hired was Ken Dircks, another young BCIT grad and a chemical engineering technologist.* His role was mainly as an instrumentation expert. He took the assembled cells and cell stacks, hooked them up to hydrogen and oxygen supplies and put them on testing stands. Then he ran them for hours, days, weeks at a time, monitoring them carefully, measuring the results and recording everything for evaluation. When the fuel cell began to get attention, Dircks was often the point man, the one who showed it off in the lab to visiting scientists, government officials, and corporate types. For kicks he would use the fuel cell to zap his lunch in a microwave oven.

The fourth member of the early fuel cell team was not a technical person at all but the marketing manager, David McLeod. With a flair for witty stories and the thickest set of eyebrows west of Scotland, McLeod uses as an e-mail moniker "Mcibrows." He enjoyed the personal confidence and support of Geoffrey Ballard and had virtual free rein to visit Ottawa at company expense and lobby for support. He usually accompanied Watkins to technical conferences to glad-hand the scientists and steer them in the direction of Watkins' displays of impressive fuel cell results. He called their song and dance the "David and David Show."

As the Ballard fuel cell advanced, McLeod became an increasingly important player. "My day-to-day contact was mainly with Watkins," recalls DND's Chris Gardner, "but the other person who played a really active role was David McLeod. He kept tabs on everything. Without McLeod the later contracts probably never would have happened. He spent a lot of time beating the bushes and talking to the military people." For the technical team, McLeod was their cheerleader, their gadfly, their late-night companion, and confidant when they put in long binges of work.

---

* Dircks is the person who nearly broiled me with a bank of aircraft landing lights while demonstrating an early Ballard cell when I first visited the Ballard lab in 1989.

Raised mainly in small-town southern Alberta, McLeod left home at fifteen, dropping out of school and running off to the bright lights of Winnipeg. He spent years living as a virtual street kid, supporting himself by hustling at pool and trying to be a writer. He became an office boy at a large insurance company and, on the side, worked at a men's clothing shop. He came to work so well dressed that the insurance company president asked him where he got his clothes. "That must be how I got into marketing," he laughs. "It's all about style."

But his path to marketing was anything but direct. One day he walked into the computer room at the insurance company. Captivated by the technology, he soon became a junior operator, learning how to work the IBM 1401. It was the early 1960s, when the computer was housed in an air-conditioned inner sanctum and cranked its way through thousands of punch cards to digest data. "That's where I learned the basics of what later became computer science," he says. "At that time, you couldn't even take a degree in it." He was so good around computers, and so turned on by them, that they took over his life. "But what I really got good at was explaining computers to people. And that's where I started to make the transition from being sort of a technical weenie to being more of a systems guy and eventually a marketing guy."

In 1967 he married for the first time and moved to Edmonton to take a better job in computers. Pretty soon, though, he was drinking excessively. He never actually got fired from a job because of booze, but it was often a close shave. "You cannot drink as I did and maintain much focus for long. The only thing that saved my ass," he says, was moving on just in time. To a new city. To a new job. To new friends. He calls it the "geographic cure," but, of course, it didn't work. By the time he reached Toronto and got a job with Digital Equipment, he was a "full-blown drunk." Eventually, he says, "you run out of friends, you have no family, you have nothing," so you make a "very basic decision" to give it up and enter a recovery program. "I did that in 1977 and I haven't had a drink since."

Next McLeod moved to Vancouver and started life over, with no material possessions and two young children. He moved from job to job, trying "goofy things," such as directing over one hundred women who were trying to sell dresses through Tupperware-style "party" events. Eventually, he got back into what he knew best, computers.

Meanwhile, through a private connection, he got to know a fellow resident of Vancouver's North Shore, Geoffrey Ballard. One thing they had in common was that Ballard, too, had given up drinking. In the business world, he had found himself often taking a drink at lunch and again at dinner. "I was drinking too much by my standards," Ballard says, "and it was affecting my judgement." In 1979 he gave up alcohol completely for ten years, but today is a social drinker.

By the time McLeod met Ballard, Ballard Research had the battery contract with Amoco but was trying to find new lines of work. The Amoco contract was profitable—funding was running at about $3 million a year—but not secure. The Ballard partners worried that if Amoco cancelled the contract, which eventually happened in 1987, they essentially had no business. Sitting together in a White Spot restaurant one day, McLeod told Ballard about his computer marketing work. It happened that computers were one of the new areas of technology Ballard was considering. "Why don't you come and work for me," Ballard said. "See if you can help us to diversify. I think you've failed often enough that you probably now know what to do. The measure of the man is whether you get up and try again. Maybe now it's time to hit one out of the ballpark."

McLeod was touched. "Geoff was the first person who ever gave me credit for failing. Everybody else gave me shit." Ballard came to treat McLeod with almost fatherly affection, and like Chris Gardner, he gives McLeod a lot of credit for the early success of the fuel cell team. "He had a lot of energy and encouraged them" at every stage, says Ballard. His enthusiasm and drive "spurred them on." Like the others, McLeod, was eventually given a generous bonus in Ballard shares. But first, years of hard work lay ahead.

The project began with David Watkins learning all he could about fuel cells. Martin Hammerli passed on his own knowledge of PEM cells and found that Watkins absorbed it "like a sponge." Hammerli found him to be "a very fast study, and one of the few people I've met in my career who was not afraid to learn from someone else." Watkins also delved into the existing literature on fuel cells and began to see ways they could be improved. Hammerli calls him a "tremendous engineer and innovator. His mind works in a very creative way." With Watkins busy sopping up information or away on trips to fuel cell conferences, much of the day-to-day work was left to Danny Epp and Ken Dircks.

The first challenge was simply to master the state of the art. This meant studying what had been done by GE, trying to duplicate the earlier results and then seeing what could be done to engineer it better. Watkins quickly came to the same conclusion as James Huff at Los Alamos. "My first three months," he told *The Toronto Star*, "I read all this crap on them and decided, 'Hell, no one's done any engineering'" on them.[17] But he not only read. DND had supplied him with an old GE fuel cell that he could take apart and study. Ballard Research also bought one of the cheap Sammer PEM cells that were being sold for lecture and demonstration use.

To build their own fuel cells they bought a sample of the commercially available polymer membrane made by Dupont and sold under the trade name Nafion®. When it arrived, the Ballard team knew so little about it that a comical scene ensued. The government scientists, Gardner and Hammerli, happened to be visiting for the first design review. The Ballard team gave them a tour of the tiny lab. There was precious little to see, just a few workbenches, tools, and a fume hood. To justify the visit and kill time, they decided to unpack the membrane material, which had just arrived, and look at it together.

The Nafion®, a clear plastic, came rolled up in a shipping tube and was itself wrapped in plastic. "We pulled it out of the cardboard tube," says Epp, "and unrolled a sheet of it. And we cut a piece of it off. We all looked at it and felt it and passed it around. 'Yeah, that looks like pretty nice stuff,' we agreed." It was flexible. The edges were not sharp. It seemed easy to cut. "Then we all left the lab and concluded the review meeting." When Gardner and Hammerli were gone, Watkins and Epp went back to the lab to get down to business, planning to use a piece of the membrane to make the first fuel cell of their own. They began to cut another piece off the roll, and as they tugged at it they realized it was just the polyethylene wrapping that came to protect the Nafion®. Epp laughs at the absurdity of admiring something not very different from a very thin plastic report cover. "We had been showing polyethylene to everybody, and we all thought it was wonderful stuff." Watkins, who was appalled, said to Epp, "Don't you ever dare tell anyone."

Soon they were building their own cells. The first step was to make the membrane electrode assembly. "That's the heart of the fuel cell," says Epp. They were by no means reinventing the wheel. "There's sort of a recipe for making these things. It's in the literature, in the patents. It's explained." The assembly consists of a piece of membrane sandwiched between electrodes on each side and then bonded together.

To make the electrodes they took pieces of porous carbon fibre paper and coated them on one side with platinum. They bought the precious metal in the form of so-called platinum black, which is a powder that is so finely divided it has an extremely large surface area for a given weight. They mixed this powder with a binder, which was essentially a form of Teflon®, painted it onto one side of the carbon paper and baked it so the platinum black was well attached. Next, the platinum side of each paper electrode was placed against the Nafion® membrane, and the thin sandwich of materials was again baked to bond it into a single unit.

"What you're trying to do," explains Keith Prater, "is create a situation where the platinum black is connected to the carbon paper, because that's where the current is going to go. That's the way the electricity flows." At the same time, "the platinum black is also in touch with the Nafion®, because that's where the hydrogen ions, the protons, are going to go. And the gases come through the porous carbon paper" from the side that is away from the membrane.

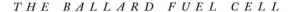

T H E   B A L L A R D   F U E L   C E L L

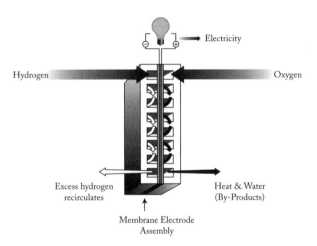

Hydrogen

Oxygen

Electricity

Excess hydrogen recirculates

Heat & Water (By-Products)

Membrane Electrode Assembly

Cell uses either pure (gaseous) hyrogen, or a hydrogen-rich fuel, such as methanol, which must be processed first before the resulting hydrogen is fed into the cell. Hydrogen and oxygen are combined electrochemically in fuel cell to produce electricity. Only by-products are heat and water.

The gases—hydrogen comes in on one side and oxygen or air on the other—are fed to the membrane electrode assembly through tiny channels in the flow-field plates, which are pressed up against the carbon paper. In the Ballard fuel cell these plates also conduct away the electric current. In GE's Gemini fuel cells the plates were made of niobium, but Ballard's task was to design a low-cost device, so sheets of graphite (solid carbon) were substituted. Danny Epp machined fine grooves into the electrode side of each plate to distribute the gases.

The other components of the early Ballard test cells included Plexiglas end plates to hold the units together, wicks made of polypropylene to draw off the water created by the reaction, and O-rings pressed up against the membrane electrode assembly on each side to seal the unit. For the very first attempts, Watkins and company relied in part on pieces of hardware they had cannibalized from the small GE lecture cells. "I took some of those components," says Danny Epp, "and modified them to make our own little single cell."

"Little" was no exaggeration. The first one they built measured only about seven and one half centimetres (three inches) on each side. It looked like a toy and was easy to take apart and reassemble. It ran at ordinary ("ambient") atmospheric pressure and a temperature of about 55°C. To keep the experiments simple, it was first fed extremely pure hydrogen and oxygen.

Small it may have been, but this toy delivered the goods. They hooked the wires from the cell to a tiny light bulb and opened the valves on the tanks of gas. Hydrogen and oxygen flowed into the cell and—*voila!*—the light bulb glowed. They laughed and grinned and slapped each other on the back. "The first time we got electricity out of it, we were all ecstatic," Epp recalls. "I mean, we were pretty thrilled. Because, you've got to remember, none of us had ever seen a fuel cell work before." Fred Steck, the polymer chemist working next door, heard the commotion and came running in to see what was up. By then a tiny dribble of water had leaked out onto the work table. "The droplet of water was the first product from the fuel cell reaction," he says. "And indeed, to have a little light bulb glowing— that was a breakthrough. I think Dircks still has the cell in his office."

They called their first cell design the Mark I. To nobody's surprise, when Dircks hooked it up to his test equipment it put out very little power. "All we were trying to do was to establish the state of the art in Canada," says Epp. To do that, and to learn more about their cell and its quirks, they made more of them and tried them in different configurations. Some were run on pure hydrogen and oxygen, others on hydrogen and air. Still others were tested using a hydrogen-rich gas that simulated what would result from liquid methanol that was reformed by existing techniques. (DND ultimately wanted a fuel cell that could run on liquid fuels.) This gas contained traces of carbon monoxide and a fairly high level—twenty-five per cent—of carbon dioxide.

Besides varying the gases, they made cells with smaller and smaller amounts of platinum on the electrodes. The ones with large amounts, comparable to GE's Gemini cells, worked well. With reduced amounts of platinum, though, the cells often worked nearly as well for the first hundred hours or so; then performance began to drop off significantly. They saw how crucial it was to run their trials for long periods. In one trial, after 120 hours the power output was still ninety-six per cent of the original "baseline" figure. After 1,500 hours, though, it had dropped to seventy-three per cent. With slightly higher amounts of platinum, the cell gave ninety-eight per cent of its power after 243 hours but dropped to eighty-seven per cent after 886 hours.

Other labs' experience suggested that the catalyst on the anode was being "poisoned" by trace amounts of carbon monoxide in the hydrogen flow. Tests confirmed this. The solution was to use a catalyst on the anode that consisted of a mixture of platinum and ruthenium, another noble metal. After running such a cell for over 1,000 hours they found that it still put out ninety-four per cent of its baseline power. They were learning, and fast.

They moved on briefly to a cell with a slightly different shape, or "geometry," which they called the Mark II, but it was fundamentally the same. Next came an attempt to duplicate the performance of the GE cell of the 1960s. They had access to an internal report from GE and Los Alamos showing the design. "So we copied that," says Epp, "and called it Mark III. And the Mark III worked just as badly or as well as GE's performance data suggested. It was a slight variation on what had flown in Gemini, but essentially that state of the art."

With Mark III they were getting serious. It had an active surface area nearly twice as large as the earlier cells. It ran at a higher temperature, up to 71°C, and under pressure, which could be controlled by a pneumatic piston set into one of the end plates. To accommodate this pressure, the end plates were made of aluminum instead of plexiglas. The Mark III was a big step forward, delivering roughly twice the power of the Mark I. By the end of their first year, they were already producing about the same power as GE had done after many years of development.

Next they bolted groups of matching Mark III cells together, like slices of bread in a loaf, and made cell stacks. But this brought complications. In single cells heat dissipated easily, but inside a stack of cells it tended to build up to an unacceptable level. They had to insert plates with cooling water channels into the stack at regular intervals to draw off the excess heat. Another challenge was to make sure the flow of gases to each cell in the stack was adequate and nearly uniform. This required feeding the gases through a properly designed manifold, just as a branching manifold distributes gas from the carburetor to the cylinders in a conventional car engine. They tried a five-cell stack and soon moved on to one with eight cells. Running on pure hydrogen and air, it produced 130 watts of power, which was already higher than DND had specified in its contract.

The Ballard founders were elated with the progress. None of them took a hands-on role in the development, though. The three partners were much more focused on running the much larger battery side of the business. But because it was such a small company, there were plenty of opportunities to discuss the fuel cell problems and suggest solutions. Geoffrey Ballard and his partners frequently got together with the fuel cell team informally and threw ideas around, often over a cup of coffee. This fit Ballard's overall philosophy and approach to science management. "Yeah," he says, "I'd go down to the lab, put my feet up and let them tell me what they were doing. Rather than having them come up to the office and report."

To David McLeod, this casual approach and informal atmosphere is just what was required. In 1989, he expounded on how the fuel cell technical team was given the freedom to pursue the technology without bureaucratic shackles. "The personality of the head man, Geoffrey Ballard, created an environment" in which this rapid advance could take place. "You've got to have the ability to try things without having to compare five reports as to why you want to do that and fifteen reports to cover your ass when it didn't work." You go into very large research houses, he says, and the cautious, paper-burdened approach is evident in the labs. "Everything is managed administratively, but many times little attention is given to the technology."

The fuel cell team enjoyed a large dose of encouragement from the top as well. "Passion drove David Watkins," said McLeod. "He couldn't let this device sit. It haunted him. It drove him nuts. He had to understand it, know what to do with it. And that's what was created in this building by Geoffrey Ballard. He understands that kind of guy. He gives him license. He lets him go." McLeod saw Ballard's own passion and zealotry as a positive force. "He's crazy in a lot of respects, because you have to be. You have to have this absolute, blind commitment to the thing that transcends everything. There's skill in giving a Watkins what he needs. You've got to stroke these people, make them believe that what they're doing is really important stuff. And, of course, if that ingredient exists, miracles happen."

Geoffrey Ballard was not alone, of course. Paul Howard was the administrator and held the purse strings for the project, but in his modest way he is quick to credit his partners. "Keith understood the science," he says. "And Geoff is no slouch either, in electrochemistry or mechanically. He has a good understanding of it. He digs in, too, and he challenges. He can challenge even the mechanical designs of things, because he's a practical kind of guy, too." As for Howard himself, "I'm more a details kind of guy, and I've got the patience for it. So, as a result I can relate more to Danny and the others."

Since the work involved mainly Howard's specialty, mechanical engineering, he often dropped into the lab to discuss the technology. "Paul would come through more than anybody else," says McLeod, "because he always walked through both labs. He was really keen on having the lab in nice shape," in case somebody came in from outside the company to look at the technology. "He prided himself on clean floors and things like that. He didn't like clutter." Howard did not have to play the heavy very often, though. It was enough that everyone knew he might suddenly show up. "Yeah, I was the neatnik," Howard admits.

The rapid progress being made was not a result of big money being thrown at the technical problems. Quite the opposite. The fuel cell budget was so tight that the technical team had to cut corners wherever possible. Instead of ordering specialized, top-of-the-line equipment from scientific suppliers, whenever possible they walked a few blocks down the street and bought off-the-shelf stuff—usually made in Hong Kong—at Canadian Tire, Canada's leading automotive and hardware retail chain. Before heading for the store, Danny Epp often scrounged first through the trash bins at the battery building.

Part of Epp's task was to design and cut the grooves in the flow field plates that channel the gases to the electrodes. This was precise work that could best be done by a computer-controlled engraving machine. Here again, top-of-the-line equipment would have been prohibitively expensive. But Epp knew of some very small computerized machines used for engraving trophies and signs. "We couldn't afford to buy such a machine, so I went to one of the trophy manufacturers here in town and asked if we could borrow one of theirs." He paid for his time on the machine of course. "But after a few hours of working with their machine I ran out of money. So I made a barter deal with them. In exchange for its use I would design and build—here in our shop—equipment for them to hold signage and trophies." He did that, he says, in his spare time.

Spare time for the technical team was an oxymoron, though. For the first few years they literally ran themselves ragged, putting in killing hours, working weekends, threatening their home lives and marriages. They all had keys to the building and regularly stayed on late into the night, or even right through it.

For Epp, some of the longest work binges involved machining the grooves in the flow field plates and trying to find the best design. In the GE cell, which the Ballard team copied, the grooves formed a pattern of parallel channels. They all branched off at right angles from an intake channel along one side of the cell, crossed the middle of the cell, and then joined up with a similar outflow channel along the other side. This did not work very well.

The water created in the fuel cell reaction was the problem. "In fact," says Epp, "as soon as you opened up the cell—after you had operated it—you could literally see where water was covering large portions of the active area of the cell. You could see large areas that were obviously inactive, because they were flooded." The basic design of the flow fields was flawed.

It was Ken Dircks who first came up with the idea that led to a solution. "Instead of making a whole bunch of parallel paths," Dircks suggested, "why don't we make a single path that zigzags in a serpentine pattern, thereby ensuring that we force the water out using the pressure of the air or oxygen, rather than a wick." To make this work even better, Watkins later explained to a journalist, "You blow a little bit more oxidant than you need through the cell to remove the water."[18]

Even with this new concept, there were many possible patterns, and some worked better than others. Epp became engrossed in optimizing the design. He would spend hours making a pattern and trying it in a test cell. If it did not work to his satisfaction, he would order some pizza or Chinese food and stay late in the lab, engraving a new pattern of zigzag grooves in the pure, black graphite. Geoffrey Ballard recalls dropping in at the fuel cell lab long after business hours and finding Epp busy at his machine, with a cup of coffee to keep him awake. "Danny just played with the patterns," says Ballard, "and if one didn't work, he'd be there till midnight trying a new groove pattern." Even when Epp did go home, he often found himself lying awake at night, picturing the maddening lines in his mind.

"We came and went nights, weekends, as we pleased," says Epp, and it certainly added some stress to his marriage. Unlike Ballard's motel in Arizona, they did not have a couch or place to take a nap. But there was no point in sleeping, says Epp. "We were always doing something. If you were going to sleep, you might as well go home."

And then, "when we achieved really high performances, we stayed even longer to make sure that we weren't fooling ourselves, that these were real numbers."

Changing the flow field design proved to be a crucial innovation. "Presto!" says Epp. "We immediately doubled and quadrupled the performance of the cell, within only a couple of weeks. That was probably in 1985 or early 1986. And that was a breakthrough." The patents on the flow fields were eventually issued in Epp's name, and they still reside in his office at Ballard. He takes down the elegant patent plaques and shows them off with unabashed pride.

Other changes in the fuel cell also came rapidly. It was just the way they worked. "Every day we would look at the results of what we had," says Epp. "We would sit down and do some modifications to the design of the hardware. I would remake something, experiment with something, give it to Ken and he would test it." They could see the results promptly and make further changes. "We had very quick—what we call 'hardware iteration.' We were able to assess, redesign, remake, and test in a very fast cycle. We could do that in a couple of days."

This was one of the real pay-offs from having a small group and very little bureaucracy. Unlike at big corporations, the Ballard team did not have to file reports with the head office. "And we didn't have to go through a funding cycle," says Geoffrey Ballard. In large corporations, when someone gets a good idea they often have to write it up and wait for the next year's funding. "It's absolutely incredible, the checks and balances" at giant companies. But the Ballard technical team could just get on with the work and experiment with new ideas, all right there at the workbench. Small, in this case, really was beautiful.

"They went from an idea to a working product in only a year," says Ballard. Part of the explanation was inherent in the PEM fuel cell itself. "It has been a very forgiving technology. From the very beginning. Every time you touch it, it lends itself to what you're trying to do. And the system gets simpler, not more complex—which is the other measure of a good technology." This was very different from his experience with the rechargeable lithium battery, which kept presenting obstacles and getting more complex at every turn. "A technology that is going to become commercial is one where, every time you tackle it, you get further insight and it becomes simpler." One success leads to another. "And it's very exciting when you see that happening."

The experts from DND and the NRC dropped in to check on things every four to six months. And Watkins filed regular reports to them. "David was most talented," says McLeod. "He had a very good way of writing reports that were concise and simple." Watkins was also extremely thorough and conscientious about the results, never exaggerating the achievement. "He'd never show a voltage or power curve that did not have the caveats of how many hours it had run and under precisely what conditions. He was very specific." And that differentiated Ballard from other companies. "In later years, for example, Watkins would not publish anything unless it had run for 150 hours. He had a very tough template on that."

By mid-1986, shortly after the end of the first contract, Ballard had built a twelve-cell stack that produced 280 watts of power. This was far better than the fifty to 100 watts that had been foreseen in the contract. The project officials in Ottawa were understandably very happy with the progress. "They did a tremendous job," says Chris Gardner, "right from the start. The performance that they were achieving by the end of the contract was a lot more than we had ever expected." Gardner goes even further. "It was definitely a high point of my own career, that's for sure. You certainly don't get involved in many projects that are as successful as this one. So, it was pretty exciting, just watching it develop. It was a lot of fun."

Three Guys
and a PRAYER

For the fun at Ballard to continue there would have to be steady funding after the first contract ended. Initially, "it was a pretty low-level project," says Danny Epp. "The future looked quite precarious." The initial government money had come from a source—the National Energy Program, channelled via the National Research Council—that had dried up entirely. But Ballard had delivered substantially more than expected, says Keith Prater. "DND was surprised, and they scurried around to find enough money to hold the thing together for another year while they figured out what to do with it." What DND came up with was a one-year follow-on contract providing $248,000 to keep the work going. This was not hard for Ottawa to justify.

Ballard's early success, delivering roughly double the anticipated power levels, was highly unusual. "In most such contracts with universities," says Geoffrey Ballard, "the researchers never quite get to

the results, but they always need more money to try and get there."
David McLeod is more scathing about the frequent lack of results
in such contracts. For many companies and labs, especially in the
US, he says, "fuel cells were basically just a source of perpetual
funding. There was no incentive to deliver a product, because if
you did, you'd lose your funding." Typically, he says, "in the wonderful world of government-sponsored research, you can be soft on
the deliverables."

With funding for another year in place, the technical team carried
on. Outside of Canada, PEM was still barely recognized as a fuel cell
technology worth developing further. In the US virtually all the R & D
money was going into other types of fuel cells. Within a few more
months, though, Ballard was to make fuel cell history, achieving power
levels never before seen and putting the company and its PEM technology front and centre in the international fuel cell world.

A primary goal of the DND contracts was to find cheaper materials
and lower the cost of PEM cells. One way was to reduce the amount
of platinum required. Another was to find a way around the high
price of Dupont's Nafion® membrane.

Dupont had put many years and umpteen million dollars into
developing its membrane. Its production required at least nine complex chemical reaction processes, some of them quite hazardous and
demanding tight controls to ensure workplace safety. Dupont was
manufacturing it in relatively small quantities mainly for use in the
industrial-scale electrolysis of sodium chloride to produce chlorine
gas. Overall chlorine plant investment was so enormous that the cost
of the membrane was a comparatively minor consideration. Nafion®
was also being used by the US Navy to generate oxygen through the

electrolysis of sea water on board submerged submarines. (The oxygen was breathed by the crew and the hydrogen was vented.) In military applications, too, cost was a secondary consideration. Hence there was no market pressure on Dupont to lower its selling price and little prospect of such a reduction. In search of an alternative, Watkins, the leader of the fuel cell technical team, looked elsewhere.

Dow Chemical had developed an experimental polymer membrane of its own, also mainly for industrial electrolysis. It had a lower electrical resistance than Nafion® and would be shown to permit a higher power density. In the mid-1980s it was still at such an early stage that its properties varied unpredictably from batch to batch. Although the membrane had not yet been released for sale, Watkins and McLeod visited Dow and obtained a sample. But Watkins had no particular expectations for the Dow membrane. Busy with building and testing other cells using Nafion®, he did not immediately substitute the Dow membrane for the Nafion® and test it. It sat around the lab for several months. In late 1986, though, Watkins finally got around to taking a piece of the Dow membrane and putting it into a single cell.

When Dircks hooked it up and tested it, the Ballard team could hardly believe what their instruments were telling them. The cell seemed to be kicking out four times the current of the Nafion® cells. Watkins was so excited that he phoned McLeod at his nearby North Vancouver home. It was 10 p.m., but late hours were nothing unusual. He asked McLeod to come right over to the lab. Dramatically, he placed the little cell in McLeod's hand so he could feel it as it ran at this totally unexpected level of power. Watkins, McLeod recalls, "was just beside himself. And we sat there damned near all night, talking." They knew right away that this power level changed everything for the PEM fuel cell's market potential. "I've done my job," Watkins told McLeod, "Now it's time for you to do yours."

In reality, Watkins' job was just beginning. The next step was to try the Dow membrane in a multicelled stack. They assembled one with six cells. Possibly because it *looked* just like the previous stacks, they took no special precautions. Hooking it up to their standard test equipment, as they had done so many times with earlier stacks, they left it running. Within a few minutes it generated so much power that the finger-thick electric cable leading off it got incredibly hot. As they watched, mesmerized, the bare strands of copper began to melt and fuse like liquid solder close to the end of the cable. Eventually, the cable burned right through. They hooted and jumped around in delight. Fred Steck heard them and came running in to see the burnt-out cable and distorted battery clamp that connected the cable to the cell. When David McLeod got there, the cable was still smoldering and an electrical smell pervaded the lab.

Watkins was so surprised by this result that he did not immediately announce it even within the company. The news diffused through the main building by word of mouth. Keith Prater, who was away at the time, only heard about it a few days later. "That was a reflection of Watkins' personality," Prater says. "Perhaps he didn't quite believe it himself. Perhaps he was afraid it might turn out to be not quite what he thought it was. So it wasn't a big eureka. It just sort of oozed through the building." Still, the Ballard partners were fully aware of the significance of this power boost. Geoffrey Ballard was also away at the time. When he returned, Prater grabbed him. "You've got to see this, Geoff," he said, dragging Ballard down to the lab.

Soon they were building twelve-cell stacks with the Dow membrane. These confirmed that the Ballard PEM technology was in a league all its own. "This is by far the highest reported performance of any solid polymer fuel cell that I am aware of," Watkins told the publication *Chemical Week* a few months later. The implications were clear to him. "These power densities and overload capabilities could make the electric automobile happen."[19] This was not just the idle boasting of one proud engineer. To Keith Prater it also changed the fuel cell playing field, opening up entirely new market prospects, especially in transportation. The company was soon to be on the lookout for venture capital, and its ability to find money "was in large part on the basis that we had gotten this fourfold improvement in power, and we could now extrapolate the power we could get out of the fuel cell to something that could run a car."

Even when the Ballard team was sure the spectacular results were real, they did not rush out to announce them to the world. In part, this was because of a delicate problem with Dow Chemical. "We could not technically publish those results without Dow's approval," says McLeod as he warms to the tale. "There's a whole story behind it, because we'd actually bootlegged the bloody membrane." Watkins and McLeod had gone to visit the Dow laboratory in Houston, Texas. Watkins had heard about the membrane and approached the fellow who had it to beg, borrow or steal a sample. "This guy had to figure out first of all where Vancouver even was, let alone who these two idiots in front of him were," says McLeod. "We basically conned him out of it. We gave him quite a story about what we were trying to do. And I think at the end of the day he actually felt sorry for us, so he gave us maybe a square metre of the stuff."

The way the membrane had been cadged from Dow turned out to be both good news and bad. The good news was that it had performed so well. The bad news was that it had been developed without full knowledge of the higher management at Dow. It was part of a sort of "black program." This meant that the fellow who had given them the membrane would have some explaining to do. Ballard wanted to publish the results, of course, says McLeod, "because this was the greatest thing that had happened to fuel cells in a long time.

And poor Dow was sitting there, going, 'Where did this come from? What is it? Whose is it? And do we even have a patent on it?'" McLeod heard the story of Dow's internal problem somewhat later. "That was the first question that some of the executive vice-presidents at Dow asked: 'Excuse me, like do we have a patent on this thing?' Nobody at the top knew a thing about it."

Once the complications with Dow had been sorted out, Watkins and McLeod decided to unveil the dramatic results at a fuel cell conference in Arizona. In the course of their trip, they went first to Los Alamos. The scientists there provided a useful sounding board and reality check for the Ballard team. The Los Alamos group had, after all, helped Ballard launch its project and were still virtually the only other people in North America actually working on PEM cells.

Watkins revealed that Ballard had boosted PEM power by a factor of four. While he was still speaking, Byron McCormick, the head of the fuel cell division at Los Alamos, asked McLeod to step outside and join him in his office. "I don't think you appreciate what it is you people have done," he said, "but you've made the electric vehicle possible. This is the most significant breakthrough in fuel cells that I've ever seen." McCormick suggested that Ballard should immediately join up with a powerful American industrial partner. He mentioned a few possible companies, including Allison Turbines (a division of General Motors) and Lockheed, the aerospace giant. (Today McCormick is in charge of fuel cells and other alternative energy programs at General Motors.)

Another person who listened in amazement that day was James Huff, the man who had offered advice and help to Keith Prater in 1983, when Prater was preparing to bid on the first DND contract. Huff had been doing studies on the potential of fuel cells for automobile transportation, mainly using computers to model the power and performance required. But none of the existing fuel cells was powerful enough. "In our feasibility studies," he recalls, "using the performance that was available when we did them in the early 1980s, we were right on the hairy edge of being feasible. We were hanging by our fingernails, because every design that we did had the fuel cell operating at its maximum performance capability."

This had led Huff and others to conclude that in many cases a fuel cell vehicle would only be feasible if it was a so-called hybrid system, with a large supplementary battery to provide peak power for hills and acceleration. (In 1997 Toyota unveiled just such a prototype hybrid car, and Opel followed suit in 1998.) But the Ballard results changed Huff's perspective. "Now all at once, we were no longer doing feasibility studies on the very edge of credibility. What it meant was, I was no longer designing at maximum performance. I now had some leeway."

At the fuel cell conference in Arizona, nearly all the participants were from the US, Japan or Europe. Watkins was not even on the agenda to give a formal talk or presentation. Instead, he and McLeod were relegated to a corner of the hall for a poster session. But the David and David show had something impressive to flaunt. Watkins set up a display with the graphs and power curves showing the Ballard achievement. People came by, saw the results and were utterly astounded. One of the top people from the US Department of Energy took one look and told McLeod, "My God, we've been backing the wrong technology."

The US government had been putting most of its transportation-related fuel cell money into phosphoric acid fuel cells (PAFCs). Although they were further advanced at that time, PAFCs are inherently less well-suited for transportation than PEM cells. They operate at a much higher temperature (around 200°C), which gives them a long warm-up time. And they run best at only partial power, which means they do not respond well to the demands of immediate start-up, intermittent operation, and sudden changes in power demands. By contrast, PEM needs little warm-up time, can begin operating at around room temperature (20°C), and reaches peak performance at temperatures below the boiling point of water (100°C). It can also change its power output almost instantly.

But the US continued to back PAFC for many years, although the results were feeble at best. As late as 1992, PAFCs were still typically operating at only about one-sixteenth of the peak power attained by Ballard's PEM cell five years earlier. The US government financed a prototype bus program based on PAFC technology, largely because it was considered to be a better understood and more mature technology that could be brought to market quicker. This, too, proved to be quite wrong. And it gave Ballard time to gain a solid lead over the competition.

Ballard's strong showing at Los Alamos and Arizona put Vancouver on the international fuel cell map. Scientists began to call up Paul Howard and ask to be shown the Ballard cell. At first it was only tentative. "Gee, that looks interesting," they would tell him, "but are you sure about it?" Howard attributes the doubts to the fact that nearly all work on fuel cells was being done elsewhere. "We're not a hotbed of technology here in Canada. People felt, if anything happened in fuel cells, it sure as hell didn't happen in Canada. And if it happened in Canada, it sure as hell didn't happen in BC. And if it happened in BC, it sure didn't happen in a garage in North Vancouver."

Still, people were curious. "So we said, come to Vancouver and we'll show you. We won't tell you how we did it, but we'll show you the lab bench, and you can check and make sure there's no hidden wire bringing power from another source." Howard enjoyed watching the scepticism dissolve over the next few years. "So that was the deal. And people did come. And they would look at the volt and amp meters, and they'd kind of scratch their heads and say, 'That looks real.'" In the beginning, he says, it was one or two scientists, who then went back and told others. Through the late 1980s and early 1990s, people kept coming to see what Ballard was doing. "First it would be a lowly scientist. Then it might be a scientist and his boss. So, over a five-year period, word began to pass that these guys have done something that is real. This is not just smoke and mirrors."

Meanwhile the technical team slowly grew. As the surprise meltdown of the cable showed, Ballard was weak in its understanding of the electrical side of the technology. As McLeod explains, they knew so little about electricity that they did not foresee the results. "They fried a lot of things," he laughs ruefully. "The load banks were rudimentary. You have to attach the device to something that pulls off the electrical load. We didn't really understand what we were doing." The meltdown occurred because nobody had calculated that the stack was going to put out several hundred amperes. "No one said, 'Gee, I think we're going to melt the cable.'"

One new recruit was Jim Blair, who knew electricity and electronics and joined at first as a consultant, becoming a salaried employee only a couple of years later. Blair moved in his workbench and tools and took over the job of designing and building test stations. "He came out of the movie industry," says McLeod. "Lighting, special effects. One of these hands-on inventor types. Really quite talented."

They built ever larger fuel cell stacks. This meant designing better ways to manage the water and humidity levels. "If you let the membrane dry out," says Martin Hammerli, "the resistance goes up and performance goes down. If you flood it, with too much water accumulating, then the gases can't get through to the membrane and electrodes to react. So there's a fine balance between those conditions." The Ballard team learned how to strike that balance. By early 1987 they had a stack that put out up to 1,500 watts.

But soon their second contract, the single-year one, would be running out and they would again need money from the Canadian government. Fortunately, with the Los Alamos and Arizona visits, says McLeod, "we really knew we had something." But it was something that had to be protected. McLeod's job was to secure additional funding for further fuel cell development and for patent protection as well. This meant moving higher up in the military hierarchy in Ottawa, or what McLeod calls "the food chain." He was also eager to get Ballard some battery work for the Canadian and US military establishments.

Geoffrey Ballard groomed McLeod thoroughly for his task. Working in government-funded science was Ballard's background, "so he really knew how to talk to these people," says McLeod. "But he couldn't handle doing it himself. He'd lose it." Ballard could easily lose his temper or offend someone. On the other hand, he was a patient teacher who enjoyed coaching McLeod on how to talk to the civilian bureaucrats and the military brass. He alerted McLeod to the importance of showing interest in the specific jobs people did and giving them a chance to explain themselves. "Always ask them what they do, David," he said. "That's how Ballard used to start one-on-one conversations," says McLeod. "*Well, what is it that you do?* I had many people in the system come back to me and say, you know, nobody's ever asked me that."

Then there was pure technique. Ballard showed McLeod how to use the whiteboard properly, how to use a marker and talk at the same time. He taught him how to get people's attention quickly. Then, says McLeod, you've got to hold their attention and use it properly. "You can't talk down to people. You have to talk their language. And if you don't know it, you've got to learn it, because that's the game. And you've got to make them as comfortable as possible."

Ballard also drilled McLeod on the science involved. "I didn't even know the language, for God's sake. I didn't know electrochemistry or batteries. I mean, what the hell *is* energy? I'd never spent fifteen minutes in my life thinking about it. And Geoff was able to educate me in things like that. Later, people in Ottawa actually used to come to my presentations just for fun, because it turned into a show." Teaching, McLeod muses, was one of Ballard's main talents. "And what still annoys me at Ballard is that there's no recognition of that. You know, Geoffrey wasn't really a gee-whiz science guy, but he was a *hell* of a corporate guy. He had insight that really worked, particularly with engineers. And most of the bureaucrats that I talked to were scientists or engineers."

Geared up for the challenge, McLeod laid siege to the Canadian bureaucracy. High on his agenda was to protect the Ballard achievements. He certainly did not intend to take the advice of Byron McCormick at Los Alamos and try to snag an American partner. "We were still a tiny company, just three guys and a prayer, as we used to joke. I knew we needed help and a partner. But I sure as hell didn't want a US partner before we even knew what to do. Because we would have lost it, right away." This was to be a Canadian success story. "So I went back to Ottawa and convinced people to take a much more proactive role in assisting us in doing the patents. Because we had no money to file patents. It wasn't something we had built into the contract. And we certainly didn't have that kind of war chest." Under the contract with DND, he says, "you had the obligation that any licence or patent gets filed on behalf of the Canadian DND."

McLeod's lobbying led him to the office of Major-General George MacFarlane, who was associate deputy minister at DND. McLeod told him about the recent boost in power and the way people had reacted at Los Alamos. "And he got so excited he could hardly sit. Because he believed me. He said, 'By God, you're right. This is a significant thing. What are we going to do?' And that's when a lot of things started to get discussed, such as what the strategy should be. It raised the visibility of that tiny little contract, and what we were doing, right to the top."

McLeod pauses for effect. You've got to realize, he says, that in the area of sexy technology "Canada had never had anything even to talk about since the Avro Arrow." The Arrow was a Canadian-designed and built, high-performance jet fighter-bomber program that was cancelled by the government of Prime Minister John Diefenbaker in 1959. (The prototypes were physically scrapped, and the Canadian Air Force bought American aircraft instead, leading to accusations of betrayal of the national interest that can still be heard to this day.) "And here we were suddenly, beating the world. That was the drama behind the thing."

In public, General MacFarlane was not yet willing to commit the government to concrete steps on behalf of the Ballard fuel cell project. "I know the United States, Britain, and Germany are all working on generally the same thing," MacFarlane told *The Vancouver Sun*. "I think Ballard is at the moment ahead of them because they have a working fuel cell that can be scaled up." The military is interested, he added, because it needs mobile power and "the fuel cell is one of the few ways of making electricity mobile.... Sooner or later, conventional oil is going to run out." On the other hand, the fuel cell is not an urgent priority. "We are really taking a very long-range view. We very much want to continue the development," but the project requires a major infusion of money and "fuel cells are low on the totem pole" of DND priorities.[20] In private, though, behind the scenes, MacFarlane was much more proactive on behalf of the Ballard technology.

And so the funding for the next contract with DND came about quite indirectly by way of some slightly Byzantine intrigue. The army had no burning need for fuel cells. But in McLeod's poking around in the halls of DND he learned that the navy was interested in it. And the navy, he found, had a lot of clout. The Cold War was still raging, and the Mulroney government was looking at the possibility of buying nuclear-powered submarines. But nuclear was tremendously expensive. Some people in the navy opposed acquiring them, says McLeod, "because a fuel cell could do the same things a hell of a lot cheaper." These people asked McLeod not to mention publicly that they were opposed to nuclear, but promised that they would pull strings and make sure that Ballard got funding to continue its work.

There was just one hitch. The next contract would entail a large enough jump in the funding level that it had to be justified by tying it to a specific application, even if that was mainly a pretext. Canada did not have a lot of military production infrastructure, says McLeod, which made it important to pick carefully the areas where Canada would produce its own technology, rather than buying it off the shelf from allies. This could have made fuel cells a difficult sell. But "since the navy could not openly commission a fuel cell for a submarine power plant—and it would have been too large and expensive at this stage in any case," they got the army to "put forward the formal idea of needing a fuel cell for a four-kilowatt field generator with stealth properties." (This meant a quietly running unit with low infrared, i.e., heat, emissions.)

And so it was a combination of MacFarlane's personal support and behind-the-scenes lobbying by the navy brass that led to a new three-year contract to continue funding Ballard research and development. This provided $948,000 and was earmarked for the development of a silent, portable generator unit for the army. "You'll never get anyone to confirm the story, but it's true," McLeod insists. "General MacFarlane made that contract happen, instantly. But now, there's no paper trail. It just happened," McLeod chortles. "If I ever write a book," he adds, "that's what it will be about. The politics of technology."

Another person who helped McLeod to sell both the fuel cell and Ballard's battery technology was Simon Reisman. It was the flamboyant, tough-talking and notoriously foul-mouthed Reisman who had led Canada in negotiating the Autopact (1965) and Free Trade Agreement (1988) with the US. At their very first meeting, in one of Ottawa's better restaurants, Reisman lived up to his reputation.

McLeod showed up ten minutes late. It had been raining. His hair and clothes were a mess, and he felt on the defensive. After some small talk, McLeod said he hoped Reisman wouldn't mind if he smoked a cigarette. Reisman paused, sat back and made a big show of taking off his glasses. He let the seconds tick by, then put his glasses back on and stared at the young man from BC. "Let me see if I've got this right," said Reisman. "You've got a wife and a couple of kids and a mortgage that you can't afford? You're here in Ottawa, in a town where there are no hopes or dreams, and that's all you're selling? It strikes me that you *need* a fucking cigarette."

"That was when I knew I liked Simon," says McLeod. Once the ice was broken, Reisman got down to business. "So tell me, what is all the talk about this thing," the Ballard fuel cell. "Who the fuck *are* you?" McLeod replied, "Well, you *signed* the Autopact. I'm actually *doing* it." The Autopact provided for cross-border reciprocity between the US and Canada in the automobile industry. Reisman looked at him and said, "That's a pretty bold-assed statement." "Well, it's the truth," McLeod parried. "You, as a bureaucrat, just put the paper together. I'm actually trying to do something with it." He explained Ballard's vision that the fuel cell would power the automobile of the future. "That's how our relationship started."

Ballard was seeking funding and contracts from the Canadian government and from the US as well. Reisman proved to be quite useful. "Simon Reisman was very well connected in Ottawa," says Geoffrey Ballard, "and we desperately needed to have Ottawa connections, because we were a West Coast company, and it was easy to put us down." So they offered Reisman a directorship, which he accepted, serving a two-year term. By Reisman's own admission, says McLeod, he never delivered any money. "But he delivered other things," especially "a wealth of information that was very, very helpful."

Geoffrey Ballard also thinks Reisman did an excellent job. "He would make comments to the right people at the right time. About how Canada ought to be paying attention to the fuel cell and funding it. He told people he thought it was a good thing for Canada, in fact another Avro Arrow. And his judgement was considered good." It opened a lot of doors for Ballard. The small BC company soon scooped up some prime battery contracts for the US military and also landed fuel cell work under a US government program to develop a low-emissions car.

Reisman guided McLeod through some of the mysteries and intricacies of the government bureaucracy and coached him on ways of approaching US institutions as well. "It was Simon who gave me insight into how to deal with some of these idiots across the line." McLeod was at first intimidated by the size of Washington and its style of doing business, but Reisman's advice bolstered his courage. "Because he was never afraid of the Americans," says McLeod, "I felt, why the hell should I be?"

Nugget
of GOLD

General Electric's first PEM fuel cell went into space. Ballard brought it down to Earth, building it out of much cheaper materials and making it run on air and impure hydrogen. But the first *practical* Ballard fuel cell, one that had to generate power outside the laboratory, went under the sea.

Around the time that Ballard got to work on the military field generator, the company received its first order from a private customer. The buyer was John H. Perry, Jr., a flamboyant Florida entrepreneur and multimillionaire with a flair for self-promotion. His family tree goes back to Commodore Matthew Perry, whose US Navy squadron entered Tokyo Bay in 1853 and forced Japan to open trade with the West. John Perry attended the elite Hotchkiss School and Yale University, and inherited from his father a chain of small newspapers and radio stations, including many in Florida. He settled eventually in Palm Beach, acquiring major interests in the printing and cable television industries.

Perry also took more than a passing interest in American politics, coming to know personally all the presidents from John Kennedy to George Bush, who is, he says, a "kissing cousin" related to Perry on his mother's side. Perry did not just know them. He bombarded them, and any congressman or senator who would listen, with advice on how to put the nation's finances in order. He came up with a pet solution, his "national dividends plan," and spent over $10 million lobbying for it.

Although born into wealth, Perry has never been one of the idle rich. Always a tinkerer, as he says in his autobiography, *Never Say Impossible*, he loved machinery and enjoyed working on his own car from high school on. Soon he stepped up to airplanes, constructing a plane of his own in the family garage. "I built it—but then I had the sense not to fly it," he quips.[21] He did learn to fly a commercial biplane, though, and in World War II he served with distinction in the Civil Air Patrol flying coastal patrols and scanning the sea for the periscopes of German U-boats.

After the war Perry's interest in submarines took a different turn. Living in Florida, he came to enjoy boating, fishing, and spearfishing. Once while diving in the Bahamas, he was chased by a shark and nearly nabbed. He made it back to the boat, pulled himself aboard, cocked his spear gun to take a shot at the marauder and wounded himself. "Sidelined," he says, "I began thinking that there ought to be a way for hunters to safely hunt sharks underwater. 'There ought to be a small, not-too-expensive submarine for such work,' I reasoned. When we got back to Florida I decided to build a prototype."[22]

Perry searched for information on small submersibles and prowled the local stores for building materials: plywood, fibreglass, wire. Then he set aside space in his garage and went to work. His young son Henry enjoyed watching and pitching in. The result, he admits, "looked a little like a cross between a kayak and a blimp—unwieldy, yet light and watertight. Full of confidence, I carried the vessel to the nearby inland waterway, put it in the water and prepared to submerge. Happily, the thing didn't work. If it had, I'm sure I would have become an accident statistic. As it was, I learned some good lessons and I was still alive."[23]

Soon Perry was approaching the challenge with a higher level of professionalism. He moved out of his garage to a small industrial building and hired a skilled welder to build him a proper pressure hull of steel complete with battery power. Again he took his submersible to the inland waterway. Together with an associate, he checked everything, shoved off and put the controls into dive position. The craft went down a few feet, crept forward, then surfaced. He was elated.

Suddenly, though, he felt a thump. He had struck something. Perry threw open the hatch and saw that he had bumped into a small fishing boat. Both boats checked for damage, and everything seemed OK. Perry apologized profusely and returned home, considering his experiment a great success. Then the phone rang. It was the Coast Guard asking whether he knew anything about a collision between a fishing boat and some kind of submarine. Perry owned up to his part in what he thought to be a minor mishap. "Well," said the guardsman, "that fishing boat sank."[24]

But Perry was not deterred. He hired more knowledgeable assistants and built better submersibles. At the time, the late 1950s and early 1960s, oceanographics and undersea research were booming fields. The US Navy was willing to fund research and buy enough small vessels to make the business an attractive one. Meanwhile, Perry and some associates had acquired a private island in the Bahamas. It was an ideal base for undersea research and experimental aquaculture ventures.

By the mid-1960s Perry Oceanographics was building submarines that made headlines. One of them helped to locate a US Air Force bomber that had crashed off the coast of Spain carrying a hydrogen bomb. Perry also worked with the navy to build Hydro-Lab, an underwater laboratory in which scientists could spend extended periods of time.

Throughout the 1970s and 1980s, Perry and his company were at the forefront of minisubmarine construction. Some carried people, others were robot subs operated by remote control. His boats carried such notables as Britain's Prince Charles on demonstration rides, helped salvage the wreckage of the Space Shuttle Columbia, which exploded just off the Florida coast, and made cameo appearances in James Bond movies. At its peak, the company had more than 250 employees.

In 1987 Perry approached Ballard to have a PEM cell stack built to power one of his submarines, called the PC 1401. It was about the size of a small car and was built to carry a crew of two, who could look out the front through a large Plexiglas bubble. The idea was to replace the battery system with something that took up the same space but could give it much greater range and time underwater. Perry needed a two kilowatt fuel cell system, to be operated on pure hydrogen and oxygen. He wanted it quickly, with delivery in only three months, and was willing to pay $50,000.

The Perry order was a unique challenge for Ballard. With the Mark IV technology then available, the system would require two fifty-four-cell stacks, whereas Ballard had only been building stacks of six and twelve cells. "We had never built that many before," says Paul Howard, who was in charge of the fuel cell team. "But it was an order. We wanted to respond to it. They had money on the table. I'm sure we didn't make a profit," but that was not the point. It was the first Ballard stack that had to operate beyond the controlled conditions of the laboratory, and with people's safety at stake to boot.

"We figured we would at least cover material costs," says McLeod, "but the real question was whether or not we could do it. And there was a lot of concern, because we had never built anything that big. Yet everybody understood the significance of why we would do it, and it wasn't to make money. It was to prove that this technology was a lot more advanced than anybody had ever given it credit for."

Keith Prater, too, recalls that building the Perry system involved a major and problematical scale up from the small test cells Ballard had been building. The Perry system required a sudden jump to dozens of cells stacked together, with gas manifolds feeding hydrogen and oxygen to all of them efficiently and evenly, to get the required power. "So that was a leap of faith," says Prater. "Could we actually plumb this thing and make all the cells work? And in the case of the Perry stack, they actually needed two of the things, side by side, put into a round pressure vessel to avoid leaks and so forth."

But Ballard took the contract and built to Perry's needs. When the stacks were delivered and installed, it was a historic moment. "That was the first real application of the PEM fuel cell in anything since Gemini," says David McLeod. When the stacks got to Florida, though, all did not go smoothly. "The installation of it went as expected. There were problems. They originally wired it backwards. They put the oxygen on the hydrogen side." Eventually, though, it ran and performed well. McLeod and one or two others flew down for a test dive.

But this was not the end of the story. The sub could use even more power, and the Ballard fuel cell was progressing rapidly. In 1989 Ballard replaced the two Mark IV stacks in Perry's submarine with a single, much more powerful stack of new Mark V cells. This cranked out four and one-half kilowatts but fit into the same space as the system that had totalled only two kilowatts. A year or two later, Ballard would regret supplying Perry with this improved stack, but in the late 1980s, Ballard proudly displayed photos of the Perry submersible in its company brochures.

Unlike the earlier boost in power that came from switching to the Dow membrane, the improvement from Mark IV to Mark V was not due mainly to changes in electrochemistry but to a series of refinements in the cell design. The most important was accomplished by more than doubling the cross-sectional surface area of each individual cell. Not all of this area takes part in the actual electrochemical reaction; some of it is "wasted" on equipment such as bolts and gas manifolds. But a doubling in surface area did not require a comparable increase in the amount of space taken up by these other features. So the *active* cross-sectional area of the cell, and with it the power output, increased much more than proportionally. As happened at several stages in the development of the Ballard fuel cell, it was good, painstaking engineering more than novel science that made the difference.

Soon after the first Perry system was delivered, Ballard made a second important sale, this time to a much more prominent and prestigious buyer, Britain's Royal Navy. This came about through a contact that the indefatigable McLeod made at one of the fuel cell conferences he attended together with Watkins. "We ran into a guy from the UK Ministry of Defence," says McLeod, "one of the back-room guys out of Bath, England. And he was looking at advanced power systems for submarines. He actually had a request for proposal (RFP) in his hand that he was wandering around the floor trying to get people to bid on. I basically ripped this out of the guy's hand, went and made a photocopy, and said, yes, we'd be delighted to bid on it."

In fact, just making the bid was an enormous challenge, because the Royal Navy wanted to work towards a system large enough to run a full-size military boat. "This was for a full-up power plant," says Keith Prater. "The proposal was to scale up the stack and build first, I think, a forty kilowatt unit, and then an eighty kilowatt unit," and then to gang several of those together to provide enough power for a real submarine. (More recent Canadian government studies of fuel cell submarines foresee a power plant of four hundred thousand kilowatts.)

"It was the first time," says McLeod, "that any of us had sat down and looked at what the development strategy would be to build something of that size." But Ballard decided to pour its resources into the proposal, spending around $50,000 of its own money. It was a valuable exercise. McLeod calls it "the best fifty grand that we ever spent. David Watkins and I spent days in my office in the heat of summer putting this bid together." The briefing document turned out to be three inches thick.

Prater, McLeod, and Ballard flew to England to meet the senior Royal Navy brass. "We made our pitch and impressed the Royal Navy," says Prater, "but then they had a funding cut." Not that the money went to someone else. The project simply never went ahead at all. McLeod says there were other complications. The person who had circulated the RFP did not actually have the blessing of key people in the UK Ministry of Defence. "We surprised and embarrassed a whole bunch of people," says McLeod. "Nobody in the system really knew who we were, and we suddenly showed up and did a presentation about the potential of a fuel cell in a submarine, and basically made them look really stupid."

But the effort had its benefits. The Royal Navy did have some interest in fuel cells. Its research establishment came up with $50,000 to $75,000 to acquire a pair of Ballard stacks like the first ones that went to John Perry. These were installed in their laboratory and tested, says McLeod, "so they could confirm the data and get a feel for it." Ballard was quite satisfied with the outcome. "We were really able to leverage from it," says McLeod. Senior people throughout the military establishments in the UK and the US got to hear about it. "So this gave us a *lot* of credibility very quickly." It may even have helped with Ballard's battery business.

Just as greater attention was being paid to the fuel cell, the battery side of the company also got a major boost in the form of a series of sizeable military contracts. These were to lead, indirectly, to a financial connection that was a turning point for fuel cell development as well.

Amoco had long sponsored Ballard's ongoing research and development of the rechargeable lithium battery. But the future of this contract was insecure at best, and Ballard was free to manufacture and sell the single-use version of the lithium battery on its own. These were high-powered and complex batteries that operated under pressure and had dangerous chemicals in them. They had to be disposed of carefully and were extremely expensive, which restricted their market almost entirely to the military. To make and sell them, the parent company, Ballard Technologies, had established a battery production subsidiary that was called BTC Engineering and later Ballard Batteries.

As first constituted, Geoffrey Ballard was its president, but it was actually run by three other men. One was the chief scientist, electrochemist Lynn Marcoux, who had known Keith Prater in Kansas and Texas and had played a role in the original Ballard-Schwartz battery work for John Horton in Arizona. Another was Greg Patterson, who became chief engineer. The third was Keith Prater's father-in-law, Brian Yeoell, an Englishman who had trained as a civil engineer and gained managing and marketing experience working for oil companies in North Africa. Yeoell had immigrated to Canada, where he worked some years with the BC Institute of Technology. By the mid-80s he was semi-retired but was interested in Ballard and offered to help out marketing the single-use batteries.

Because the threesome of Ballard, Prater, and Howard had worked so well together, says Prater, "we thought, hey, let's create another troika. And those three people were in some ways mirrors of Geoff, Paul and me." One (Yeoell) was somewhat older and would handle the marketing and entrepreneurial side. One was an engineer. The third was a scientist. "So we thought they could sort of break down the work the same way. But in a sense they were being pushed together, whereas Geoff and Paul and I were attracted to each other."

The personal chemistry did not work. "Nobody was really in charge," says Prater. "The three of them were continually battling. Eventually I took over as CEO of this subsidiary." In the meantime, through his lobbying in Ottawa, David McLeod had heard about an opportunity for Ballard to supply batteries to the Canadian military.

Canada was buying hand-held sniffers that detected poisonous gases and other chemical warfare agents. These portable chemical agent monitors were being manufactured in England, and they ran on a cell that was about twice the length of a largish cylindrical flashlight battery. The Canadian military preferred to buy its batteries from a Canadian source, and Ballard had the capability of making long-lasting lithium batteries to power the devices. After some discussion, the Ballard people felt they had an understanding that an RFP would go out, but that Ballard would in fact be the only available Canadian supplier and was a sure bet to get the contract. Based on this expectation, Ballard began looking for money to set up an assembly line.

Meanwhile, though, the situation got complicated. Yeoell and Prater made the mistake of writing a letter to their contact in Ottawa thanking him for setting up this "sole-source contract." When the letter was seen by others, the contact had to deny that any such exclusive guarantee had been made. "We had made a balls of it," says Prater, sheepishly. "But we kept getting signals or indications that we were going to get this contract." So planning for the assembly line went ahead, which was wise, because the contract eventually did come through.

Before the Canadian contract was in the bag, though, Ballard landed another contract, this one from the US military to manufacture 60,000 much smaller "button type" lithium batteries for night vision goggles. Ballard still had the technology and much of the needed equipment from the Ultra Energy smoke detector battery days. But to go into manufacturing mode would take capital. Up to this point, Ballard had mainly been funded by a large single customer, Amoco. Suddenly, it needed an independent source of money, and quickly. Feelers went out in the Vancouver venture market. This led to a long and intimate business relationship with one of Vancouver's most respected venture capitalists, Michael J. Brown.

Mike Brown had taken an economics degree at the University of British Columbia and gone on to Oxford as a Rhodes Scholar. He also had a unique financial pedigree. His grandfather, Colonel Albert Malcolm ("Buster") Brown had founded a Vancouver-based investment company in 1923, and his father, Thomas (Tom) Brown, had become one of the principals in the prestigious local firm of Odlum Brown Ltd. After graduating, Mike Brown first went to work for Odlum Brown but then joined a couple of partners in an independent financial consulting firm.

In 1973 Brown became a founding partner in Ventures West, which managed venture funds that invested in "young technology companies." By 1987, Ventures West was the leading venture capital company in western Canada, administering $85 million invested in 37 companies, including such successful firms as MacDonald Dettwiler and Associates, Mobile Data International, and Nexus Engineering. In a town dominated by the scandal-ridden Vancouver Stock Exchange (VSE), which was infamous for sleazy deals in which naive investors lost their shirts, Ventures West stood out for its high ethics. "Some say Ventures West is everything the VSE should be and isn't," intoned *Fleecing the Lamb*, a book that exposed these scams.[25] Any company backed by Brown and his firm enjoyed a prima facie seal of approval and probity.

In early 1987, Brown was sitting in his dentist's waiting room thumbing through the magazines when he came upon an article in *Popular Mechanics* on fuel cells. Brown understood the concept of the fuel cell and remembered the high school experiment in which hydrogen and oxygen were produced by electrolysis. He had a strong interest in science and technology and a personal commitment to environmental protection. In 1990, for example, he was a member of a City of Vancouver task force on atmospheric change. "I had a concern about global warming," he recalls, "and started writing papers and letters" about it around 1987 or 1988. "I look at things in a fairly long time frame, and I certainly have an environmental bent."

A few weeks after reading the fuel cell article, Brown got a tip. A financial industry colleague talked to one of Brown's partners about Ballard's need for capital to set up its battery production line. Brown hopped into his car, drove across the bridge to North Vancouver, and met with the Ballard principals about their needs. While there, he was given a tour and shown the latest Ballard fuel cell stack. This experience, along with the quality of the Ballard team, whetted his interest in the company. "It was originally the technology that got me excited," he says, "for sure. But no technology is of any value without people."

Intrigued by Ballard's growth potential, he persuaded Canada's Business Development Bank (BDC) to take an interest as well. Brown got the BDC to ante up around $500,000, while Ventures West came up with some $800,000 for a total of $1.3 million, the first significant infusion of private venture capital in Ballard. Brown took a seat on the company's board of directors, just as he takes an active role in many of the firms for which he provides seed money. For many years to come, he would be paying the piper and calling the tune. "It's... worth remembering," he told *BC Business* magazine "that Ventures West doesn't just dish out money. We like to live with a company we finance. That means at a minimum being represented on its board, in some cases even becoming active in its management."[26] Brown himself, for example, served as chair of Mobile Data International (MDI), a connection that was to lead to a key personnel change at Ballard.

Most of the initial $1.3 million was to be spent on setting up the production line for the Canadian and US military batteries. But Brown generally only invests in companies that have the potential to become leaders in their specialized field. Usually the product or service being provided also has proprietary elements that will give the company a long-term competitive advantage. In Ballard's case it was the fuel cell that really grabbed Brown. Paul Howard heard him call the fuel cell his "nugget of gold," the part of the company that had true future potential. But there was a basic problem. "You couldn't write a business plan for what we had" on the fuel cell side, says Keith Prater, which at that time was still little more than just "dabblings at the back of the lab. So it had to be an investment in holding the thing together and helping the battery company make money" while the fuel cell made further progress.

Mike Brown remembers how difficult it was to justify investing in the fuel cell, because it was such an unknown technology. "When I did my due diligence to decide whether we should make the first investment, the question was, who should I phone to find out whether these guys were on the right track or not. Well, the answer was, there was *nobody* to phone." There was really no one who knew enough to help him much. "I talked to a few people who sort of set themselves up as experts. A guy at the University of Texas at El Paso. And some guys at Los Alamos. And someone at the Argonne National Laboratory in Chicago. But it was pretty sparse stuff."

Brown likens the situation to someone having to decide whether or not to invest in the first microcomputer or computer chip. "Who does he phone to see if this thing makes any sense? And the answer, of course, is, you *don't*. And I don't think that comparison is wildly invalid. I think the Ballard fuel cell may have as big an impact on the world around us as the Intel chip." Not that this view is universally shared, even in the late 1990s, although the media have certainly made the comparison between Intel and Ballard's potential. "Even now, people think it's wildly arrogant to speak that way. But think about what could happen here if decent hydrogen storage systems are invented for the car. This thing is going to turn out to be cheaper to make than the internal combustion engine. It's going to be nicer to drive. It will certainly be more reliable. So people are going to want to have it. I've invested in some other things that you could call loosely related to trying to solve environmental problems," but the Ballard fuel cell "is pretty extraordinary." It must be special to him; Brown has a large colour poster of the Ballard cell stack hanging on his conference room wall.

He sits back to mull it over. "I've got grandchildren," he says, "My view is that my grandchildren, and certainly their children, will regard fuel cells as standard, normal things, the way you and I look at the internal combustion engine." But he insists that it is not important to him whether his grandchildren are aware that he played an important part in the fuel cell's development or not. "I don't care if anybody else knows. I can sit around in my dotage, talking to myself and dribbling at the mouth, and *I'll know*."

Going
for BROKE

A year after the first infusion of venture capital, Mike Brown's nugget of gold was gleaming brightly. Ballard was already the world leader in PEM fuel cell technology. The first privately sold Ballard stack was taking John Perry's minisubmarine deep into the waters of the Florida coast. Another stack was being built for sale to the Royal Navy. A contact that Keith Prater made was leading to a deal to lease a two-kilowatt stack to Germany's prestigious Daimler-Benz corporation. A much larger ten-kilowatt stack, for stationary power generation, had been commissioned for sale to Dow Chemical's chlor-alkali plant in Sarnia, Ontario. And the power density of the Ballard cell just kept on improving.

The battery side of the business was also doing well. A humming production line was cranking out thousands of the high-tech lithium-sulphur dioxide batteries for the US and Canadian militaries. This provided a cash flow that the Ballard partners diverted, as much as they could, to the fuel cell. But it was never enough. "Funding was always a problem," says Geoffrey Ballard. "Getting enough money to do things at the right speed was always a problem, because the [Canadian] federal government had limited resources. They might renew the contract. But to pursue a technology, your demand for funding just goes up exponentially." The Ballard partners could see that they would soon be in a money bind again. When they discussed the fuel cell and the great potential it was showing, they agreed that they should finance its development with a second instalment of private capital, even if this meant diluting their ownership of the company.

By this time the firm had a new president and CEO. Geoffrey Ballard had served as first among equals for nearly ten years, but he did not believe in clinging to power for its own sake. "I've always tried to work my way *out* of a job," he says. "Every time I get a job my first reaction is, who do I train to take over, so I can go on and do something else. I think that's a very sound management principle. It gives depth to the corporation." Just as he had taught David McLeod how to talk to the military brass and civilian bureaucrats in Ottawa, he had encouraged Keith Prater and Paul Howard to carry their share of the burdens of management. In 1986, for example, Prater had become president and CEO of the battery subsidiary BTC Engineering. "Geoff would counsel us and advise us and teach us," says Paul Howard. "He likes teaching. And we would listen to him. He had the experience."

Eventually, Prater went to Ballard and said that he wanted to step up to the position of president and CEO of the larger parent company, Ballard Technologies Corporation, soon to be Ballard Power Systems Inc. "That's great," Ballard had replied, "I've been waiting for you or Paul to say that, and I'm glad that you did." Ballard remained chairman of the board, but the change freed him from some of the daily responsibilities. However, as Prater says, "Geoff was a very strong chairman, and the company was still controlled by the three of us, so it was still very much a partnership."

Together they had to face the cash-flow crunch. They asked for a meeting with Mike Brown and put the situation to him. Prater recalls that he made a proposal to Brown "for another million dollars or whatever, for some percentage of ownership, I don't remember exactly, but something less than control. And Mike essentially said, thanks but no thanks." Brown's position was that just a small amount of extra money was not going to solve Ballard's problems. "So it was on my shift," says Prater, "that I put forward a recommendation that we bite the bullet and go after a big chunk of money to support the fuel cell, recognizing that in the process we were going to lose control of the company." Geoffrey Ballard and Paul Howard agreed. "And it was then that we went back to Mike and began negotiating the next round of financing."

Diluting their ownership so that they lost control of the company was a big step, they thought. But Mike Brown had a much more drastic agenda in mind. Prater had a conversation with Brown about money. "We agreed," says Prater, "that the fuel cell was sufficiently exciting that we ought to go out and get eight to ten million dollars. He and I talked about what the future company would look like. We talked about what Geoff would do and what Paul would do. And when we came to CEO, Mike was gentle but firm in making clear to me that there was no way of raising eight or ten million with me as CEO. The financial community wouldn't find me credible."

As Brown tells it, "in the fall of 1988 the Ballard company needed more money. And, together with my partners, we reached the conclusion that a new kind of leadership was required to make the company proceed." The Ballard founders, he thought, had certain skills and abilities, which were perhaps appropriate for a small contract research house, but not for a rapidly growing company that required massive infusions of capital. "It is very rare," says Brown, "for the founders to carry a company right through to great success and fruition. So it's not unusual for the founders to move aside and do something else." Typically, he says, there is something lacking in the capabilities or experience of the founders. "In this case, what was missing was a real good understanding of how to position the company compared to the big companies we were going to have to deal with." Brown was already looking ahead. He could see that if the Ballard fuel cell was going to become a significant energy technology, the company would eventually need major industrial partners and have to enter into joint ventures.

The Ballard partners were not happy to hear this news from Brown. *We brought it this far*, Geoffrey Ballard said to himself. *Was that nothing?* And Brown was aware of their sensibilities. "To begin with," says Brown, "when I put it on the table that we had to have a change, they thought I was a real bad guy. They hated it, absolutely." Brown could tell right away that their feelings were hurt. "And I can absolutely understand that. I deal with entrepreneurs all the time. It's my life. And the entrepreneur who doesn't get upset when you make that suggestion is probably not a guy you want to back in the first place. So it wasn't a big surprise to me that they were upset, and it obviously took them a while to accept."

For his part, Geoffrey Ballard could see it from Brown's side as well. He had, and retains, fond feelings and a lot of respect for Mike Brown. "We needed more money, and Mike was willing to put some money into it. He liked the technology and what the Canadian government thought about us. We had a very good reputation. However, Mike felt that if he was going to put money in, he had to have a return for his investors, and the company had to change." Ballard was still mainly a contract research corporation that took a percentage mark-up for overhead and profit. "Mike Brown felt that sort of modus operandi or mental set was not the kind of thing he wanted to invest in. He wanted something that moved towards marketing and production and manufacturing. So, to put money in from Ventures West, he wanted us to choose a CEO who had marketing experience, and who would move towards product and manufacturing."

The Ballard partners went home and discussed the options with their wives. They agonized over it, slept on it, and came back to the office each day to hash it out among themselves. In their minds, they still had a choice. They could reject Brown's suggestion and scrape up the money to continue operations at a modest level. They could remain small, retain control of the fuel cell technology, and quite possibly be a successful small company. Or they could accept Brown's advice and guidance.

To Geoffrey Ballard it was not only a personal and financial choice. Taking a broader view, it was a choice between aiming the fuel cell at small niche markets, on the one hand, and going for broke on the other. Or, as he likes to put it, "setting out to change the way the world thinks about power." The small market niches for the fuel cell included such things as the military field generator, wheelchairs, golf carts, lighthouses, and other remote navigational aids such as aviation beacons and marine buoys. Taken together, these were by no means negligible. One advantage of niche markets was that they require relatively little investment. There might also be a fairly high level of profits on these specialized applications, and the company would be able to grow slowly and incrementally. "I felt very comfortable about taking care of the small path, the market niches, and to grow that way," says Ballard. "But I recognized that it was an entirely different skill set the other way. We didn't have the expertise to tackle the marketing of this idea simultaneously on all the fronts that utilize fossil fuels and the internal combustion engine."

The other obvious advantage of the niche market approach was retaining corporate control. The danger, though, was that at some point a giant company like General Motors might recognize that the fuel cell was the wave of the future and simply take it over. In theory, the company could be protected by patents, but in reality, says Ballard, "you won't have had the money to *have* a big patent portfolio. They'll work around you." Patenting is terribly expensive. "Stay small and you don't cover yourself. There are all the little details. You don't have enough resources. Even today we turn down three out of four patents that we could do. We only file about twenty-five per cent of them because of the high legal fees, the process itself, the whole package."

The alternative that Mike Brown was offering meant pushing the fuel cell forward rapidly into the biggest world markets. Perhaps that way, Ballard and his partners could enjoy the thrill and pride and satisfaction of seeing the technology that they had babied along for years actually begin to change the world within their lifetimes. As it turned out, this approach also made them all quite wealthy. But that was by no means guaranteed when they faced the crunch and a decision had to be made.

A big part of the decision came down to the fact that the fuel cell was the only technology on the horizon that held out the promise to solve some of the world's most serious problems. "It was so needed and the world was so ready for it," says Ballard. "Oh, Los Angeles is just dying. Vancouver is going to be eaten alive by its own smog very shortly. It seemed like the time to go for broke." Ballard foresaw that the fuel cell could ride along on the green wave that was sweeping the world. Of course, he had been personally committed to alternative energy since quitting his job in Washington and giving up his career with the US Army. But now more than ever, it just seemed that all the pieces of the energy technology puzzle were coming together so neatly that the decision to go for broke almost made itself.

"There's just a surge which you can feel happening," he says, "when everything is falling into place. The way the public responds. The way the technology responds. The fuel cell was like that." For one thing, the advances in fuel cell technology were coming on so rapidly. "It looked to me like this was going to be a real humdinger. Right from the beginning. Oh yeah. The technology was just too good. It was an easy technology, forgiving. And you could go all your life and not find a forgiving technology." Most of the time, he says, as with the rechargeable lithium sulphur dioxide battery, you struggle with complexity. But here was the fuel cell achieving power levels that made replacement of the internal combustion engine look possible just as people were becoming more aware of environmental problems throughout North America. "You can tell when that happens," says Ballard. "There's a momentum."

Far beyond the shores of North Vancouver, the thinking about energy and power sources was changing, which augured well for the Ballard fuel cell. In the United States the Department of Energy spent $34 million on fuel cell R & D in 1988. Japan budgeted $39 million in 1987. And in California a regulatory push was on to require low and zero-emission vehicles.

Recalling this turning point, Ballard sits back, looks out the window and smiles. "Shakespeare was quite right when he said—how does it go?—that there is a 'tide in the affairs of men, which, taken at the flood, leads on to fortune.'" To Ballard, this was just such a time, and just such a tide, and he was determined to ride it. "We *knew* the technology and we didn't think there were ten people in the world who knew it was going to dominate the world. You knew it was. You could just feel it. Perhaps I more than anyone. I just had a sense." This still left the question of how to proceed. "In fact, there were two questions. What was the path to bring the fuel cell to the forefront of hydrogen technology? And would Ballard Power be allowed to play a part? The key thing was to participate."

Not that Geoffrey Ballard was a clairvoyant who predicted the sequence of events perfectly. He didn't. For one thing, he thought the automobile itself would be one of the last areas of technology in which the fuel cell would find a mass commercial market, rather than one of the first. "The automobile is socially and physically the most difficult thing you can possibly do," he says. Socially, because we have woven the conventional automobile into our style of living so completely that it is extremely difficult to get people to change their habits and expectations. But physically, too. "It is the smallest package and the most demanding. You've got to put that thing under the hood and leave room in the trunk for clothes and put six people in as well."

Mike Brown agrees that no one really expected the fuel cell car to come on so fast. But along with fuel cells for stationary power it had to be a main target. "We knew that the endgame was the car," he says. "I can remember a board meeting where we discussed opportunities to get into some niche markets, like wheelchairs. And we said, no, no, no. If we do that and actually get some revenues and some earnings, that's probably good, but it's going to deflect us from our end target." So they decided to pass up the niche markets entirely. "All we're going to do is go after the two biggest markets in the world. Nothing more," he laughs. "The car and electrical utilities, that is stationary power plants. So there we are. We're going after the two biggest market places. And on the way we're going to abuse what is actually the world's *biggest* industry, which is the oil and gas business."

Brown is quite aware of how crazy that must have sounded at the time. "Well, gosh, when you're sitting there, and maybe twenty-five people are working on the fuel cell, and your vision is to do this, you have to be regarded as just a little nuts. And we all were. We were all a little nuts. I mean, we didn't know how hard it would be to do it. And if we'd ever figured out how hard it really would be, it would have been so daunting that we never would have started." But that's the history of most entrepreneurial start-ups, he says. "Most people who have a great vision don't really know how hard it will be to accomplish. And if they did, they'd be so scared that they couldn't do it. They've always got a beneficent view of the future."

The Ballard partners mulled the situation over among themselves. They agreed that they had only two choices. "We could have stopped taking venture money and continued being a contract R & D organization," says Prater. The alternative was to take the big plunge into accepting additional venture money and have the possibility of becoming a "truly successful" company. Simple arithmetic told them that they would lose control of Ballard by taking the next chunk of venture capital. "But that was our choice. And having made that choice and then talking with Mike, it was absolutely clear to me that we were going to have to find someone else as CEO. And I accepted that." The entire discussion and wrenching decision took only a week to ten days. "We were running to the end of the money," Prater laughs. "Like being hanged the next morning, that tends to focus one's thinking."

Mike Brown had several people in mind as candidates for the position of president and CEO. Among them was a thirty-six year old executive named Firoz Rasul. He was of average height and build, with a serious, no-nonsense demeanour and salt-and-pepper hair and mustache that have since gone white. Born in Kenya to an Ismaili Muslim family, Rasul had strong backgrounds in both technology and marketing. He had taken a bachelor's degree in industrial engineering from Hatfield Polytechnic in England and then a Master's of Business Administration at McGill in Montreal. After gaining business experience working for General Foods and Black and Decker, he became vice-president of marketing and sales for Mobile Data International (MDI), a Richmond, BC, manufacturer of data-collection devices.

MDI had been funded by Mike Brown and Ventures West and was one of their great success stories. In fact, Brown himself had served as chairman of the board from 1978 until MDI was sold to Motorola in 1988, so he had worked closely with Rasul. "I joined MDI pretty much from inception," says Rasul. "I was employee number thirteen." Apparently this did not bring him bad luck. During his seven years at MDI, its sales grew from about $2 million to $42 million and its employees to around 425. Brown credits Rasul with a large part of this achievement. "I knew Firoz well and had a huge regard for him. Firoz is very hard working, totally honest, very smart, and a really good positioner of companies. He had learned a lot during the course of the MDI thing. And I learned what a really good marketing guy looks like."

When MDI was sold to Motorola, Rasul had accumulated a nice little pot of gold from its employee shareholder plan. He decided to leave because he did not like the big company atmosphere. He was looking around for some new challenge when Brown invited him to lunch and told him about the Ballard situation. Rasul's first question was, "Why do you want me to become the president of a company that has no money and probably won't have any revenue for a long period of time?" Brown told him, "Firoz, you and I will raise the money. Because I think there's enough of an idea here. Because Geoffrey, Paul, and Keith have brought this thing to a certain level where it's credible to believe that we can cause this revolution." Mind you, Brown added, "a few things have to go right along the way. We probably have to raise huge amounts of money. And we probably have to team up with somebody much, much bigger than we are."

Rasul was intrigued. As he said in early 1989, shortly after taking the top position at Ballard, "I was attracted, first of all, by the strength of the fuel cell technology and its performance relative to the nearest competition, like United Technologies and others. Its performance is about ten times as good as theirs. Today. Right now." Second, he was attracted "by the quality of the people. The Ballard people have been together for the past fifteen years and have extensive experience in high-performance power systems, because they are used to doing work for the military, which requires high reliability, high performance, high-quality power systems." Last but not least on his list of reasons was "the attractiveness of the opportunity, in that this technology has come about at a time when the world is looking for solutions for both power and the environment. You look at the environment and see the problems that contribute to the declining quality of the environment today, and inevitably you come back to power sources. The biggest culprit is power. Whether it's the internal combustion engine in a car or a central generating power station that runs on coal or oil. I felt the time was now for the world to be introduced to this new power source."

Rasul was only one of several people that Brown introduced to the Ballard partners. "I did not insist that they hire Firoz by any stretch of the imagination," says Brown. "In fact, what happened was that Firoz spent a good bit of time with the three guys, getting to understand what was going on. He even went to Europe with them on one occasion, if I recall, in the fall of 1988. And, in the end, the deal was struck with Firoz by Geoffrey, Paul, and Keith. They did it. They're the ones who enthusiastically decided that he was the right answer."

It took the Ballard partners a while to accept the new situation, Brown says. "But, by golly, when they did, they decided to do it properly, and they made Firoz an equal partner" with an equal share of stock in the company. "And they agreed that Firoz would be the guy who was in charge of the strategic direction of the company. They agreed, in effect, to report to Firoz." Unlike so many entrepreneurs, who get so wrapped up in their companies that they cannot let go, the Ballard partners were able to keep their own personal preferences in perspective. "I mean, this is amazing, actually. And it's one of the things for which they've got to get a huge amount of credit. That they figured out their own limitations. They understood what Firoz could bring that they didn't have. They understood the sense of vision that Firoz could create and the possibility that he could go and do some of these mega-deals."

Geoffrey Ballard agrees with Brown. "It was hard for my ego. But it was the right thing to do, because the company had to move forward from being a research organization to being oriented to worldwide marketing. We needed strategic partners, and we needed someone with that negotiating skill set. Firoz clearly had those skills."

For the Ballard partners, though, there was more to the decision than being forced to turn their company over to a savvy marketing whiz kid. Rasul immediately made a favourable impression on them. For starters, he was articulate and well coiffed. David McLeod joked that Rasul's hair was probably neat even when he got out of bed. "Firoz was a very young man and very energetic," says Geoffrey Ballard. "We liked the cut of his jib."

What struck them most was Rasul's personal ethics as a Muslim and follower of the Aga Khan. "We liked the idea that he was an Ismaili," says Ballard. "He had strong family ties. Something like twenty per cent of his income was tithed out to things like a hospital in Pakistan. He fit the morality that we liked in our business." Remember, Ballard adds, "we were a very strong family company at that time. We weren't bloodthirsty, cut-and-dried people. We nurtured each of our employees. If people got in trouble, we helped out, we would make loans from the corporation to our employees. We wanted someone who had a moral responsibility to employees."

Keith Prater and Paul Howard shared this commitment. "That's why we get along so well," says Ballard. "We would solve most issues and questions on the basis of what was right, not what was best for the company. If employees had a complaint, it came down to what was right." This was understood by all the employees, he says, "and it generated a tremendous loyalty. And some of that still flows through Ballard today, even with the much larger employee base. Many loans never got repaid. We wrote them off. If somebody got sick, we'd bend the rules and make sure the family got what they needed. It was our brand of socialism. All three of us felt a very strong responsibility that comes with power."

Ballard has a favourite story that illustrates how unusual his company was. "One time," he chuckles, "we were looked at by a company that was going to invest in us." The company sent a prominent management consulting firm to do an analysis of the Ballard corporation. "And eventually a memorandum was leaked back of what they said about us. Basically, to paraphrase it, they'd said that Ballard Research was really a family-run company that was expressing Geoff Ballard's social responsibilities. And as such, it did not have the proper attitude to compete effectively in the give and take of modern business."

If they had to turn over their business to someone new, the Ballard partners agreed, let it be to someone who shared their values. "Firoz has a fundamental moral bent that is much stronger than that of the average person in business," says Ballard. "It was the key point that attracted us."

For his part, Rasul is also clear about this ethical side and how it carries over into the corporate culture at Ballard Power. "I'm a Muslim," he says with quiet pride. "And sharing is a big part of what I was taught as a child, in my family. The values I espouse and practise come from that. Moral values are part of the culture we have here at Ballard. It comes from sharing. From sharing the glory, but also sharing the success and the failures. And it comes from knowing that a community, or a group of people will succeed as a collective entity, rather than as an individual."

Rasul moved into his new office on his thirty-seventh birthday, at the beginning of January 1989. By then, Ballard had moved into a new, larger building in North Vancouver, one with room for the battery assembly lines. The fuel cell team was also brought into the mainstream of the company. Geoffrey Ballard retained an office down the hall and stayed on as chairman of the board. Keith Prater became vice-president for technology and later for intellectual property with key responsibility for patenting. Paul Howard was vice-president for finance and later for transportation.

Part of Rasul's agreement in taking over was that he could still back out if the next big instalment of money could not be raised. Tackling the venture capital market was his first challenge, and he hit the ground running. He and Mike Brown drew up a list of about fifty potential investors and sent out proposals. Based on the response, they whittled down the list and flew off together with Keith Prater to visit some thirty companies for follow-up presentations. There were several hectic trips around North America and one to Europe.

"It was a lot of hard work," recalls Prater. "We would get up in the morning and have four or five of these meetings in a day. Sometimes we'd fly from one city to the next to make the next pitch. Sometimes we spent the day driving all over town in a rented car." Once, while trying to get back to the airport in New York, they strayed from the main highway and found themselves lost in the clogged streets of a grim and intimidating ghetto neighbourhood. *Oh, oh,* Prater thought to himself. Three suits in a shiny new sedan seemed awfully conspicuous and vulnerable. "It was the sort of experience that established a bond, certainly between Mike and Firoz and me. We worked well together. It began setting the tone for the expanded partnership that was going to evolve over the next five years."

When the campaign to raise funds began, Prater was still technically president and CEO. He was also the one with the greatest scientific understanding of the fuel cell. "Because it was a technology sell, in the hour or so we would have to make our pitch, I was probably doing forty-five minutes of it." But at the same time, Firoz Rasul was introduced to potential investors as the company's golden boy and heir apparent. "Of necessity," says Prater, "we were selling two things. One was the hope of the technology. The other was that we also had acquired this individual with the experience necessary to take this thing further. And an investment would not have been made without both."

For his part, Brown was not just along for the ride. In fact, his role was crucial—to reassure investors about the company and its secure future. As Prater says "There were a number of investors who, because they were geographically so far away, would only—could only—have invested if they believed that there was someone closer whom they trusted to keep an eye on the investment. And Mike was that person."

"We are 3,000 miles away and it is a long trip," Bob Shaw told *PROFIT* magazine. His company, Arete Ventures Inc., of Rockville, Maryland, was one of those that anted up the cash. "Essentially, we depend on Michael Brown as lead investor to look after the investment. We have an extremely high regard for him."[27]

The Ballard team were surprised to see which of the venture companies they targetted actually decided to join the syndicate and which declined. "It seemed," says Prater, "to be very much a matter of the enthusiasm of the individual that we got ahold of." They visited Xerox corporation, for example, which had a venture capital division. The person in charge there really liked the technology, but the guidelines at Xerox called for investing only in technologies that were somehow related to Xerox products. So this key individual had to twist things a bit and imagine something rather silly, says Prater, such as a fuel cell-powered copying machine. "But he really wanted to invest, and so he managed to, and they were a very good early-stage investor."

"On the other hand, we went to a couple of funds that were nominally environmental funds, and we thought: Hey, if anyone's going to invest, these guys will. Well, it turned out that the environmental funds mainly invested in landfill sites and didn't understand the technology at all and weren't interested. That's what the environmental funds did," says Prater in a flabbergasted tone, still amazed years later. "They were into remediation, not into the prevention of environmental harm."

In the end they were successful, even leaving some money on the table because the investors did not seem to be a good fit. By the middle of 1989 they had lined up a blue chip roster of investors and a total of $7.5 million. Besides Xerox Venture Capital, Arete Ventures kicked in cash on behalf of twelve US and European gas and electrical utilities. There were also Metropolitan Life Insurance, British Gas, Motor-Columbus Techinvest of Switzerland, and Advent International Corporation of Boston, one of the largest venture funds in the world. In addition, Ventures West and the federal Business Development Bank of Canada increased their own investments to 14.8 per cent and 9.3 per cent respectively of the total stock.

The new arrangement left Ballard's employees with 38.3 per cent of the shares. Of this, just under half was held by the top people: Rasul, Ballard, Prater, and Howard, plus the original fuel cell team of Watkins, Epp, Dircks, and McLeod, who had all been given large stock holdings in recognition of their pioneering work on the technology. As share prices soared in the mid to late 1990s, some of them indulged in the outward signs of financial success. McLeod and Epp, for example, became the proud owners of beautiful sailing yachts. Prater and his wife bought themselves a large piece of semi-rural property where they could keep horses, and built themselves a new home.

It was a promising start for the new, expanded company, henceforth known as Ballard Power Systems (with its subsidiaries, Ballard Battery Systems and Ballard Advanced Materials, and later Ballard Generating Systems.) One measure of the success, Keith Prater points out, was that all of the original investors proved willing to put in more money later. There were two more rounds of venture funding before Ballard went public in 1993, a $4.6 million private placement in 1991 and another the following year for $2.5 million. "And they all played," says Prater. Not that this was by any means automatic. "Each time there was a new round of financing, there were debates and discussions." Ballard's financial team had to go around and visit investors again every round. "Oh yeah," Prater muses, "Any time you've got a situation where people are investing in something which has no definable value, the negotiation over what they are willing to pay for the next bit of it is always an interesting experience." Additional investors came in as the company grew, "but each of the original investors did, in fact, continue to invest. And that was seen as an important show of faith to the new potential investors."

With its new capital base, Ballard Power was off to a good start in its ambitious campaign to spearhead the fuel cell revolution. Yet it was still a tiny company on an unimposing back street in a small Canadian city that hardly anyone had ever heard of. People who walked into the building would have had the impression that the company was mainly interested in manufacturing batteries. Only two fuel cell stacks had actually been sold, and a few more were being leased out.

But these facts are deceptive. Already in 1989, the Ballard fuel cell was far ahead of the competition. Anyone who knew how big, heavy and noisy a portable gasoline generator could be would have been impressed by the tiny device only a bit larger than a car battery putting out the same level of power cleanly and quietly, and with no moving parts to wear out. Who could doubt that this thing would eventually sweep the world?

Certainly not David McLeod, who had been watching this device evolve for five years. "We've created a very good case for replacing the internal combustion engine," he said back then. Slipping into his marketing pitch, he rattled off the advantages of a fuel cell. It had never yet powered a car, but he was already describing its driving properties. "It gives electricity instantly. When you're driving and put your foot to the floor, it's instantaneous. It's load following to such a degree that we talk in microseconds." Moreover, he added, the fuel cell is a "manageable technology, something that lends itself to high-volume manufacturing, to simplicity. And that's why there's all this excitement about it." As for who might want to buy it, "the market," he insisted, "is everywhere, from a five-kilowatt tactical field generator at one end to the car at the other, and everything in between. So, at this point it's merely a matter of getting the cost down."

On
the ROAD

Ballard Power entered the 1990s with new sources of financing in place and a clear goal, to commercialize the fuel cell and introduce it into the largest power markets. But if Geoffrey Ballard thought he would be able to work in harmony alongside Firoz Rasul and continue to play a decisive role in running the company, he was mistaken. Downstairs in the laboratory, rapid progress continued on fuel cell development. Upstairs, though, along the corridor of executive offices, seeds were planted that soon sprouted into robust personal rivalries. There would be harsh words and hard feelings that quietly festered over the years and evolved into contending claims to credit for the company's achievements. By the time the fuel cell was making headlines in the mid-to-late 1990s, these barely concealed personal tensions would undermine the pleasure and gratification the principal players should have felt in their time of glory.

Given the personalities of Ballard and Rasul, and the situation—an ambitious younger man moving in on the turf of a proud older one—the friction and contention were perhaps inevitable. David McLeod watched the conflict unfold with a sense of sadness. "When Firoz came in he was confronted with problems because Geoffrey had this presence." Ballard had a big ego, and everyone in the company was accustomed to listening to him. In McLeod's opinion, "you can't have two CEOs in a building. You just can't. However, having said that, it's unfortunate that Firoz was never able to use him as a mentor. Because Geoffrey was tough. A lot tougher than Firoz. He could make decisions and would live by them, right or wrong."

It took about a year before the first signs of trouble appeared, a year in which Firoz Rasul lost little time in putting his own personal stamp on the company. One move was to bring in new people—recruited by him and with no previous association with the company's founders—high up in the organization. Yet he realized that it was important to maintain a sense of continuity in such a period of transition. And if he had forgotten, no doubt Mike Brown, who held the purse strings on the board of directors, would have reminded him. "I thought it would be a disaster," says Brown, "if we lost the three founders." And so, the Ballard partners stayed. So did the original technical team. "Watkins, Dircks, Epp—they were all kept on," says Rasul. "I did not want to lose any of them. But there were also new people coming in, with skills that would take us further. It was a change, but nobody left."

Still, the old guard was gradually eased out of the most powerful positions, a process that continued through the mid-1990s. Rasul turned to his old firm, MDI, for two new executives. Robert Fleming became vice-president for marketing, replacing David McLeod, who became vice-president for government and military and remained active in his role as lobbyist with the federal government in Ottawa. Avarham Elarar was brought in as president of the Ballard Batteries subsidiary. These appointments were part of a trend towards recruiting experienced specialists for management positions. As McLeod told *BC Business* magazine, "Avarham didn't know a battery from anything, but he knew production."[28] Keith Prater stayed on as vice-president for technology and later for intellectual property, that is, patents. Paul Howard took on the title of vice-president for programs and later for transportation systems, which in practice mainly meant taking charge of the company's program to build a series of demonstration fuel cell powered buses.

The most significant personnel change came in early 1990 when Rasul hired a powerful new chief financial officer, vice-president and corporate secretary, Mossadiq Umedaly. Like Rasul, Umedaly was an Ismaili Muslim born in East Africa, in his case in Uganda. "I'm Iranian many generations back," he says, "but my grandparents were born in India." In fact, he had met Rasul when they were both sixteen years old at an Outward Bound school at Mount Kilimanjaro. But after that, they did not meet again until 1989, when Rasul asked if he wanted to come and help him "build this company."

Umedaly is a short man with a round face and deceptively soft cherubic features. He came to Canada in 1975, took an undergraduate degree in business and then an MBA at McMaster University. He began his career as an accountant, working for Price Waterhouse in Toronto and Rome, and then joined the Aga Khan Foundation in 1980. The Aga Khan is the progressive spiritual leader of the twelve to fifteen million strong Ismaili sect of Shi'ite Muslims. Umedaly describes him as a "Muslim with a particular bent for Third World development," including health, nutrition, and education. "That's his passion in life." The Aga Khan has businesses, such as insurance companies, banks, and tourist resorts, that earn money, mainly in the West. Then he spends "phenomenal amounts, virtually all that money," says Umedaly, "in the developing world on projects that are designed to improve the quality of life of people there."

One of the projects Umedaly is most proud of was when he, together with seven other people, helped to set up the Aga Khan university and teaching hospital, a $400 million (US) project in Karachi, Pakistan. Umedaly was there from conception to completion and operation, and calls it "a world-class institution whose objective was to set standards that would be emulated throughout the Third World." He found the work fascinating and enjoyable. "It was the first time that I'd done something in my job that was really worthwhile. You know, if you work for a big company like Price Waterhouse, you can only do things that make small improvements." He was only twenty-nine when he joined the Karachi project and gained great experience as chief financial officer and chief planner. "How often," he asks, "do you get to do something like that from scratch?"

"I'm very lucky," he says, "because I got the chance again here at Ballard. When I joined Ballard, just after Firoz, it was a very small company, really just a blank piece of paper." The Ballard founders would hardly agree with that assessment, of course. They felt that they had already brought the technology and the company a long way in the right direction. In addition, Geoffrey Ballard simply could not stand Umedaly, and the feeling seems to have been reciprocated. There was none of the mutual respect that existed between Ballard and Rasul, at least at the beginning. To Ballard, Umedaly was Rasul's right-hand man and nothing more.

When Rasul asked him whether he wanted to join Ballard, Umedaly's first concern was that it might be too early. Sometimes an invention can come too soon, he says, when the market is not yet ready for it. Is it worth waiting a while, he asked himself, just keeping it cool for a time? "But then we felt, no, we only live once, we're going to go for it and try to see what we can do to change the world. We knew right from the beginning that it had the potential."

Umedaly saw not only the business potential, but the dire need for the fuel cell as a clean technology. He had been a car enthusiast all his life. In East Africa his parents used to race cars, and he himself had driven high-performance sedans in African automobile rallies. He loves the car as a machine but hates its impact on the environment. "If you live in Rome or Karachi or London or Paris," he says, "you realize what a mess this internal combustion engine makes, and that sooner or later we've all got to find a solution."

The key thing, he adds, is to find an alternative that does not impinge too strongly on people's set ways. "There are many environmental technologies that require people to change their lifestyles. And until human beings come close to a major problem staring them in the face, they won't change." On the other hand, if you can find a way to solve the problem that does not force people to change their lifestyle, "then you've got a solution that's viable. And, in fact, that's what a fuel cell does. Whether it's in a stationary power plant, or an automobile, or a bus, you can operate it the same way as you do today. Get the same range. Get the same performance. So there's no compromise in these regards. And that's why we think it will fly."

Under the new management, Ballard continued expanding the fuel cell side of the company, which grew from a few dozen people at the end of 1989 to 107 by the end of 1993. Meanwhile the battery side of the company also grew rapidly through 1991. The early Canadian and US military battery contracts were followed by a larger $30 million one for the US Army. Battery-related employment peaked at 174 as the large contracts were fulfilled. Then in November 1992 the US Army cancelled two out of three multi-year supply contracts due to excess inventory and over purchasing. Employment on the battery side dropped to only 36 by the end of 1993. In 1995, rather than put additional money into Ballard Batteries, Ballard Power sold its shrinking battery subsidiary for $3.7 million to Bashaw Holdings Limited. (Now called BlueStar Battery Systems International Corp., the spin-off company is based in Surrey, BC.) The Ballard company had decided to focus fully on fuel cells, including those for stationary power.

One of the earliest major fuel cell contracts, beginning in 1988, was to develop the largest PEM stack built by anyone in the world up to that time, a ten-kilowatt unit for Dow Canada. Jointly financed by Dow and the Ontario Ministry of Energy, and costing $600,000, the stack was designed as a stationary power source to run on hydrogen that was a by-product of Dow's chlorine plant in Sarnia, Ontario.

Stationary fuel cells do not have quite the same requirements as a power source as fuel cells for transportation, and in some ways they are a simpler engineering challenge. A stationary fuel cell may not need to start up quickly, for example, and it can be designed to run at a fairly steady power level. It does not have to be as compact or lightweight as a fuel cell for transportation. Its initial cost per kilowatt generated can be somewhat higher, since it will operate over a much longer period, typically thirty years or more.

On the other hand, stationary PEM cells face stiff competition. Other types of fuel cells, including solid oxide and molten carbonate ones, which operate at much higher temperatures, are serious contenders for many stationary applications. Among other factors, the time required to bring them up to optimum temperature—it can take hours—is not a serious drawback for a plant that may run non-stop for months at a time. Moreover, the extra heat produced can be captured and put to use. Hence high temperature fuel cells can attain somewhat higher overall energy efficiencies than PEM. How the contest between PEM and the other types will shake out in the stationary energy market remains very much an open question.

When Ballard set out to "change the world," it had its sights firmly set on both stationary power and transportation, and it has retained this dual focus. Today Ballard has a subsidiary, Ballard Generation Systems, with a separate facility in Burnaby, BC, devoted entirely to stationary fuel cells, as well as a number of industrial partners exclusively interested in this side of the business. Its commercialization plan through the end of the 1990s has entailed spending nearly $100 million over three years mainly on marketing 250-kilowatt units the size of a shipping container suitable for specialized power needs such as hospitals and remote housing subdivisions.

Transportation, especially automobiles, looked initially like a tougher nut to crack. "We thought the automobile would be the last frontier of the fuel cell," says Geoffrey Ballard. "We didn't think it would be the first. It's sociologically the most complex, infrastructurally the most difficult, and it's controlled by a very small group of very powerful companies. We essentially went after stationary fuel cells first." But soon events beyond Canada's borders made the transportation market look better and better.

The most encouraging developments came from California, which had the worst air pollution problem in the United States. Even in the mid-1990s, long after measures were introduced to ameliorate the situation, southern California still averaged about one hundred days a year in which ozone levels exceeded federal health standards. (The next worst US city, Houston, averaged thirteen such days a year, while New York and Philadelphia had only four days a year.) In 1995 the greater Los Angeles area had fourteen days with particularly terrible "stage one" ozone episodes, in which everyone is advised to avoid vigorous outdoor exercise. And this was already a great improvement over the horrendous situation in the 1970s, when, for example, 1977 saw 121 such episodes.

Responding to this air pollution crisis in the 1970s, southern California established a regional agency, the South Coast Air Quality Management District (SCAQMD), that was responsible for monitoring air quality and encouraging the reduction of air pollutants from all sources. But during the early and mid-1980s it was ineffective, largely because enforcement had no teeth. "Of the roughly 10,000 businesses applying for... permits to expand operations each year," *Newsweek* magazine noted, "only 2,000 were showing that their emissions would fall within permissible limits. Yet the agency routinely granted permits anyway. Violators, if they were fined at all, paid an average of just $260 per violation."[29]

In 1987, though, the California legislature passed a bill that revitalized the agency. In 1988 it launched an ambitious twenty-year plan that not only mandated a crackdown on polluting industries, it also provided funding to subsidize the development of cleaner technologies, and regulations that would require their use, especially for transportation. From the outset the plan foresaw that vehicles purchased after 1993 in the Air Quality District for fleet use (such as buses and rental cars) would have to be low-emission types (LEVs) that could run on cleaner fuels such as methanol.[*]

In the longer run, the plan aimed to encourage "zero emission" vehicles, or ZEVs, such as battery and fuel-cell powered buses and cars. Regulations were adopted in 1990 requiring that starting in 1998 two per cent of all new cars sold in California (around 22,000 a year) had to be zero emission types, and by the year 2003 this had to rise to ten per cent. Auto companies would be penalized if they fell short. In 1995, though, as a result of intensive lobbying by some

---

[*] This was fortunate for positioning the Ballard fuel cell, because methanol is a convenient liquid fuel that can be converted to a hydrogen-rich gas and used by a PEM fuel cell. Having methanol already available at California gas stations promised to ease the introduction of fuel cell vehicles in that state. The first Ballard fuel cell powered DaimlerChrysler cars, aimed at the California market in 2004, are expected to run on methanol.

auto makers and oil companies, the California Air Resources Board, a state-wide rather than regional body, agreed to scrap the 1998 deadline. As the *Los Angeles Times* reported, "The Big Three—General Motors, Ford, and Chrysler—and US oil companies have launched efforts to roll back the mandate, including massive advertising campaigns targeting the car-buying public."[30]

Environmental groups expressed outrage. But one Air Resources Board member, Joseph Calhoun (a former General Motors employee) said that retaining the original deadline would guarantee the failure of electric cars by requiring their mass production too early, when the battery technology was not yet sufficiently advanced. "I'm convinced we have a program that is headed for a train wreck," he said, mixing his transportation metaphors. "If we go ahead with forcing the two per cent, we will really, really have a disaster."[31] A Chrysler spokesman said, "We have urged some sort of easing into the market instead of this shock approach of dumping a bunch of cars on the market and trying to sell them... You can't jam this down people's throats."[32]

In return for being granted the relief, a group of six auto makers agreed to produce at least some battery-powered electric vehicles sooner, specifically 5,000 in 1996 and 1997 and 14,000 in 1998. And they did try, with General Motors launching its sporty looking EV-1 in the fall of 1996. It ran on conventional lead-acid batteries and was initially priced at $33,000 (US). This proved to be a bit rich for a car whose battery needed to be recharged after 120 km or less. GM switched to leasing the cars, as well as a battery powered pickup truck, but still they went over like a lead balloon. Just over 400 were leased out in the first two years, and GM was hoping to market 400 more in 1998. Even with more advanced batteries that gave it about twice the original range, though, by early 1999 GM's electric car had "failed to catch on in the markets where it is being leased."[33]

Despite the abandonment of the 1998 zero-emission goal, the target of ten per cent ZEVs for 2003 stands. Under the rules, any auto company that does not fulfill its quota will be subject to a hefty ($5,000) penalty for each car below the target. Meanwhile, several other states, notably Massachusetts and New York, have introduced similar requirements. This establishes a solid future market for ZEVs and has helped to spur on Ballard's efforts. "Environmental regulations on emissions—particularly in California and Massachusetts—are a driving force for the transportation market," Mossadiq Umedaly told *The Financial Post*.[34] One measure of how fast the fuel cell for transportation has come along is that as late as 1995 an Air Quality District report stated that ZEVs effectively mean battery-powered electric vehicles, "as other zero-emission technologies such as fuel cells are not likely to be commercially available before 2010."[35] Today the likely fuel cell debut is 2004.

California's push to control emissions eventually led to direct funding of the Ballard R & D effort by the Air Quality District and was the beginning of a long-standing and close relationship. Years later a former official with the district, Larry Berg, was to become a Ballard director. But initially, interest in fuel cells in California merely gave the Ballard fuel cell enhanced international profile. Led by its new executive officer James Lents, a physicist, the district began to look at the Ballard fuel cell as an interesting technology with great promise.

In October 1988, a Ballard team flew down to southern California and showcased its latest technical achievements at an international fuel cell conference in Long Beach. People there were impressed. As a *Los Angeles Times* editorial noted, "it is no small surprise to hear serious discussion these days of what amounts to importing clean air from Canada. The discussions are serious because of technical breakthroughs in the design of fuel cells in the laboratories of

Ballard Technologies Corp.... The laboratory now thinks it can replace diesel engines in city buses with power units that would add only ten per cent to the lifetime costs of the bus.... Americans who have looked at the equipment agree that the Ballard break-through is real enough. One of them is James Lents.... The fuel cell needs more tinkering to get the cost down even further, but Lents is encouraging the company to expand beyond the labora-tory, build some prototypes of fuel cells that generate enough power to move electric buses around, and get the buses on the streets for long-term testing."[36]

Geoffrey Ballard began to feel out the BC provincial government for development money for a fuel cell bus. This led to a key but some-what contentious event in Ballard company lore. Geoffrey Ballard often played tennis with the late BC energy minister Jack Davis at the posh Hollyburn Country Club in West Vancouver. In breaks between sets, and afterwards lolling in the hot tub, they talked business and technology. They agreed that one of the biggest obstacles to the fuel cell was scepticism, bordering on outright opposition, from the oil industry and the automobile companies, especially in North Amer-ica. During these chats, Davis told Ballard that the only way to move the fuel cell technology forward in the face of such scepticism was to put something out there that actually worked and proved the big companies wrong.

Existing cell stacks were not nearly compact enough yet to fit into a car, but a larger vehicle might be viable and help pave the way. They discussed various transportation demonstration projects, including locomotives and large transport trucks, but none of these had polit-ical sex appeal. A bus, on the other hand, had the advantage that peo-ple could get on it, go for a ride, relate to it. Davis wanted to be assured that the project was feasible. Ballard thought it was. Well, then, Davis said, "give me a significant, green photo-op for the pre-mier and I will get you the funding." BC's premier at the time was

William Vander Zalm, a man embattled by foes even in his own party and soon to be immersed in a scandal that forced his resignation. He needed all the favourable publicity he could get. Ballard agreed that a fuel cell-powered bus, developed with provincial money, would look very good politically.

Ballard quickly discovered that his optimism and priorities were not widely shared at his company. Even his closest colleagues thought he was a bit nuts. "They literally all deserted me," he says, recalling this lonely time with a touch of bitterness. "The bus was my baby because no one else wanted it, even at Ballard. They were all against it. They were afraid of the risk. They didn't want to do anything where failure might loom. Everybody said, you couldn't make a vehicle work."

But Ballard, with his bulldog tenacity, would not let go of the idea. He pursued the contacts with Davis and got him to provide money to prepare a detailed proposal for the provincial government. When that seemed to indicate that a bus was feasible, Ballard came back to his colleagues urging a concrete decision to proceed with actual construction of a small "proof of concept" bus.

According to Ballard, Rasul's main objection was the considerable chance that failure could turn the project into an embarrassing fiasco. At some point it turned personal. During a key meeting, Ballard recalls saying to the young CEO, "Wait a minute Firoz. You're new on the block. I've been in this business a long time and I'm not willing to give up. I want this bus thing to happen." In Ballard's recollection, Rasul replied, "Well, we're all major share holders, let's put it to a vote." And in the showdown, everyone voted against Ballard. "The rest of the guys felt Firoz's power. That's why they deserted me." He was shocked and hurt.

But Ballard still would not give up. "I said, 'OK, I'm going to do the bus anyway, but I'll do it without any funding from the company, and I'll focus on that and leave the rest of the running of the business to you.'" He and his wife had long enjoyed weekend and summer visits to their seaside home on scenic Salt Spring Island, which is a few hours away from Vancouver by ferry. Now he was determined to go into semi-retirement and live there full time. A contributing factor to this decision was a debilitating liver disease that was sapping Ballard's strength. "I'll move over to Salt Spring," he told them, "and I'll chair the board, but I won't be part of the day-to-day operations of the company except for the bus." Raising outside money, he says, meant that the bus would not be a burden on company finances or cash flow, so the others could hardly object. "It was a project that was being funded," says Ballard. "It's pretty hard to stop a project that's being funded."

Ballard had no doubt about who should be in charge of the project. "I'll get the money," he told Paul Howard, "I want you to build the bus." Howard's forte had always been day-to-day operations. He had been in charge of the project to overhaul John Horton's submarine and had been project manager on the original fuel cell project. "I had taken the submarine and made it work," Howard says. "So, as Geoff said about me, anyone who can take a complicated vessel like that and figure out how to make all the changes and make it work and manage all of that in terms of budgets and schedules, obviously knows how to get things done. That's what I'm good at. I know how to make things happen. That's why, when the bus came along, he turned to me and said, 'OK, make this thing work.'"

And that's just what Howard did. The total cost was around $6 million, of which Jack Davis got BC to put up the largest share, $3.8 million. The Canadian federal government kicked in $1 million, and the rest came in the form of services in kind, mainly labour, from the Ballard company. This labour input consisted of a technical team that varied between six and eight people.

Howard might have preferred to design and build special equipment to fit the specific needs of a small, electric-powered bus, but that was never an option. From the start he realized that, because of the time element and especially the budget constraints, they would have to buy standard off-the-shelf equipment. "We didn't have money to develop components," he says. "We had to find stuff and adapt it."

The group began by determining the preliminary design para-meters and performance goals. Based on this, they decided to aim for a smallish vehicle. They bought a ten-metre-long (thirty-two feet) twenty-six seat diesel bus made by National Coach Corp. of Califor-nia and stripped out the engine and rear rows of seats. To give it the needed power the bus would have to carry twenty-four of the five-kilowatt Mark V fuel cell stacks. But that was only the start. Next, they had to look at electric motors, radiators for the coolant water, compressors, and other electrical components. It was all a new and exciting challenge for people who were not automotive engineers and had never built a working vehicle before.

A lot of digging, learning, and first-hand research were required. In general, Howard says, "We knew what components we had to get. So we would search around." They used their fingers to do the walking through the Yellow Pages, phoned around and got people to explain how the equipment worked. It was a steep learning curve. "That's how practical engineering is done." For example, says Howard, "we would go to the people who provided the radiators to car companies and learn from them what kind of a radiator we should have."

Likewise, in the laboratory the fuel cell stacks could run off tanks of oxygen or compressed air, but the size of the compressor did not matter. For a bus, though, they needed the smallest, lightest turbo compressor available to force the air through the fuel cell stacks. Fortunately, Howard had a team brimming with talent. "These guys were very practical, hands-on mechanical and electrical engineers," he says. In the case of the compressor, for example, one of the engi-neers, Doug Strasky, happened to be a race-car enthusiast and knew that a certain type of turbo compressor was used on such vehicles. "Let's go get one," Strasky said.

And so, over the next two years Howard and his team built their bus. "And, of course, it became a success and a showcase," says Howard, smiling. The company had already built fuel cells that worked, but nothing was as impressive as making wheels actually go around. He vividly remembers the euphoria and change in atmosphere at the company the first time the bus actually ran. The schedule called for having the bus out and rolling by March 1993, but it was ready sooner than expected. The system had already been tested inside the large garage-like bay where it was constructed, with the wheels turning on a stationary dynamometer.

Even years later, Howard can rattle off the date and time that the big event took place. "It was January 27, 1993, a drizzly night, about 5 or 5:30 p.m. People at Ballard tended to work late, and somehow the word started to spread, 'I think they're going to try to run the bus tonight.'" The idea was to have only the most basic trial, to back the bus out of the bay onto the parking lot. It was not yet licenced or insured, so they could not take it out onto a city street.

Instead of going home, people hung around and waited. In the end, there were about fifty employees milling around in the parking lot, waiting. On board were the driver—Doug Strasky, the race-car enthusiast—and two or three other engineers. With the fuel cells warmed up, Strasky put the bus into reverse and slowly backed it out onto the parking lot. Then the little crowd surged forward. Strasky opened the door mainly to acknowledge them, but before he knew it fifteen or twenty of the employees pushed past him and insisted that they wanted to go for a ride. Strasky shifted into forward gear and slowly took them around the back of the building, down an alleyway and around to the front. Because Howard and his team had already run the engine inside the building and watched the wheels go around, they knew it would work. "But just to see that when you put it into gear all the pieces came together. Even for me, a kind of conservative engineer, it was so exciting."

Things began to get giddy. When the first group of people got off the bus, they were grinning from ear to ear and making dramatic statements to each other about what an historic occasion it was. Unfortunately, there was no champagne handy to celebrate with. They weren't ready or expecting anything big that night. But they were intoxicated enough already from the thrill of seeing their years of work come to fruition.

When the bus reached the front door of the building, Howard ducked inside to tell anyone else who was around what was happening. He ran up the stairs and found Firoz Rasul conferring in his office with one of the company's lawyers, Henry Ellis. "Hey, we've got the bus out and are driving it around the parking lot," Howard told them. "Come and have a ride." Rasul was nonplussed. That can't be, he said, it's not supposed to be ready for a month or so. But he and the lawyer came downstairs and joined the rest of the crowd for a quick jaunt. And when they got off the bus, Ellis the attorney turned to Rasul and said, "*Now* I know what a fuel cell does."

"And in my mind," Howard laughs, "that was one of the most significant comments I heard. Because Ellis had been our attorney for a number of years and he understood the fuel cell. We had been telling him about it for years." But no matter how often you draw the picture, no matter how much you talk, people don't get it until they see it make the wheels go around. "And that became the real importance of the bus, because the layman could begin to understand it. It didn't matter if technical people or scientists understood. The people who have influence and make decisions about money had to understand what the fuel cell did."

Mike Brown, who deals with the money people all the time, agrees with this assessment. "People sort of seize on the bus. They can actually see it. They look and say, 'Hey, this looks like an ordinary bus.' But, of course the most marvellous thing is that it looks like an ordinary bus, and it kind of drives like an ordinary bus, but it doesn't make a lot of dirty crud."

The next milestone in the Ballard bus development was the public roll-out in the presence of government officials and the media. This took place on June 8, 1993, outside Vancouver's futuristic geodesic dome called Science World. By then a new British Columbia premier, Mike Harcourt, was waiting on the podium with Geoffrey Ballard and other dignitaries to bask in the glow of the long-awaited photo-op. Firoz Rasul was away on other company business.

Paul Howard was directing the logistics, and everything seemed to be going well. The bus was idling off to the side of the Science World building, and Geoffrey Ballard was about to speak. Suddenly Howard got a call from the driver, again Doug Strasky, on his walkie talkie. "The compressor just stopped." A small bolt—not actually part of the fuel cell, but crucial—had broken. "It was the end of my life," Howard says, recalling the sinking feeling he had in the pit of his stomach. "Hundreds of people were there. My family and friends were there. I was at the centre, and the person you would look to if this thing wasn't going to work."

After a stunned moment of horror, Howard orchestrated a comic-opera charade. He went up to the podium and discreetly told Geoffrey Ballard what had happened. Ballard remained cool. Then six Ballard Power employees, hidden from view, pushed the bus until it rolled silently down a slight incline. Strasky steered it toward the podium. Because it was expected to be an extremely quiet vehicle, no one seemed to notice that the engine was not actually running.

Geoffrey Ballard launched into his speech. "We must create a commercial project that can go into production," he said. "This is not a project that industry can do alone. It will take legislation and determination," he intoned, predicting that the fuel cell would eventually replace the gas-guzzling internal combustion engines "that pollute our city." Premier Harcourt toasted the "Ballard bus from British Columbia" with a glass of water to symbolize the water that is the fuel cell's only emission. Environment Minister John Cashore likened the Ballard headquarters in North Vancouver to Kitty Hawk, North Carolina, where the Wright brothers had made their first airplane flight.

When the speeches were over and the applause died down, Harcourt said, "Now let's go for a ride." Howard's heart nearly stopped. But then he got a miraculous reprieve. The crowd closed in tightly around the bus. Reporters, thrusting their little tape recorders in his face, asked him one question after another. "They wanted an explanation of how the fuel cells worked before they went for a ride," says Howard, "so we opened the back and I started explaining things and pointing out the fuel cell stacks. I was getting asked more and more questions. And it occurred to me on the spot, *I'm just going to keep talking.* In the meantime, people were milling around. So it was becoming unsafe to drive the bus right then."

Howard made a point of answering every question in great detail. "And there really was a lot of interest, and the cameras were all there. And Harcourt had to get someplace else." There were too many people around the bus to move it safely, so the ruse worked. "Come back this afternoon for a ride," Howard told reporters. By then the problem was fixed. "It was just a little bolt that had broken, and we were very fortunate. Our engineers are very good. The media came back at one o'clock and we had a great ride. We got great PR." The event was carried on CNN worldwide. Only a lone Seattle TV station clued in and reported the glitch.

With a total peak power of 120 kW, equal to about 160 horsepower, the bus had a range of only 160 km (100 miles) and it only carried twenty passengers. Fully one-third of the space, including where six of the original seats had been, was taken up by mechanical equipment, especially the bulky fuel cells, which were twice the size and weight of a conventional diesel engine. But it was peppy enough, with acceleration and hill-climbing ability comparable to that of a diesel bus. From a standing start, it could reach fifty kilometres (thirty miles) an hour in twenty seconds, and it had a top speed of seventy (forty-five miles). Geoffrey Ballard called its performance "magnificent. It was overwhelmingly better than anyone thought the first attempt would be."

Over the next two years, the little demonstration bus was displayed in British Columbia as well as in California, where the Air Quality District was helping to fund the next, larger Ballard bus. The quiet, non-polluting bus captured public attention wherever it went. But the conflict-ridden way it came about left Geoffrey Ballard embittered toward Rasul and the others who opposed him. Of course, he says, "Once the bus was actually out there driving around, then it became the darling of the company and it became everybody's idea." Its value, he says, "was so obvious."

There are differing views at Ballard Power on just how the bus project was launched, and who played what role. Firoz Rasul has his own response to Ballard's account of the early events and the decision to build the bus. He grants that Ballard was "very instrumental in working with the provincial government" to secure the first demonstration bus funding and contract, but he is uncomfortable with characterizing the bus project as part of a deal or trade-off in exchange for Ballard's semi-retirement. "It was not part of a deal," he insists. "It was more the case that we said, 'Geoffrey, we need you to help us in this area. This is an area where you can put something together.' And he was very happy with that. Although he was not actively involved in the company, there were areas that certainly captured his imagination and where he thought he could help."

Mike Brown is not certain precisely how the dispute over the bus played out and who stood where. "There were discussions as to whether we should do the bus or not. And I honestly can't remember what my position was." But he says that he can see why Rasul and others might be reluctant to sign on to the project. On the one hand, Brown asks rhetorically, "How do you prove that the damn thing is feasible and will work without making something? It's the most obvious thing in the world that you have to figure out how to do that." On the other hand, "the problem was that we didn't have very much money. It looked like a hell of a project. And what if it didn't work?"

Failure could have serious consequences, and if Rasul worried about that, Brown says, "that's a completely legitimate issue." He points to the large colour photo on the wall of his conference room showing the Ballard fuel cell stack as it was in 1989 and 1990. "That stack right there doesn't produce very much power per litre or per kilogram of weight. It wasn't good enough. I mean, it was marginal, damned marginal. That's why we had to have a small bus. It couldn't go very fast. We were really lucky. It was a close shave, that bus, getting it so it would actually work." In retrospect, he says, "it turned out that the bus has actually been a tremendously valuable thing to have. I don't know, frankly, whose idea the bus first was. It may well have been Geoffrey. It might have been Paul or Keith. I don't think it was Firoz. It doesn't matter in my view. It got done."

Mossadiq Umedaly is less diplomatic and more caustic than Rasul in his rejection of Ballard's claim that he launched the bus project virtually on his own. "There's a little bit of revisionism there," he argues. "Everything we do is a team effort. No single individual—not Firoz or myself included—has ever accomplished anything in this company, because we just don't operate as individuals." Besides, says Umedaly, "nobody's going to go and give X number of dollars to Geoffey Ballard to build a bus. There's an organization and a system and a credibility and a marketing effort and a technology behind it, and a financial strength behind that. So there were teams that led certain things, and I think Paul Howard was certainly the early leader— with Geoffrey Ballard—on the bus. And we've gone on to the next phase in that."

As for Ballard's claim that Jack Davis wanted the bus as a photo opportunity for the premier, Umedaly scoffs at the very idea. "You don't want to print that. It's embarrassing. But I don't think we ever sold it like that. That's in Geoffrey's mind." Umedaly repeats his argument that public funding involves a far more sophisticated and rational process and that Geoffrey Ballard has drastically oversimplified the situation. "You will never sell any politician on a photo opportunity. That's a figment of people's imagination, in fact. It's very amateurish, frankly. You've got to show them real stuff. These are people responsible for public money, so they're not as frivolous as that."

Keith Prater supports Geoffrey Ballard's basic account. "Geoff was essentially told, 'If you can do this on your own, that's fine.' But the board of directors said, 'We don't think we're ready for this.' The bus was done by Geoff in spite of other people's perceptions." Paul Howard agrees. For one thing, he clearly credits Ballard with being the one who pushed for the bus project. "This is where I attribute the visionary part to Geoff. He had the vision to see that you've got to put this thing into a vehicle for people to see what it really is, a showcase." Howard also confirms Ballard's private channels into the BC government. "He knew Jack Davis and was able to get the provincial and federal governments to come up with the $5 million it was going to take to do it. And basically it *was* through his connection with Jack Davis and playing tennis at the Hollyburn Country Club. I wasn't party to it, but I believe it, because I know we got the money," he laughs.

Howard acknowledges that Ballard was making a big personal sacrifice for the good of the company by agreeing to focus on funding the bus and stepping back from his role as an unusually active board chairman. "To Geoff's credit," says Howard, "he recognized that you couldn't have two guys running the company. He had to step right aside. And I'll tell you, it was a much easier transition for Keith Prater and me, because we were going to stay on as vice-presidents. I'm sure Geoff went through a much tougher time than we did. He said to us, 'Look, for the interest of the company I'll step aside. The fuel cell is really going to go someplace. But I've got to bite my tongue when I see things being done that I disagree with.'"

Howard clearly recalls opposition within the company to the bus project and Geoffrey Ballard's push for it. "Yes, there were those who thought that putting fuel cells into a bus was a crazy idea." One engineer was eager to work on the bus, so Howard assigned him to it. "But he told me, privately, after the project was under way, 'You know, I'm kind of ostracized here. People think I'm nuts. They think what we're doing is nuts, that this is never going to work.'" There were quite a few employees, says Howard, who thought jumping from small five-kilowatt stacks to a system with over one hundred kilowatts was at best premature. "Then we began to build it. And it became the focal point. And what's that expression, 'success has a thousand fathers and failure is an orphan?'"

The first small bus, and the larger ones that followed shortly, put Ballard on the road, literally and figuratively, to the clean, green transportation future. But with Geoffrey Ballard and his supporters on one side and Firoz Rasul and his cohorts on the other, a schism split the company's upper echelons, and it never truly healed. Even in conversations with both of them many years later, there is no mistaking the edge and caustic tone in their voices when they speak of each other. Unfortunately, the dispute over the bus was only the first such irritation that would impair personal relations at Ballard and cast a pall over its emerging success.

Venturesome
but CONSERVATIVE

W hile Paul Howard and his team tackled the challenge of building a functioning bus, Firoz Rasul and Mossadiq Umedaly faced problems of their own. They had to keep the finances healthy so that the company could survive while its fuel cell program expanded. To do this they had to come up with a balanced strategy that paid attention to all aspects of the business—the technology, the marketing, the patents, the funding—so that the company was equally solid on all key fronts. And they had to snare some major industrial partners to ease Ballard Power's access to key markets and contribute to its R & D efforts.

Rasul and Umedaly devised and pursued a cautious financial plan that was designed to avoid relying on any single source of funding. One thing they shunned like the plague was borrowing money. "We will not take debt," says Umedaly, "until we have a vision that we can repay it." This carried forward a policy that had been rigorously adhered to by the Ballard founders as well. "Technologically we are very venturesome and creative," Umedaly adds, "and financially very conservative."

In the early 1990s, when Ballard was still a private company, they could divert revenues from the profitable battery division with its sizeable government contracts and put some of that money into research and development on the fuel cell. They also received infusions of government money from Victoria, Ottawa, and Washington for the first Ballard bus, for work on a US-sponsored transit bus program, and for a US-funded fuel cell vehicle program that was coordinated by General Motors.

In addition, Ballard could fall back on its syndicate of private investors. They went back to the venture capital market twice and raised an additional $7 million by mid-1992. But then, as the *Financial Times of Canada* noted, the company's "cash-burn rate" was accelerating: "Another $30 million is required to fund Ballard's R & D program over the coming 18 months. Rasul says he may tap a 'strategic partner'—a company that can bring to the alliance a low-cost manufacturing process or a profitable application. The likely alternative: a public offering of shares."[37]

In 1993 Ballard went public at a price of $8 per share, plus half a warrant, which could be exercised at $10. The initial public offering raised $15 million, and the company was listed on the Toronto Stock Exchange. This IPO fell quite a bit short of the amount Ballard had hoped for, but it was followed by a series of additional offerings over the next few years. In May 1994, for example, the company received another $10 million in equity financing, in August 1995 over $21 million, and in February and June of 1996 a total of more than $57 million.

These public offerings required that Ballard Power pay careful attention to its investors. The challenge was to keep them confident of the company's prospects over the long period of time before there were likely to be significant revenues from the commercial sale of fuel cells. As Rasul says, technically it is investment bankers that float the stock. But effectively, nobody does it for you. "You do it for yourself." And what are investors interested in? "They're investing in three things: management, credibility, and technology." Through the mid-90s, most of the Ballard stock was bought up by blue chip institutional investors, mainly pension and equity funds in Europe and Canada. He and Umedaly consciously targetted pension funds, says Rasul, "because they have a longer vision; they're not looking at quarterly results." This is particularly relevant to a company like Ballard that has no prospect of profits for many years.

But getting an institutional investor to buy a chunk of Ballard's equity was only the first step. After that came constant follow-up to massage the investors and keep them happy so they would be likely to take a part of subsequent offerings. "We're in direct communication with our investors," says Umedaly, "meeting with every major investor at least once a year and most of them twice a year." Sometimes they have problems or concerns to raise with the Ballard executives. For example, there may be items in the news that concern them, such as other technology developments that could impact on the commercial potential of fuel cells. In such cases, "they will phone us and we'll deal with those concerns. We'll find out the answers and respond to them."

Umedaly recalls the time when "a major European institutional investor called up and was worried that they had read about a fast, rechargeable battery that could potentially put us out of business." He checked with his in-house battery experts so he could reply with hard facts. "And in this case I was able to show that it was not a magic bullet at all, because it would recharge quickly only a few times and then you would destroy the battery."

Another way to gain the confidence of investors was for Ballard to establish impressive corporate standards. When Umedaly came to

Ballard at the beginning of 1990, he and Rasul reckoned they would need anywhere from $100 million to $250 million in development money over the years before they could hope for substantial earnings. That required creating a high degree of credibility. "So from Day One, the company had to be impeccable, with the highest standards in everything we did. We got the best advisors, the best consultants, the best internal systems that reflected a substantial public company, not the private company it still was. We took the high road all the way."

Next, it was essential to establish milestones and demonstrate concrete progress along the way to commercialization, which they realized meant a ten-year time horizon. "Usually," Umedaly says, "you can hardly visualize three years out" because the technology changes so rapidly. "But we *had* to look ten years out, and it was a very good thing that we did. Not simply from the point of view of showing the public, but as an internal focus." The Ballard leadership took what was an external requirement—to keep the finances flowing—and turned it into a series of in-house targets for passing specific milestones within fixed time periods. The targets included such things as achieving specific improved power densities or particular reductions in cost.

This was not a common way of doing things in industry. "In the early days," Umedaly says, "there was a lot of tension about this approach, because the scientists and engineers were not used to working that way." They were accustomed to doing "good work" and thought that "in the fullness of time something would emanate" from it. The technical people expected that the business people would then take the technical advances and market them. "Well, we turned that upside down and said, 'if we're to take people's money, this is the time frame in which things *must* happen.'" Even the annual reports were laid out with yearly time lines of goals to be met a year or two ahead, and with little check marks indicating goals either fully or partly achieved. The 1995 report, for example, set as a goal for 1996: "reduce cost of production fuel cells by implementing low-cost flow field plates." Another goal was: "develop advanced methanol fuel processor." The 1998 report set as goals for 1999: "Secure orders for next generation heavy-duty fuel cell engine for transit buses," and "demonstrate next generation fuel cell automobile engine with partners."

Any scientist you meet at Ballard, Umedaly says, will tell you "that it's been a very good focus for them, and that you *can* plan, even in scientific endeavours. As long as you have a vision of where you want to go. As long as you can see the light at the end of the tunnel." The point is to have a concrete target and try to get there "in a certain time frame, and do it within a certain cost figure."

Once the targets or milestones were established, the Ballard management would show them to the investment community to build confidence. "We took that vision to the external, financial world and said, OK, this is our long-term plan, these are our long-term milestones." And it worked marvellously. "As we achieved these milestones, people recognized that, Yes, they are on the way to commercialization, one step at a time. And we've consistently hit these milestones, plus or minus six months or a year. And that's why we've been successful in raising a lot of money."

The most dramatic demonstration of Ballard's progress has been the repeated doublings of power density. Calculated in terms of kilowatts per cubic foot of volume, Ballard fuel cell stacks went from roughly one kilowatt in 1987, to two kilowatts in 1989, five in 1991, ten in 1993, twenty-eight in 1995 and fifty in 1997.

Raising new equity financing was only one leg of what Rasul and Umedaly like to picture as a three-legged financial stool. Another leg was government funding, which had begun as the most important source of funding and continued to be significant even after the company went public. In 1994, for example, Ballard received $6 million from BC, the Canadian government, and California's South Coast Air Quality Management District for the second phase of its bus program. That same year there was also $3.7 million from the Canadian Department of National Defense to develop fuel cells for submarines. In 1995 there was $6 million (Cdn.) from the US Department of Energy for the second phase of its program to develop a hybrid fuel cell electric automobile engine in collaboration with General Motors; also $8.1 million (Cdn.) from the US Department of Transportation to develop methanol fuel cells for buses to be built by Georgetown University; and $8 million (Cdn.) from the Chicago Transit Authority for a test fleet of three fuel cell buses. The following year (1996) brought another $8.6 million for three BC Transit buses. But after that, especially with the 1997 mega-deals involving Daimler-Benz and Ford, worth hundreds of millions of dollars each, government funding became relatively a much less important element in the financial planning. Ballard's management welcomes the shift. "Our objective," says Umedaly, "is to be independent of government. And eventually, revenues will take over. Just straight revenues. Selling fuel cells."

The third leg of Ballard Power's financial stool, and an increasingly important one through the mid-1990s, was the funding provided by strategic partners. But the reasons for courting major industrial partners went well beyond the money they could bring to the small BC company. As the 1994 annual report states, "These alliance partners help us in three ways: 1) ensure our access to substantial markets; 2) provide an understanding of market needs, so that the products we jointly develop will meet user requirements; and 3) provide complementary technology and manufacturing expertise which accelerate the commercialization of Ballard fuel cells."

Waxing eloquent on why strategic partners were so crucial, Rasul leans back in his chair and starts ticking off his fingers. "Our strategy says that, one, we are a very small company with limited resources trying to play in a *very* big market. Two, the product that we make is a component—it fits into something else, such as a car—it's not an end-user product. Three, it uses unconventional fuels," which carries with it the problem of providing an infrastructure or network. Gasoline may be available everywhere, but the fuel cell will probably require a supply of natural gas, hydrogen or methanol. "Four," he continues, "it's a new technology trying to displace a technology that's been around for 100 years," namely the internal combustion engine. "Five, the game is going to take a *lot* of money to be successful. And six, it needs a lot of complementary development in other technologies, which are associated with and ancillary to what we do but which are also important to our success." He mentions membranes, catalysts, fuel reformers, and hydrogen storage.

"Now," he adds, "we can't do all of these things, but they will have to happen for us to be successful. So our strategy was to create important relationships with players in each of those markets. With companies who will buy our products, or design the complementary technology, or provide the fuel, or provide money—including government money—and so on."

The first step was to convince those companies or institutions of the effectiveness of the Ballard technology. "When we started out, we had shown the technology in the lab. People said, 'Well, that's great. It works well in the lab. But it's your engineers who are working it and it's in your lab. Why don't you get some independent view of whether this technology is as good as you guys claim it is?'"

"So we identified about twenty different entities. There were commercial organizations like auto companies and power companies. There were national labs. There was the military. And we delivered units to each of those, in exchange for money. Now, we didn't sell these. This is another part of our strategy. We leased them, so the ownership and intellectual property stayed with us." Among the earliest auto companies that leased the cells to test them were Daimler-Benz, General Motors, and Mitsubishi. Since then, nearly every major auto company in the world has leased Ballard stacks, put them onto test stations, run them for hundreds or thousands of hours, and monitored their performance.

"They evaluated the technology," Rasul continues. Meanwhile, many of these companies had their own fuel cell programs, although most were much smaller and lagged far behind Ballard's. "So they were able to benchmark what we were doing against what they were doing. And they were watching how quickly we were moving down this path" towards greater power and reduced costs, "because they had become convinced that the life of the internal combustion engine was finite."

These leased demonstration stacks not only showcased the Ballard fuel cell and brought in much-needed revenues. They also had a less obvious benefit for the Ballard executive. The purpose of the programs was "not just so that people could tell us whether the things worked or not. We knew they worked." But as part of the lease arrangements, Ballard sent along what they called customer service engineers to set up the units and show how to run and monitor them. "Actually," Rasul grins, "they're sales people in disguise. They go right into the bowels of the company and get to know the engineers and research scientists." While there, they talk about what can be done with the cell stacks and what changes or improvements might be made to them. "So we were getting a lot of great information. We knew exactly what the other companies were thinking, where they were going." As a result, when the Ballard executives eventually got down to discussing more serious strategic partnership arrangements with some of the companies, he adds, "we knew exactly what they wanted and could have very clear conversations about where they wanted to go. These are some of the invisible things that happen that you don't want to exactly shout about."

And so the Ballard stacks were delivered to a score of companies and laboratories. As part of each deal the recipient had to sign agreements not to open or disassemble the stack. In addition, warning notices to this effect were affixed to the outside of the units. Ultimately, each of these leased stacks was to be returned to Ballard intact. This cautious approach was meant to protect Ballard's proprietary secrets, the precise details of how things are arranged and assembled inside the cell stack.

Ballard had patents on many of its most important breakthroughs, of course. "We protect our technology vigorously and aggressively," says Rasul. "We've filed patents for key inventions around the world." By 1998 the number of patents allowed or pending totalled 220 covering 70 inventions. But patents only go so far in providing protection. Not every significant detail or technique can be patented, and the entire process is incredibly expensive and drawn out in any case. Part of the solution was, and remains, to lease the stacks as "black boxes," with no right to look inside. And the stacks were to be serviced only by Ballard personnel and eventually returned. That way Ballard could be sure they had not, in fact, been opened up and studied. This policy was only adopted after the company had experienced something of a scare.

When Ballard sold its first two stacks to John Perry, Jr. for his submarine in 1987, they were made up of Mark IV cells. Eventually, Ballard replaced Perry's Mark IV stacks with a single stack of more powerful Mark V cells. Ballard got the Mark IV stacks back from Perry, but the entire deal had been an outright sale, not a leasing arrangement. Perry's company retained the new Mark V stack, Ballard's latest technology at that time. The Ballard executives were not overly concerned, because Perry seemed to be just a customer. They assumed that he would use the fuel cell in his submarine for years to come.

But then, as Keith Prater puts it, the relationship "soured." In 1990 Perry was so taken by the fuel cell and its potential that he sold his undersea research company and decided to go into the PEM fuel cell business himself, which put him in direct competition with Ballard. To get the needed technological know-how quickly, he bought the small fuel cell division of the Massachusetts-based Treadwell corporation and moved it to Florida.

Perry declined to be interviewed for this book, but in his autobiography, *Never Say Impossible*, he tells a rather incomplete story. He never mentions the Ballard fuel cell at all, much less that his company had bought two different models and gained extensive experience with them. He leaves the reader with the impression that he personally was a pioneer of fuel cells and that his group was among the first to realize that, of the various types of fuel cells, the PEM cell had the greatest promise, especially for transportation. "After intensive study our team, with good counsel from other researchers, began its work," he writes, "believing that the PEM is the leading candidate for commercial applications."[38]

Soon Energy Partners was receiving a small amount of US government money, and putting in a lot of its own, to build the $3 million "Green Car." This was actually a hybrid fuel cell and battery-powered pick-up truck with a huge bank of batteries and cells taking up most of the box at the rear. "As fuel cell technology advances," Perry added in his 1996 book, "I predict that the battery system will no longer be necessary."[39] (This was hardly a daring prediction. By then a second generation of Ballard buses was on the road, powered exclusively by fuel cells, of course. And the Ballard cell had already achieved the power density the US government had estimated was required to power a practical fuel cell car all by itself.)

What took to the Florida roads in late 1993 (a half-year after the first Ballard bus, which required no battery backup) was a rather awkward looking vehicle. The Green Car relied for its performance in part on an ultra-lightweight vehicle chassis made of exotic materials. (The Ballard buses were of conventional, much heavier but affordable, steel construction.) And its two fuel cell stacks only put out a total of fifteen kilowatts of power, compared to 120 kW for the first Ballard bus. In fact, for the cell surface area involved, it had only one-quarter to one-third the power of the Ballard stack. So, perhaps the Ballard people should not have been concerned.

Still, Perry's was the only rival fuel cell vehicle at the time. Although they had no evidence, Ballard Power couldn't help but worry about the possibility that its proprietary secrets might have been compromised. "We had no basis for getting the Mark V cell stack back," says Keith Prater, "so we lost control over it." In the future, allowing potential competitors access to the innards of the Ballard stack was something that would be granted only reluctantly, and only in exchange for important considerations, as Ballard's strategic relationship with Daimler-Benz would show.

As Ballard expanded its fuel cell program and hired scores of new employees, its new leadership was concerned lest it lose the intimate, small company atmosphere and personal incentives for hard work that had given it a competitive edge. They succeeded to an impressive degree in retaining the sharing and caring atmosphere and ethic they had inherited. Under Ballard, Prater, and Howard the company had shared its profits with its employees and rewarded the early fuel cell team by giving them major blocks of stock as a bonus. Firoz Rasul brought in a more formalized stock option and bonus program, similar to what he had been familiar with at his former company, MDI.

"Every employee is a shareholder in this company," Rasul says. "This is a large part of our success. They get stock options. Most companies have stock options just for the management team. We have stock options for everybody in the company. Egalitarian is probably not the correct word, but we have a set of rules that ensure that we are all going to have an opportunity to benefit" when the value of Ballard's shares increases, as it did dramatically between 1995 and 1998. "For me, that's a very important part of the culture here. It's something I insisted on when I joined the company."

He steps over to a window overlooking the huge, open shop floor of the modern new building. Below there are dozens of test stations, each holding a Ballard cell or cell stack that is being operated and monitored, and bustling technicians in coveralls or lab coats. "All these people share in the success of the company because they own a piece of it. But, what's more important, they created it themselves. It was not a gift. Their hard work was what caused it to be where it is today. That's one aspect of our culture—that everybody is an owner and entrepreneur and shareholder."

"The other part of our culture," Rasul says, "is that we either win or lose as a team. Our bonus plans, for instance, are set up in a way that even if there are 325 of us, and if you met your goals and I didn't, you and I suffer together. So you can't say, 'I met my goals, why shouldn't I get my bonus?' The key was that the company didn't meet its goals. We want to win. And winning for us is getting this technology to the market, getting it out there against all odds. And there are lots of odds against us. There are stakeholders, people with vested interests—and they include the oil companies, the utility companies, the automobile companies. We couldn't have picked three bigger industries in the world if we'd tried."

Ballard is like a family, he adds. "People spend more time here than they spend at home. Our wives call themselves 'Ballard widows.'" As we speak, Rasul's secretary comes by with a note telling him that his wife has called reminding him that he promised to take her and their three teenage girls to a performance of Shakespeare that evening. Rasul doesn't get away early enough to enjoy dinner at home and an evening out very often. In fact, like most of the people at Ballard, he works killer hours. "I have a ski retreat up at Whistler," he says, "but I don't think I've been there ten times in ten years."

Rasul has also carried on with the sensitive and generous way of dealing with employees that was instituted by the Ballard founders. "When people work at a successful company," he says, "they give a lot of themselves, emotionally, physically, mentally, intellectually. So you have to treat them as part of the family. We've had people who've gone through divorces, which they've had to settle. And in such cases we've paid for lawyers' fees when they couldn't afford it. Lots of times, for compassionate reasons, we've made loans so they could meet their debts. We've had our finance department sit down and help some-body consolidate or sort out their financial affairs. There are people who've been hospitalized, or someone in their family has been, and we've helped. It's part of the silent, invisible fabric of the company. It's not something we make a big deal about."

By instilling loyalty to the company, by hiring the right people, and by giving them freedom to work at their own pace, Ballard has retained the in-house creative edge and ability to make quick progress that was decisive in the early years of the fuel cell. Rasul recalls the time a major US auto company sent some engineers to visit. In the morning, they discussed an idea with a Ballard group, then broke for lunch. Nobody noticed that one of the Ballard engi-neers had skipped lunch and stayed behind. When they returned, he presented a mock-up of the idea that he had built in the machine shop. "That would have taken us three weeks," one of the Americans said, "including two weeks to book time in the shop."

That evening, the Ballard engineer skipped dinner, stayed on late, built the actual device, and hooked it up to a test stand at midnight. Only then did he go home. By seven the next morning, the test results were ready, in time for an early meeting with the American team. "This whole exercise that took you less than twenty-four hours would have taken us seven weeks to do at our facility, maybe even three months," said the Americans from the giant, more bureaucratic firm. "And it wasn't that we told this engineer to do it," Rasul comments. "I mean, this has to come from within."

But such self-direction is not suited for everyone. "A lot of people who join Ballard find it difficult," Rasul says, "because it's so demanding. It brings out things people did not know about themselves. Both good and bad." Some people do not fit in. "One individual moved here from Calgary. He was very well placed in a power company, senior and quite accomplished. We thought his experience would help us. So we brought him to Vancouver, and he started working with our people. But he couldn't quite get used to the small-company, fast-moving environment. He was hung up on procedure and wanting support. And he just couldn't adjust to the pace and how quickly we were making decisions."

In fact, the new employee was afraid to make decisions. "I remember this guy saying, 'we don't have enough information here.' And I said, 'You're right. We have a choice. We can spend three months getting more information. And once we've done that, how much better is that decision going to be?' And I said, 'Part of the skill in being successful as an entrepreneur is being able to make decisions with little information. You never have the luxury of getting all the information you want. There are times when you must have more information. And there are times when you must make a decision.' He couldn't see the difference, and he was very uncomfortable."

Rather than err on the side of caution, Rasul explains that Ballard has consciously tried to hire and encourage the opposite type, people who are just bursting with ideas and energy and ambition. "One of the first things we look for is great intellectual capacity." Some of the types he seeks out are just "whippersnappers," he says, young kids who are very bright and pushy, and who want to get ahead. Typically such a young person has "great ideas and he's bubbling over with all sorts of things he wants to do." The challenge is to "start with this energy and then harness it and channel it, so it moves you forward. I think that has been one of our biggest challenges and our greatest accomplishments." He calls it "the care and feeding of prima donnas."

Bolstered by this approach, even as Ballard grew, its ability to make rapid technological progress remained. Nowhere was this more apparent than in the improvements in power that were demonstrated by successive Ballard buses. Soon after the first small "proof of concept" bus was out on the road being tested, Paul Howard and his team plunged in with another $6 million budget (this time including $1 million from California's South Coast Air Quality Management District) to build a second-generation "commercial prototype" bus. This was a full size, twelve-metre (forty foot) long, sixty passenger bus with a range of 400 kilometres (250 miles). No seating space was to be sacrificed on this vehicle. The fuel cells would have to be made much more powerful and compact to fit into the rear engine space, just like a diesel.

Again, they bought a standard chassis, a New Flyer transit bus. To give it decent acceleration and hill-climbing ability, it needed 275 horsepower. This had to come from twenty much more powerful fuel cell stacks, each one no larger than the stacks in the first bus. The plan called for each one to put out thirteen kilowatts (compared to five for the first bus) for a total of 260 kilowatts gross power. And it was here that the team working on the fuel cell stacks were really triumphant. In just a couple of years they managed to improve the power density by over two and a half times.

As in the earlier doubling of power from the Mark IV to Mark V cells, says Paul Howard, the key to this improvement was not mainly advances in electrochemistry but good engineering. Of course, he admits to bias, being a mechanical engineer himself. And he concedes that there were some improvements during this period in the membrane and the catalyst. But these were incremental and more in the areas of cost than power improvement. "Most of the advances that Ballard made in the '90s were in what I'll call packaging—in mechanical engineering, not in science."

Whereas the previous improvement was largely due to scaling up the size of the cells, this latest boost in power density was achieved through several steps. Most involved changes in the flow field plates, the grooved graphite plates that channel the gases to the electrodes and draw off the current by making contact with the electrodes. Mainly this was done by refining the layout. Not nearly as much of the plate was given over to peripheral things such as the through bolts that held the stack of cells together, or the manifold channels that carried the gases to and from the many cells. In the plates used on the first bus, only about half the surface area of each plate was taken up by the "serpentine flow fields," the actual channels that carry the gases. "So in essence," says Howard, "we were wasting all the rest of that space," which translates into a sacrifice of power density.

Because scores of plates are stacked together, their thickness also translates into power density. The thicker each plate, the longer the stack has to be for a given output in kilowatts. "Our first bus had plates that were crude, almost a quarter of an inch thick. Today those plates are a third of that thickness and still work the same way, so you get an increase in power density." And it's here that the creativity comes in. "In the early days the fuel cell team couldn't make the graphite thinner without its cracking. Well, they found ways." With thinner plates, the serpentine flow channels could also be made finer. "Just as people learned to make microprocessor chips for computers smaller and smaller" by making the lines of the printed circuits smaller and smaller, says Howard, "in the same way, we have learned how to effectively get everything you can out of that plate by making the channels smaller and smaller, and thinner and thinner, and less deep."

In 1995, a full-size transit bus capable of carrying sixty passengers was out being tested on the hilly streets of North Vancouver.

Powered by compressed hydrogen in tanks on the roof, it had excellent performance. It was able to start on an extremely steep twenty per cent grade and maintain thirty kilometres per hour (twenty miles per hour) up an eight per cent grade. On flat ground it could accelerate from zero to fifty kilometres (thirty miles) per hour in nineteen seconds. And it had a respectable top speed of ninety-five kilometres (sixty miles) per hour. After further refinements and an even more advanced prototype, Ballard got contracts to build commercial transit buses for actual city use. In early 1998 the first three were delivered to the Chicago Transit Authority, and three more took to the streets of Vancouver later that year.

If the first small bus was exciting to the public at large, the full-size buses really dazzled people in the automobile industry and in government. A steady flow of visitors came to Vancouver to see Ballard's fuel cell program. The ones Paul Howard most wanted to impress were the corporate executives and government officials who would be making decisions about fuel cells for cars. Often they were not technically very knowledgeable, but typically they came with an engineer in tow to advise them.

Almost without exception, such people said they wanted to have a ride on the bus. Paul Howard laughs when he recalls the irony of the situation. "Let me tell you, many of those people *never* ride on a bus and couldn't care less about a bus, but they wanted to come up here and ride on the bus." And it really turned around their thinking. The conventional wisdom during the mid-1990s was that practical fuel cells were at least twenty to thirty years away. "That's what the car companies were saying." But from 1993 through 1996, Howard saw an "exponential increase" in the numbers of senior people from auto companies and government who came and rode the bus. And invariably, they would then turn to the engineers or advisors who had come with them and say, "Why are you telling me it's twenty years away? I've seen the thing. It works."

Bad
BLOOD

W hile Paul Howard was busy building the Ballard buses, and Firoz Rasul was marketing the Ballard fuel cell, Geoffrey Ballard was not content to sit staring out the window of his seaside home in the Gulf Islands. In spite of his illness, semi-retirement gave him the time he needed to get out and beat the drum for the fuel cell and the bright future of the hydrogen economy.

He served (along with David Scott and Martin Hammerli) for several years on the federal Hydrogen Technology Advisory Group, a body whose mandate was to guide the Canadian government in funding decisions concerning hydrogen and related technologies, including fuel cells. Later, Ballard became chairman of the Canadian Hydrogen Association, an industry and government group that includes representatives of most of the major Canadian corporations and agencies that have an interest in hydrogen-related technologies, such as Stuart Energy Systems, which supplies electrolytic hydrogen for the Ballard buses in Vancouver, and Natural Resources Canada, which sponsors research on hydrogen production and storage. And he frequently attended meetings of government officials and industry representatives devoted to energy issues. At such venues, he always tried to convince them that the PEM fuel cell was an up-and-coming technology that should not be given the short shrift he felt it was getting.

Ballard also drifted back into the academic science and technology network, attending and often giving talks or papers at specialized conferences, such as a world hydrogen energy conference in Germany, or one dedicated to sustainable transportation technologies in California. During this time, the US government was still putting most of its fuel cell money into backing the phosphoric acid system, which Ballard considered very poorly suited to transportation. It was a frustrating uphill fight to change people's minds, but he made it his personal crusade to give the PEM fuel cell credibility.

"The battle I fought," he says, "was to say that phosphoric acid was going nowhere because it is cumbersome and you cannot make it smaller and effective." On the other hand, there is PEM, "which *has* all the characteristics that allow us to make it small and compact and high powered." For many years, though, Ballard's message fell on deaf ears and tended to marginalize him within this specialized scientific and technological community. "This position was contrary to the accepted wisdom," he says, which made him "the odd man out."

Given his personality, Ballard did not take this scepticism and rejection lying down. It just spurred him on to be feistier and more assertive in delivering his message. But this only brought him ridicule and isolation. "Matter of fact," he says, "it was so bad that I was sort of anathema at most technical conventions. I was very much a lone wolf, because I didn't play the game."

Once, when Ballard Power was building its prototype buses in the early 1990s, he attended a transportation conference and wanted to draw attention to the Ballard program. He made a presentation about the bus and was dismayed to find that people actually laughed openly at him. "They thought it was just ridiculous," he says, that a company like his was trying to put a PEM fuel cell vehicle on the road. For ten years, he argues, people thought there was no way that a small Canadian company could beat out all the much larger players and develop a superior technology. "The consensus was that if it was any good, the big companies would be doing it. So you were a nut case. They didn't really want to know you. You were an interesting person to have a beer with, but they didn't really want to be seen associating with you."

This changed quite noticeably, he felt, after Daimler-Benz put its prototype mini-van powered by Ballard fuel cells on the road in 1996, and it was most noticeable in a different attitude taken by Detroit. The doors of the car industry "essentially opened to us in that year," he says. "The ambience changed. Firoz is now a welcome guest at General Motors. In the past, he wouldn't get past the chief assistant to the assistant chief." But until that time it was an uphill battle. And the opposition was not merely passive. It was often overt, active, and targetted against his company. The big North American auto makers, along with the oil industry, fiercely lobbied both the Canadian and US governments not to support fuel cell development, Ballard says. "They would go and tell the government not to give us money." Beyond this, they publicly ridiculed and debunked claims by people like him that fuel cells could and should be commercialized quickly.

Ballard does not want to point a finger at specific companies, lest he wind up spending the rest of his life in court. "They're the most litigious group you've ever seen in your life," he sighs in resignation. But he insists that he knows of a "dozen examples" of active efforts by big companies to undermine alternative technologies like the fuel cell. "I had lunch with the former president of a major Canadian oil company, and he told me point blank, the oil companies are ganging up on you. They're going to the prime minister of Canada and to the president of the United States and they're saying, stop funding Ballard. We don't care what excuse you use, but don't let that fuel cell come about, or you won't have money for your campaigns."

Ballard asked this executive why the opposition was so fierce. The explanation was that they're selling gasoline and they don't want hydrogen to compete with it. Ballard, whose own career began in the oil patch, was still puzzled. "Why not?" he asked, "They've got more natural gas than they know what to do with. For the next forty years hydrogen is going to be made from natural gas." The oil man told him that "nobody in the oil industry wants to lose the monopoly they have of controlling the source of energy. Right now they actually control the major production fields of the world." But methane, the main ingredient in natural gas, can also be made from biomass and other sources. "The minute fuel cells come in and hydrogen is made from natural gas, anyone can produce it and everybody will. And they lose control."

The US automobile companies were equally arrogant, in Ballard's experience, and just as active in opposing fuel cells. He found this to be true even during the mid-1990s, when they were gladly accepting US government money to put fuel cells into vehicles under the Clinton administration's Program for a New Generation of Vehicles.

Around 1995 Ballard was invited to give a talk in Victoria, BC, to the assembled energy ministers of the ten Canadian provinces. Naturally, he extolled the virtues of the fuel cell, talked about his crusade to change how the world thinks about power, and called for expanded government and industry support for PEM development. Also at the conference was an executive from a major auto company. This executive got up at the conference, ridiculed Ballard's account of fuel cell progress and said that in the area of automobile transportation, "when there's something worthwhile to bring you, *we*," and he named his company, "will bring it."

Following the talk, Ballard tore into the man. "That's a lot of crap, and a dirty blow," Ballard told him. "You're a hypocrite." Insulted, the auto executive stormed out of the room in a huff. A week later Ballard got a call from a member of his own board of directors saying that Ballard Power was having difficulty with its federal funding because of this incident. Allegedly, the automobile honcho had gone to Ottawa and demanded that the Canadian government stop all funding because Geoffrey Ballard had insulted him, and a Ballard executive had had to fly to Ottawa to cool things down.

But Ballard would not be silenced. When he gave speeches at universities, or was interviewed by the media, he routinely criticized what he saw as the obstructionist stance taken against fuel cell development, particularly by the Big Three auto makers. He told a California conference that "against all odds" his company had "brought a new technology to an industry that did not want it." Nor did he have any illusions that auto manufacturers would provide a product like fuel cells just because the public might want them. "Established industry hates change," he said. It "does not simply supply what the market wants. Industry tries to shape the market to want what is most profitable" for it to produce.

Looking back on those years, Ballard says he was actually holding his tongue. "I was a little less outspoken during that period than I usually am, because I had signed on with Mike Brown to have Firoz do the marketing, and I sort of had to give them their head." And his illness sapped his energy. If he had felt better, he says, he would have pushed even harder and confronted people in the oil and auto industries more vigorously.

Geoffrey Ballard was not the only one at Ballard Power who experienced the arrogance of the industrial big boys. In late 1986 the Ballard fuel cell team made its dramatic breakthrough with the Dow experimental membrane. This was the fourfold power boost that got people at Los Alamos and elsewhere thinking for the first time that a fuel cell powered car might be feasible. "Within weeks of our announcement," says Keith Prater, "we had a visit from General Motors. It was two guys, one from their research division and one from their acquisitions division." They wanted to know more about Ballard's fuel cell program and toured the facility, which was still housed in the tiny and very modest separate industrial bay next to the auto body shop.

At that time, says Prater, GM probably could have bought the Ballard company for two or three million dollars. After the visit nothing happened, but word eventually came back through the grapevine that they had gone back to GM with differing recommendations. "Our understanding is that the acquisition guy's recommendation was, 'Spend the two million and buy them.' And the research guy said, 'Oh, shoot, if they can do that—a tiny company like that—for two or three million dollars, I can do it in six months and do it better.'" The research guy won out, says Prater, "and GM embarked on a program that took roughly two years and cost roughly ten million dollars, at the end of which they hadn't made any electricity, and they shut it down."

But the story does not end there. In 1987, the US Department of Energy began an R & D program for fuel cells in transportation. At first it focused mainly on subsidizing the development of phosphoric acid fuel cells, mainly for a hybrid fuel cell and battery powered bus to be built at Georgetown University in Washington, DC. By 1990, though, with the Ballard fuel cell showing such progress, the DOE also decided to put funds into PEM cells. It launched a multiphase program to develop PEM technology for transportation using methanol as the fuel. A General Motors division, Allison Turbines, was chosen to be the "prime contractor" responsible for integrating all parts of the system. Under this program, GM began leasing fuel cell stacks from Ballard.

Around the same time, says Prater, GM also started up its own in-house fuel cell program again, which made him uncomfortable because of his concern about patents and proprietary knowledge. "It always was, and probably continues to be, a bit of a challenge to work with GM, because we know that they've got their own parallel activity." Yet the Big Three never had to do truly pioneer fuel cell work because of their perception that if the fuel cell ever came on strong as a technology, and they were forced by government or market pressures to accept it, they could always obtain it through their financial muscle.

Prater waxes sarcastic about how GM thought it could reproduce Ballard's progress on its own in six months. "The relationship with GM has always been one in which they said, 'If they can do it, we can do it.' We've yet to see evidence of that." But the concern about patent protection is always there. "I'll suggest that big companies like GM tend to believe that, when push comes to shove, their economic might will be such that if they want to essentially force another company to license them technology, they can do it."

This was a concern that Ballard Power had from the beginning, and it was one of the factors that encouraged Ballard to form the strategic relationship with Daimler and subsequently with other companies. The financial resources of a big backer were urgently needed, Prater says, "to provide the muscle necessary to resist, or to fight, a big company that decided it was going to infringe. We recognized that tiny Ballard wasn't going to be able to stand up to General Motors. I mean, if they chose to come out with a product that did, in fact, infringe, it would cost us a lot to fight it. We never could have defended the patents on our own. We didn't have the deep pockets."

Here Prater is expressing his critical opinion at a time when he is no longer a Ballard executive, and when the big auto companies are finally committed to fuel cell commercialization. But Geoffrey Ballard was doing this in the mid-1990s, when he was still board chairman at Ballard Power. Inevitably, this often meant ruffling feathers at the very companies with which Ballard Power was actively cooperating on fuel cell projects. And he sometimes did it in ways that seemed gratuitously provocative.

By his own admission, Ballard comes on pretty strong in one-on-one situations, especially where he suspects that a person in authority has not done the proper homework or, perhaps worse, is faking it. He does not suffer fools gladly, especially when those fools are people who should know what they are talking about, but do not. At one point, he says, he found himself in a social situation with a senior executive from a British auto company. Ballard switches over to a pretty fair Colonel Blimp imitation, gurgling his words as if he has marbles in his mouth. The Brit told him that he had "always thought fuel cells would be the next great thing that it was important for the world to have." Ballard looked him in the eye and replied, "Do you have any idea what a fuel cell is?" Clearly, the man hadn't a clue. "Oh, hah-hah, huff-huff, hoo-hoo," was all this supposedly high-powered executive could say. "Why don't you have dinner with somebody else!" Ballard shot back. Looking back at the incident, he laughs. "I mean, I don't mind talking to Lord Frumpety Frump, but I don't like being patronized."

Ballard's opinions, and even more so the strident and even pugnacious way he sometimes expressed them, contrasted sharply with the soft-spoken, salesmanlike approach preferred by Firoz Rasul and Mossadiq Umedaly. In fact, they look almost visibly pained when they discuss his way of going public and accusing the auto and oil industries of retarding, rather than advancing, the fuel cell cause. They see themselves as fighting to get into the big leagues, not scrapping to embarrass the big league managers.

Umedaly is especially critical of how Ballard went out on his own to trumpet the benefits of the fuel cell. He also rejects Ballard's allegation that the big oil companies twisted arms in Ottawa against government funding for Ballard Power. "No," he laughs, "I don't believe it. I don't think people are so stupid as to go and be so specific. My feeling is that these things are done in much more sophisticated ways." Once more he guffaws. "But again, when you're a lone ranger, when you're a small guy fighting the big guys, or trying to get into the arena with the big guys, you have all these imaginations." On the other hand, he does not entirely reject the notion that the big oil companies opposed the fuel cell. "I wouldn't say it's not true. They have a vested interest and would like to see everything remain as it is."

But far from crediting Geoffrey Ballard with having the vision and spunk needed to bring the fuel cell to practical reality, Umedaly suggests that Ballard oversold the fuel cell in technology circles. "The fuel cell," he says, "has been around a long time. And one of the challenges was that it had no credibility as a technology. Frankly, none!" And why did it lack credibility? "Because all these cuckoo clocks had been talking about fuel cells for so long. And Ballard was one of those cuckoo clocks." So people would say, "Here's another person talking about this thing. And the question was to give it credibility. And the way to give it credibility was not to *talk* about it, but just to do it. And to show through actions, show through results, show through achieving goals and milestones, that this fuel cell was a serious one. That, in fact, we didn't just have a fuel cell, we had a fuel cell which we were going to get to the market."

Firoz Rasul is more diplomatic. Asked about Geoffrey Ballard's claim that Rasul could barely get past the lower levels of the major auto companies at first, he partially concedes the point. "Yes, that's true," he says. Initially the big auto companies were very resistant. "They were sceptical. Daimler-Benz was one of the few exceptions." The others "were not as proactive in looking at it. They said, 'Yeah, the government is forcing it on us, so we'd better look at the newer technologies.' But they were never really serious about it. And Geoffrey's right. Certainly in the last two years people have realized that those regulations are not going to go away. And after we did the deal with

Daimler-Benz the level of awareness and interest and activity went up quite dramatically."

However, Rasul rejects Ballard's description of the Big Three auto companies as overtly arrogant and dismissive. "My background is in marketing," he says. "I'm a salesman. I know how to get into doors, to get into organizations and so on. Geoffrey had an awful difficulty with this. But Geoffrey was not in the room when I made my presentations. They never actually turned us down or threw us out, or closed the door in our faces. It wasn't quite that way. They were very subtle. They were very pleasant, but we didn't get much further. But they never publicly belittled us or insulted us. That never took place. And neither did we seek confrontation."

Part of leasing cells and exploring joint ventures and strategic alliances was continual back and forth and interaction with the large auto companies. "Whenever we went to these meetings we'd say nice things, such as we know they're looking at new technology and we think they'll be convinced that what we have is useful." And whereas Ballard chafed at how long it took to convince the auto companies to come on side, Rasul sees it differently. It did take a long time, he says, "but patience is everything. We had to learn to be patient. But we also learned how to position ourselves so we could get into some of these programs."

As for the large oil companies, Mossadiq Umedaly views them not as obstacles but as a challenge. "I respect the people who lead these companies," he says. "They also see—and there are enlightened ones among them—that you can't just go on using a technology that is so inefficient, that is so polluting when there are other options that meet the requirements that are coming to the horizon. So my feeling is that you'll see leaders among them. We obviously have them among the auto companies—the Daimler-Benzes, and General Motors and Ford and others that we are working with, Honda and so on—leaders in the business who are testing this, understanding it and now

starting to adopt it. And you'll get the same from the fuel infrastructure side, because if the technology is going to work, it needs fuel."
He points to methanol as a fuel for automobile fuel cells and mentions
that Ballard has a working agreement with Methanex, the world's
largest supplier of methanol. And he predicts, "eventually you will
see other oil companies get into that business." This is precisely what
has happened in California in 1999, where ARCO, Shell, and Texaco
have joined Ballard, DaimlerChrysler, Ford, and the State of California in a major project to demonstrate about 50 fuel cell cars and buses
between 2000 and 2003.

Most likely none of these conflicts over dealing with big industry or
over Ballard's personal style would have amounted to much if it had
not been for deeper rivalries over control of the company and over
recognition for its success. Ballard had agreed to step back and let
Rasul run the company, but in his heart he never really accepted playing second fiddle. For his part, Rasul may have held most of the levers
of power in his hands, but Ballard, who was chairman of the board
and had a name that was synonymous with the company, continued
to reap most of the credit for the company's achievements. Rasul
would never get out from under Ballard's shadow while Ballard was
still around.

No matter how successful Rasul was in marketing the fuel cell or
making money for Ballard shareholders, the kudos that came to him
would be mainly from the world of business and money, the arena
where the players are MBAs, financial people, investment specialists.
But the Ballard fuel cell was also making waves in the larger worlds
of science, government, the environment, and academia. Geoffrey
Ballard, as a distinguished scientist with a Ph.D. and government connections going back decades, was comfortable moving in these circles.
He spoke at universities and conferences, received honourary degrees,

was named to government advisory groups and was invited to chair the Canadian Hydrogen Association. (His partners, too, have gained considerable recognition. Keith Prater has served as chairman of the US-based National Hydrogen Association, and Paul Howard recently chaired the organizing committee of a major Canadian Hydrogen Association conference.) Inevitably, the public spotlight focused on Geoffrey Ballard, ignoring Rasul. This only aggravated the struggle for actual decision-making power within the company. The situation was like two scorpions trapped in a bottle. It was bound to lead to conflict, and it did.

First, there were the early doubts about building the first Ballard bus. Rasul may have won the initial round, but Ballard, with his social standing and connections in government, was able to obtain financing for the project and make it happen. It was Ballard who stood on the podium with the premier of British Columbia when the first bus was unveiled. And it was he who felt personally vindicated when the bus, and subsequent buses, proved to be such a success.

Then came an event that left a legacy of bitterness and uneasiness within the company. As Ballard tells it, there was a meeting at which Rasul and Umedaly accused him of once calling them "hired guns." Ballard denied to the assembled group ever saying this, but they stuck to their claim. "You certainly did," they insisted. Ballard says that he "sincerely apologized" and told everyone present that although he had no recollection of treating his two colleagues that way, it would be a "ridiculous" thing to say and he was "utterly apologetic" about it. Looking back at the incident, Ballard is still not sure. "It sounded as if this was going to get thrown up at me every time I turned around. I honestly had no recollection of ever saying it. But it's the kind of thing I *might* have said."

Whatever the truth of the matter, says Ballard, Rasul found a way to respond. Soon after Rasul had joined the company and recruited some of his own people, Ballard claims that he and his two co-founders began to receive less and less timely information. "We did not know what he was doing," Ballard says. "We would ask him and get one-word answers." They could never be certain whether they were getting the whole truth about what was going on within the company. Ballard says he and his partners were kept far enough out of the decision-making loop that often they did not even know what questions to ask. "It was a knowledge-is-power type of thing." You might hold the title of vice-president, for example, as did Prater and Howard, but "you aren't effective, because you don't have enough information on what's being done, or what's being said, or what's being negotiated."

The most important example of this in Ballard's view involved the evolving relationship with Daimler-Benz. Ballard, who was still chairman of the board, would have liked to "interface" with Daimler-Benz, he says, when the details of the relationship were being worked out. "If I had been getting information in a timely fashion," he says, "I would have been visiting with them as part of the negotiations." Instead, he says, "I was presented with a fait accompli."

This was so extreme that, according to Ballard's recollection, during important stages of the negotiations he never actually got to meet the key executives from Daimler-Benz. "Firoz was very careful," he adds. It appeared to him that Rasul "did not want me to meet anybody at Daimler," so Ballard tried to insist. "It was to the point where I would say, as chairman, 'Look, I *want* to be involved. I want to meet the Daimler people.' And Firoz would set up meetings, for us to go to Germany. And then, all of a sudden, I would get a note giving a set of reasons why he had had to go a week early. And he didn't have time to contact me. And he was very sorry that it didn't work out, but that the meeting had already taken place."

As for himself, Ballard was becoming progressively sicker. "And I just didn't have the energy to fight it. To have fought Firoz on these things and to have stayed in control and in touch on these things would have taken almost a fourteen-hour day, six days a week. That's how much effort it would have taken, and I just didn't have the energy to do that, or the desire."

Ballard still had some power as board chairman, but when he used it, it only served to aggravate the conflict within the company. This showed up particularly in a bitter, long-running feud with Mossadiq Umedaly. Whereas Ballard has considerable respect for Rasul and his talents, and had been instrumental in selecting him from among the people Mike Brown had proposed to run Ballard, this did not extend to the young vice-president and chief financial officer. Ballard flatly dismisses Umedaly as someone who was mainly useful for doing the jobs of internal management at Ballard which Rasul couldn't or wouldn't do.

Umedaly was VP and chief financial officer, but he was not a director of the company, and thus not involved in such crucial matters as determining salaries. "Firoz insisted that Mossadiq be secretary to the board, because no one else was willing to take and write up the minutes," says Ballard. "And whenever there were salary discussions or sensitive things like that, I would ask Mossadiq to excuse himself for the discussion. There was no way that I wanted anyone who is not on the board to be discussing other people's salaries, saying why they did not think a person should get a raise, or even hearing what the others said."

Understandably, Umedaly seemed to feel insulted and perhaps demeaned by this apparent lack of trust. According to Ballard, on occasion Umedaly would overreact to the situation, audibly complain to Rasul and even threaten to quit. One time when he did this, says Ballard, Rasul had a plane to catch in a few minutes, "and it was one of the few times that I ever saw Firoz distraught. And I said to Firoz, 'I'll speak to Mossadiq, and there won't be a problem. And if he wants to quit, he'll quit, and we'll accept it. He's an employee, for Christ's sake.'"

But Umedaly stayed. Rasul wanted him and needed him, and so the feud festered. When the company moved from North Vancouver to the new building in Burnaby, Umedaly was in charge of allocating office space. On the floor where the top executive offices were to be, most offices had outside views that let in daylight. There was a clearly inferior one, though, that had a protruding steel beam and looked inward over the shop floor. "Well, Mossadiq assigned that office to Keith Prater, one of our founders," Ballard gasps, expressing disbelief even years later. Ballard was outraged and expressed his anger to Umedaly in no uncertain terms.

But the company executive, with Rasul and Umedaly at the top, still controlled the agenda and were able to get their way in the long run. Within eight years of their coming to power, none of the founders was still actively employed with the company. Another way they showed their control was in the annual reports, which gave their version of the company's history. In most of these reports in the mid-1990s, virtually nothing about the development of the PEM fuel cell was deemed worth mentioning between the time of GE's Gemini program in the 1960s and 1989, when Rasul took over and the commercialization of the Ballard cell began. The early years of the fuel cell, 1984 through 1988, when such revolutionary technological advances took place, were essentially ignored, while the later years were documented in great detail. A shareholder would have no reason to think that anything important had happened during that time, or that much had been achieved by the company's three founders or the early fuel cell team.

But Firoz Rasul argues that it is the commercialization of the fuel cell, not the early technological breakthroughs, that are Ballard Power's real success. When he came in "there was a technology, an invention. But an invention is not a business." To create a successful company, he says, the technology is only one element in the puzzle. "All the other pieces have to come together, so the company is successful on a number of fronts. Technology is only one ingredient. There are lots of companies with great technology that haven't gone anywhere. I've seen lots. Microchip technologies, software products, communications technologies, biotechnologies. They get sidetracked because they forget that for a good technology to be successful, a number of things have to be looked at."

He continues. "First, you have to think of it as a business, not just as a research and development project. And then you have to look at *all* the aspects of the business. Technology development is one. You also look at how you're going to make it. You think of marketing, how you're going to sell it. You have to think about financing, and how you're going to survive until you are able to sell this thing and how you're able to get this money. Part of Ballard's success is that we've been innovative in all of those."

How, Rasul asks, does a company that is not yet making any money in sales manage to attain a market capitalization of several billion dollars? "The key," he answers, is that, "you pay attention to every single piece of the puzzle." Switching metaphors, he likens the situation to a stool that stands on four legs: technology, marketing, finance, manufacturing. Or to a house of cards. "Take one or two cards away and it collapses."

Mossadiq Umedaly, too, is eager to explain why he thinks Ballard Power has been so successful. He considered the company something of a blank slate when he came in shortly after Rasul. "One thing we knew from the outset is that we had to raise a substantial amount of money, over a long period of time, without having a cash inflow." He and Rasul estimated that it would take anywhere from $100 million to $250 million. "That's not the vision of the founders, but Firoz's and my vision." And he argues that no other company, except in the field of biotechnology, has had to invest so much money in R & D over such a long period of time before its likely break-even point, which he hopes will come soon after the year 2000. In that sense, he thinks, Ballard Power has been unique.

Umedaly also plays down the state of the technology when Rasul and he took over. It still had a long way to go, he claims. "In the early days we were having a lot of problems with reliability." This included everything from membranes to the sealing of fuel cell stacks to prevent leaks. "We put a lot of money and a lot of focus into solving those problems," he says. "And we certainly could not go out and raise the kind of money we did, or attract the kind of strategic partners—investors who are very knowledgeable about the use of the product—until those types of problems had been solved."

Today fuel cells are being taken seriously, Umedaly says "and the reason for that—I think with great humbleness—is our achievements." Umedaly's *"our"* clearly refers to the later management of the company. "We have brought this thing to some sense of reality." The technologists, he says, always loved the fuel cell, of course, because it gave them a little budget for research. For the techies, it was a "wonderful thing," and a "great game to play." But "our objective was to get it out of the lab and into the mainstream of business, and I think we have been successful."

Even though he feels Geoffrey Ballard was the person with real vision, Paul Howard agrees that Rasul and Umedaly are entitled to recognition. "Firoz and Mossadiq are extremely dedicated," he says. "They've put a great amount of energy into this company. I've got to credit them. I may not always agree with their ways and approach, but they work very hard and they're very bright people." As for their claiming the greatest share of kudos for taking a tiny company and turning it into one that is worth billions, "They're right," says Howard. "I say the same thing to my wife, who sometimes feels that I'm not getting enough credit. I try to take the other side with her. When Firoz and Mossadiq came in, we weren't worth the kind of money that we are today. They had a very significant role. And I think that's where Firoz is coming from. We, the founders, did *not* do everything. That's why Firoz wants the credit spread around. Because it's very true. There are many good ideas that don't go anywhere."

But Geoffrey Ballard continued to reap the lion's share of credit, especially in public. In February 1999, for example, *Time* magazine named Ballard a "Hero for the Planet" and profiled him as part of a series of articles on individuals who have contributed to a better environment.[40] And in the summer of 1999 he was made a Member of the Order of Canada.

"Understand," says Ballard, where the "bad blood" between him and Firoz Rasul comes from. "Because I am absolutely certain of this." The main problem was that Ballard's name was "on the door," which meant that attention inevitably gravitated towards him, not to Rasul, no matter how long Rasul remained president and CEO and no matter how well the company did.

"With my name on the door," says Ballard, "every time the premier of the province came, or the prime minister of Canada came, he'd always walk over to the Ballard of Ballard Power. And Firoz would turn green. He'd literally turn green. He couldn't stomach it." And Ballard himself could well understand why Rasul might take it badly to have his important contribution to the company ignored. "There were many times when the reason that they were there was because Firoz had done an excellent job of marketing. And he certainly was entitled to recognition."

The most dramatic example of this was in 1996 when Prime Minister Jean Chrétien visited to help celebrate the opening of the company's new building, and to announce a $30 million infusion of federal funds for Ballard's stationary power subsidiary. Geoffrey Ballard recalls sitting at the head of the table in the conference room. Chrétien came over to him, pulled up a chair, faced Ballard, put his feet up on the table and began a conversation. "Everybody else sort of drifted away, because he was getting private information," says Ballard. Rasul was forced to hover around at the fringe of the action.

Strategic
PARTNERS

F iroz Rasul's commercialization strategy relied heavily on drawing in large and powerful industrial partners. One company that seemed to be a natural match was Dow Chemical. Dow had developed the experimental membrane that promised far higher power density than the Dupont Nafion® commercial product.* Its Canadian subsidiary had been the first to acquire a Ballard fuel cell designed for stationary power generation. In 1993 Ballard and Dow Chemical entered a "strategic collaboration agreement" to commercialize fuel cells for stationary power applications using natural gas. "After looking at the competing technologies," said Dow's director for energy, Kenneth Koza, "we see Ballard fuel cell stationary power plants as the product of choice in tomorrow's energy market." Dow also wanted to develop a market for its membrane

---

* The Dow membrane did not quickly displace Nafion® because it was not commercially available for many years, there were quality control problems that gave each batch different properties, and Nafion was acceptable where extremely high power density was not crucial.

technology. The two companies put a combined team of sixty people onto the project with the ultimate goal of developing 250-kilowatt units about the size of a cargo container.

But the partnership fizzled after only a couple of years. In the diplomatic wording used in Ballard's 1995 annual report, "Dow and Ballard were unable to agree on a business arrangement for the second phase of our collaboration, and we agreed to end the relationship." Ballard eventually paid Dow $3.5 million (in Ballard shares) to purchase equipment used in the collaboration and went looking for other partners in the stationary power field.

What happened with Dow, says Keith Prater, is that from the start the relationship was a "strange" one. Dow wanted to get into the business of selling complete natural gas power plants. But they were also interested in supplying the components of such plants. So they wanted to be at "both ends of the food chain." Ballard took the position that it was fine for Dow to sell complete power plants, and that Ballard would work with them on integrating the components. However, as Ballard's vice-president for intellectual property, Prater told them, "the fuel cell stack development is totally ours, so we're not going to let you into the stack." In other words, Ballard was not willing to share its proprietary secrets with Dow, or give the American company access even to the specific stack that was being developed for the stationary power plants. It was not a fully open relationship, because the focus of the joint activity was not to develop stack hardware but to integrate the stacks with other components.

This presented problems, Prater says, because Ballard was trying to get the best possible membrane from Dow. "They were still developing the membrane, and we were having difficulties because the properties of the Dow membrane were different from those of Dupont's Nafion® membrane. So we were having to re-engineer the stack to some extent to take advantage of the Dow material and also to support the membrane's requirements. It was physically, structurally different." Ballard could not just use one membrane in place of the other and get optimum results.

Eventually, the testing of the membrane in the Ballard cells became an issue and Ballard had to bend its own rules. Dow would formulate a slightly different version of the membrane and send a sample to Ballard. Ballard would test it, report back to Dow that some property of the membrane was not quite right, and suggest changes. This approach was cumbersome, so Ballard sent Dow a single Mark V fuel cell (similar to those used in the first Ballard bus) so that Dow could take it apart and test its membrane on the same equipment that Ballard was using. "At that point," says Prater, "they had a capability of looking inside." But by then, Ballard had already moved on to more advanced fuel cell designs. For the stationary power plant, Ballard was scaling up to much larger cells and cell stacks than were required for transportation, "and they didn't get inside those things," says Prater.

The partnership, limited though it was, might still have been beneficial for both sides if Dow had accepted Ballard's position in it. But some of the Dow people became excited enough about the fuel cell business that they wanted to be more than just assemblers and sellers of the complete power plants. "They wanted to vertically integrate, all the way through," says Prater. In other words, they wanted to be more involved on the fuel cell end than just supplying the membrane. "And their business plan began sounding a lot like Ballard's business plan. So then it became a question of, 'Gee, Dow, if you want to do all this, what's left for Ballard? Are you suggesting that you essentially want to buy us out?' And the answer was, 'Well, not really, or certainly not at anything approaching the value which you think you have.'" Negotiations went back and forth about how this impasse could be resolved, but nothing emerged that was satisfactory to both sides. "And so," says Prater, "it was agreed to split and go our separate ways, and that was done very amicably."

An area of technology where Ballard felt it had to make great strides in the mid-1990s if it was going to commercialize its fuel cell was the catalyst. The cost of the platinum required had to be brought down quite drastically. Although Ballard had some in-house catalyst expertise of its own, in 1994 it entered into a strategic relationship that continues today and has succeeded in reducing the amount of platinum or other noble metal required at least tenfold.

The British firm Johnson Matthey, with 8,300 employees and operations in thirty-seven countries, is the world's leading producer of catalysts for the catalytic converters used to reduce pollution in conventional automobile emissions. It is also the world's top supplier of noble metals for fuel cell electrodes of all kinds, which includes other types besides PEM.

A major problem with Ballard's early cells was that they used so much platinum on each electrode that the cost of that alone for a single fuel cell car might run to a prohibitive $10,000 or more. The early electrodes were coated with platinum in the form of platinum black. This is a finely powdered metal made in such a way that each particle has an extremely high surface area, which maximizes its chemical effectiveness. With platinum black, says Keith Prater, "all the various facets," or sides of the particle, "are pointing in different directions." The reason it looks black, instead of being shiny, is that the rough surface does not reflect light well. The problem, though, is that the catalytic effect of the platinum occurs only on the surface of the particles. "The platinum that is inside those particles doesn't come in contact with the hydrogen," to produce the electrochemical reaction. "So it's just providing structure, and it's pretty expensive structure."

The theoretical remedy to this problem, which was worked on largely at Los Alamos National Laboratory and Texas A & M University, was first to attach much finer particles of platinum to somewhat larger particles of carbon, so-called carbon black. Then these platinum-studded carbon particles—picture them as scoops of ice cream with chocolate sprinkles all over their surface—were used to coat the porous carbon fibre electrodes. With this so-called supported (or "dispersed") platinum catalyst, a much larger effective surface area of platinum is achieved with the same amount of metal. By the time the Johnson Matthey-Ballard partnership began, the amount of platinum required had been reduced by around seventy-five per cent.

But greater reductions were still needed, and a practical mass production method had to be devised. This is where Johnson Matthey's expertise came in. A joint Ballard-JM team was assigned to the task. No significant money changed hands; each company paid for its own share of the work. But Ballard supplied its standard test stations and Mark V fuel cells. These cells were no longer state-of-the art, which mitigated the problem of revealing proprietary secrets. Moreover, as in the Dow partnership, most testing at that time had been done on Mark V cells, so they provided a convenient baseline for making performance comparisons. Much of the practical catalyst work was done at JM's research centre in England.

JM used its own proprietary method of making the "supported" catalyst, that is, attaching the minute particles of platinum to the particles of carbon black. The average size of the platinum particles was only two nanometres, or two hundred thousandths of a millimetre across. To give some sense of this size, the period at the end of this sentence is about one hundred thousand times as large in diameter as such a particle. The supported catalyst was then made into a kind of ink and printed onto electrodes made of carbon fibre paper or carbon cloth. Printing allows the catalyst to be spread very evenly and in an incredibly thin layer. Next, membrane electrode assemblies (MEAs) were manufactured from this paper or cloth using both the most advanced Dow membrane and the latest Dupont Nafion® membrane.

The resulting MEAs were first tested in special laboratory devices, then put into Mark V single cells, and finally tested in multicelled Ballard stacks with all the realistic complexities of temperature and water management. Whole series of tests were run during the mid-1990s using catalysts spread on the electrodes in varying concentrations, or catalyst "loadings." Researchers quickly discovered that very low loadings of platinum worked as well, or very nearly as well, as much higher concentrations of the expensive metal. Both the Dow and the Nafion® membranes produced acceptable results.

To simulate the realistic conditions of fuel cells that may have to run on impure fuels, such as hydrogen from reformed methanol, cells and cell stacks were tested on gases that included varying amounts of carbon monoxide. Carbon monoxide tends to "poison" the electrode on the hydrogen side of the cell, leading to a drastic fall-off of performance over time. The JM team found that by using a mix of platinum and ruthenium on this electrode this poisoning effect could be greatly reduced.

By 1997 JM and Ballard achieved a tenfold reduction in the catalyst loading without a significant reduction in performance. The catalysts had been tested for over 3,000 hours without serious signs of degradation. A pilot production facility had been established at JM that could produce 50,000 electrodes a year and could be scaled up much further to accommodate increasing demand.

The catalyst cost problem was largely solved. JM and Ballard estimated that fuel cell stacks could be made using only about $5 US worth of catalyst per kilowatt of electricity generated, or about $300 for a small car needing a sixty kilowatt stack. And this cost may fall even further. An authoritative California study projects eventual catalyst costs in the range of only $2 to $3 per kilowatt. Moreover, at the end of the car's life the precious metal can be recovered and recycled. The Johnson Matthey partnership with Ballard has delivered what was hoped for and was formally extended in 1998.

Another potentially prohibitive cost in PEM fuel cells, though, was the membrane. In the mid-to-late 1980s, Dupont's Nafion® was priced at around $800 (US) a square metre, or about $100 per square foot. This was acceptable in the chlorine industry, for which it was designed, but far too high for transportation. In some ways, Nafion® was "overdesigned," made to last for 100,000 hours of use in an industrial plant running round the clock, whereas an automobile is built to run only part-time and for a total of only 5,000 to 10,000 hours in its "lifetime." Most estimates from the auto industry indicated that the membrane had to come down into the range of $5 to $15 per square foot before a fuel cell engine could compete with a conventional engine. Ballard set out to develop its own, much cheaper membrane and assigned its in-house polymer expert, Fred Steck, to the task.

Steck came to Ballard at the time the first fuel cell team was being assembled, but he was not hired mainly to work on fuel cell membranes. Ballard was actively trying to diversify into new technologies and product areas to reduce its dependence on the Amoco battery contract. One area it considered was polymers for electrolysis, in the electronics industry, as adhesives in composite structural materials, and for the medical field. "A lot of specialty polymers were being used for heart valves and such things," says Geoffrey Ballard. "We were aiming our business at the small-scale production of specialized polymers which we would tailor-make for markets that were too small for a major company such as Dow or Dupont to put up a production line."

In 1983, when Keith Prater went on his fact-finding trip to prepare the bid for the first fuel cell contract, he included Calgary as one of his main stops. Steck had earned a chemical engineering degree in Switzerland and had just completed a doctorate at the University of Calgary working on polymer membranes for chlor-alkali electrolysis.

He had no intention of remaining in Canada after completing his degree. He only planned to stay another half year and then return to Switzerland to pursue an academic career.

Prater went to Calgary to discuss membrane chemistry with Prof. H.L. Yeager, who was supervising Steck's research. But he also met the young Swiss chemist and was so impressed that he asked Steck to come down to Vancouver and give the Ballard people a talk about membranes.

When he did so, Steck emphasized the importance of the membrane to the PEM fuel cell. "The membrane is the heart of the fuel cell," Steck says. "Of course, I'm biased." After the talk he told Ballard, Prater, and Howard that if they were serious about fuel cells, they really should have someone at Ballard who knew about membranes. "I said it quite unselfishly," he insists. "I wasn't thinking about myself. I thought I'd be going back to Switzerland. But then, at the end of the day we got to talking, and Geoffrey said, 'Why don't you join us.'"

Steck was tempted. Of medium height and athletic build, he had always loved hiking and fishing in the mountains of his Swiss home. In Calgary, he liked heading off to the Rockies for fishing, hiking, and climbing, and Vancouver was similarly attractive, tucked up against the mountains as it is. Then there was the challenge itself. At Ballard he would be able to pursue his research in a largely independent way. In Calgary Steck had been developing new membranes for electrolysis. The work had gone so well that people in the Canadian government, particularly Martin Hammerli at the National Research Council, suggested that he try to commercialize it in Canada. Steck even brought to Ballard his own separate project funding, courtesy of Hammerli, who was also the unofficial scientific authority on the first Ballard fuel cell contract.

At Ballard Steck enjoyed (and still does) a somewhat unusual status. He was an employee not of Ballard Technologies but of BTC Membranes, which later became Ballard Advanced Materials. "Even now," he says, "I have a dual function." Steck is president, CEO, and a major shareholder in Ballard Advanced Materials (which owns the membrane technology, but is in turn owned by Ballard Power Systems to the tune of about eighty per cent). At the same time he is vice-president for R & D of Ballard Power Systems.

Steck set up a small laboratory of his own in the same building as David Watkins and his fuel cell team, but separate from the main building where the battery work was being funded by Amoco. It was a smelly place with fume hoods everywhere. Several assistants worked under his guidance. Just as the fuel cell team was working under a DND contract with money from NRC, so Steck was using NRC money to continue his work on membranes for electrolysis. This was not radically different from what was required in a fuel cell, except that the electrolysis membrane had to be porous, while the fuel cell membrane had to be a dense film. "It's just how you make the film—the processing—that was different," says Steck.

During Steck's first years at Ballard, though, the fuel cell team was using Nafion®, and later the Dow experimental membrane as well. Steck's advice on preparing the membranes to put into the fuel cell was useful. But it was only after the big leap in power with the Dow membrane that his own membrane work took on great importance. Starting in 1988, the goal was to create a much cheaper membrane that Ballard would own and be able to manufacture itself. "A high-performance, low-cost membrane was really needed," he says, looking back at those years. With the expensive ones made by Dupont and Dow, he "did not see that you could make a commercial product out of the fuel cell."

Steck jumps up to the chalkboard to illustrate how he approached the challenge. "These Dow and Dupont products are called perfluorinated membranes," he says, drawing a complex, branching molecular diagram that looks a bit like the new international space station. The backbone of the molecule is a plastic similar to what is marketed as Teflon. Branching off from it are side chains or clusters containing the element fluorine. "This ion cluster morphology," he says, "is excellent for proton conductance." But it is also inherently expensive, and Steck thought the fluorine might not be necessary. He set out to create a proprietary membrane polymer minus the fluorine in the clusters.

Producing any such polymer from scratch is also expensive, he explains, "so to keep the cost low, first we took whatever bulk, commercial polymer we could find." Then he and his team modified a batch of the polymer, adding the clusters, which they knew were needed to make protons diffuse through the membrane well.

As with the Ballard fuel cell itself, the work was an all-consuming challenge, not a job you could limit to normal business hours. For one thing, Steck and his co-workers had to be extremely careful. "The last thing we could afford was an accident." And making the actual polymer was tricky. "Polymerization is a chain reaction. If you don't control it, it can get too hot and the glass beaker can blow up." In fact, the entire procedure can take a day or even two, "and then you have to be there for forty-eight hours. If you do a chemical reaction, you cannot just interrupt at five o'clock and go home. So you plan it."

Fortunately for him, the fuel cell team who shared the premises were working punishing hours themselves, which meant that Steck could often find company even at the oddest times. "David McLeod lived close by, so he was often there at 2 a.m. He would be in his small office, dreaming about markets, and I would go and talk with him through the night." Steck wasn't married yet. Had I not been a bachelor at the time, he laughs, "I probably would have ended up divorced, because of the time we spent at the lab. We ate pizza and Chinese food, ordering out and staying up all night with the help of the coffee machine. We were tough individuals, with lots of stamina." They were much younger then, as well, and were excited about the work. "We wanted to see the results right then and there. So, if you had made the polymer and you were totally exhausted, you'd go home and sleep a little bit and come right back."

In compensation for the long days, Steck's membrane team sometimes took days off to go hiking in the mountains. "The beauty of it was, we were a small company. I could say, 'Hey, today's a beautiful day. Let's go fishing.' If you have 5,000 people, you cannot necessarily do that. But we could do that. And I made sure, even at Ballard Advanced Materials, that they got shares. We're all shareholders. So they also are part of the success."

Making a batch of some new polymer was only part of Steck's task. "That doesn't show you anything yet, because you still have to make a film" out of it and put it into a test cell to ascertain its performance. Making a film involved dissolving the polymer in a solvent and casting it on a glass plate. This meant going into the dust-free "clean room," pouring a beaker of polymer onto the plate and drawing a sharp-edged "knife" across the plate to spread it evenly. "It dries relatively quickly, but exactly how fast was important. To get a good film you had to control it." Once it dries, it looks just like this, he says, holding up a clear plastic report cover.

The first two generations of membranes Steck designed—without fluorine in their side clusters—gave excellent performance, but they turned brittle or tore easily and failed after 350 to 500 hours in the test cell. This was not nearly good enough for a fuel cell vehicle. He eventually realized that a lightly fluorinated membrane was needed for stability, a compromise between what he had been trying and the fully fluorinated Dupont and Dow products.

Meanwhile, the pace of development had become a consideration. Under Firoz Rasul's management, to keep investors happy and the finances flowing, the company was establishing target dates for specific improvements and trying to attain them, one after another. Steck sat down with two of his organic chemists to discuss how long it should take to develop this third generation membrane if everything went just right. Of course, he laughs, normally in real life "it never works out as it does on paper." The reaction does not work right, or the yield is low, and then changes have to be made. Trying to stick to a schedule is not the way R & D work is usually carried out. "Generally, someone would say, You're crazy. You can't plan research like that." But this was Ballard Power Systems. The Ballard management had its time lines and wanted results. "We came up with the number—six months. Six months, from starting on a new polymer to the time of getting data from the fuel cells. And it took us five months to get there, because the whole group was so fascinated by it. We all believed we could do it."

When the third generation membrane was ready, they put it into test cells and awaited the results. At first, says Steck, "it performed exactly as well as the second generation membrane had done, which was the best-performing membrane in the world, at that time." He had little doubt that it would have greater longevity, "but still, you have to prove it. So we put it into a test cell and let it run," beginning in 1992. He and his technical staff kept checking the read-out on the test station. Reassuringly, it showed a flat performance curve. "Of course, we were happy when it achieved the first 500 hours with no signs of decay." Then, when it hit 1,000 hours, they celebrated by breaking out a bottle of champagne. At 5,000 hours they opened another bottle of champagne and at 10,000 hours another. By then it was 1993. At 15,000 hours they again drank a bottle of champagne and considered the effort a resounding success. Steck had a shelf full of empties, and Ballard had its own durable, affordable membrane, which it then patented.

Four years later Ballard was still just at the early stages of commercializing its proprietary membrane and setting up a pilot-scale production line to make it in sizeable quantities, over 9,000 square metres (100,000 square feet) a year. "It takes that long," says Steck, but then he emphasizes that this was actually remarkably quick. Think about Dupont and the Nafion® membrane, he says. "It took them around ten to twelve years at a cost of $100 million plus dollars. It cost us about two to three million dollars." Once again, small, nimble, and creative Ballard had done something in a fraction of the time and at a fraction of the cost of the big corporations.

Company
with a DIFFERENCE

Through the mid-1990s Ballard Power made great strides in reducing the cost of the fuel cell's membrane and catalyst. It also grabbed a few headlines with its succession of impressive buses. Its management kept investors happy by meeting one technical target after another. And it was able to keep up a steady flow of government money to supplement its equity financing. But none of these had the overall impact of the decisive strategic partnership that it formed with an automobile giant, Germany's prestigious Daimler-Benz (DB) corporation.

When Ballard set out to change the world, says venture capitalist Mike Brown, they knew they needed some big partners. "We were like a little mouse in the jungle, and we knew that we had to associate ourselves with a pack of big jungle animals. Because, as soon as our pack understood what was going on, other packs would form in other places. So we'd better have our own elephants and tigers and rhinos, whatever."

Compared to Ballard, Daimler really was an elephant. Even before its 1998 merger with Chrysler, DB had 290,000 employees and annual revenues of around $70 billion (US). DB has long been best-known in North America for its top of the line Mercedes Benz cars, but these are actually a relatively small part of its overall business. The proportion of auto sales may change as Daimler enters the low-cost car market, as it did in 1998 with the launch of its small A-Class cars in Europe. Meanwhile, DB is the world's largest manufacturer of buses and trucks. It also has sizeable marine and aerospace divisions. And it is well known as a company that strives to be at the technological cutting edge, which made it the ideal partner for Ballard.

From the start the Ballard leadership sensed that DB was different from the big US auto companies. "The people at Daimler-Benz, in our experience, were a cut above," says Firoz Rasul. For one thing, the quality of their engineers was very high. Even more important, "They were motivated. They were convinced that this technology had promise. They knew it had a future. They really put their best resources forward." In addition, Rasul says, there were the more subtle things. "The people chemistry was right. We worked well with them, and they worked as a team. The feeling was right."

Fred Steck, Ballard's membrane specialist, also found DB to be a company with a difference. They always strive to take the lead in new technology, he says. "They were the ones who developed the Anti-lock Braking System. They're always in the forefront. It's their culture. In that sense there's no doubt that they're different from other companies."

Ballard's first contact with Daimler came about almost inadvertently back around 1988. The Ballard technical team was using a lot of hydrogen in their laboratory testing, and were having problems getting a supply of the pure gas in the Vancouver area. The Ballard partners thought it might be a good idea to buy or lease electrolysing equipment, so they could manufacture their own hydrogen on site. Keith Prater heard through the science grapevine about a small company in Belgium that was making electrolysers that used PEM technology. While on a trip to Europe, he dropped in to talk to them about acquiring one.

Prater told the head of the company that Ballard was making and testing PEM fuel cells. The Belgian was surprised and intrigued. "Well, my goodness," he said, "I have a contract to deliver a PEM fuel cell to Daimler-Benz." He explained to Prater that Daimler had been experimenting with a hydrogen-powered internal combustion engine automobile for some years. But there was a problem. Compressed hydrogen occupies a relatively large volume for the amount of energy it provides. Fuel economy, therefore, was a major issue for the Daimler engineers.

"What they discovered," says Prater, "is that the automobile, and particularly the luxury automobile, has a tremendous electric power requirement." There is all sorts of auxiliary equipment, such as electric windows, as well as such standard devices as fuel pumps and heater fans. "And by the time you hook up an inefficient alternator to an inefficient internal combustion engine, you're looking at only four, five or maybe six per cent efficiency in making electricity." What Daimler wanted was a much more efficient way of making electricity. And the fuel cell seemed particularly well suited, since the car would be carrying an on-board supply of hydrogen in any case.

The Belgian company had subcontracted the fuel cell to another firm, but the second company had not come through. Was there any chance, the Belgian asked Prater, that Ballard could build and deliver such a cell? The first Perry system, using Mark IV cells, had already proven itself. The one for the Royal Navy was also in the works. Meanwhile, the Ballard team was moving forward and developing the Mark V cell, which was more than twice as powerful. This meant that a two-kilowatt, twelve-volt stack required only twenty cells (compared to the fifty-four in the first Perry stack) and could be made as compact as an automobile battery. Prater was confident that Ballard could deliver the goods and agreed immediately.

Compared to building the much larger second Perry stack it was child's play. In 1989 the stack was delivered to Daimler under a leasing arrangement and tested for about eighteen months. This made Daimler the first automobile company to acquire and experiment with a Ballard fuel cell system. It worked well. In fact, says Prater, Daimler was pleasantly surprised at its performance and reliability. The German giant soon dropped its hydrogen automobile project, though, and the stack was eventually returned to Ballard.

But Daimler had not forgotten the small company in far-away British Columbia. In late 1992, David McLeod took a phone call from two Daimler scientists who were interested in PEM fuel cell technology and were touring North America to look at who was doing what. At the time, Daimler had recently acquired the Dornier aerospace company and was still integrating it into its overall company structure. The Daimler men, Werner Tillmetz and Guenther Dietrich, were both from the Dornier side of the company, where all the electrochemistry research and development, including fuel cells and batteries, was being done.

They showed up on a Friday afternoon, and McLeod got the impression that they did not expect much from their visit to Ballard. "They were your typical German technology people and were quite arrogant, of course" about what they thought Daimler was capable of. McLeod talked to them alone at first, and then showed them around the lab and introduced them to the top Ballard people. The Daimler men, he says, were immediately impressed. It was a great meeting of the minds. "After about fifteen minutes, they realized that we were a completely different group of folks than they had ever imagined." Fred Steck, the membrane specialist, also recalls the visit vividly. "After they walked through and talked with us," he says, "it was clear to me that they wanted to work with Ballard."

Soon McLeod was off to Germany with Firoz Rasul to meet the Daimler top brass and take the measure of the German fuel cell project. McLeod felt right away that the two firms complemented each other and could develop a great relationship. "We were very creative," he says, "and they were highly disciplined." Perhaps more important, the Germans were convinced that fuel cells could actually be made to power a car in the near, and not merely the distant, future. They were probably the world's first auto company to arrive at that conviction.

But McLeod was surprised to see just how small the Daimler fuel cell effort was at that time, and how far it was behind Ballard's own technology. There were just a few people working under Dietrich on single cells, he found, "tiny things, almost like what they were doing at Los Alamos." And like Los Alamos, the Daimler effort was very much focused on basic science, not engineering. "Dietrich is the one who actually took the first big hit," says McLeod. "He thought he was one of the world's authorities on these fuel cells, but it turned out that he really did not know how they worked. He did not have that experience. So he was our first tough sell. And by the time we got through with him, the rest was easy."

Keith Prater also saw how far Daimler lagged behind. When they approached Ballard they had "probably only half a dozen people" who were doing work somewhat related to fuel cells, he says. Their management had asked them to build a fuel cell in a fairly short period of time. In Prater's view, "the guy in charge, Tillmetz, eventually said to himself, I've got a few electrochemists who know something about fuel cells. And I've got a few engineers. But none of us has any real experience, certainly not in building this kind of fuel cell. I don't think we can do it in that time frame." Prater is ninety per cent certain that the Daimler people had not made a PEM fuel cell themselves before they got involved with Ballard, "or if they had, it would have been a tiny lab-scale thing to dabble in the technology."

If Daimler was going to move ahead rapidly on fuel cells, it needed the expertise and well-developed proprietary technology that Ballard already had on hand. But negotiating a joint venture was not easy. McLeod remembers going for long walks in the woods of southern Germany with Tillmetz to talk and "make sure we understood what it was they thought they were going to get, and what it was that we thought they needed." What Daimler needed most, says McLeod, was "someone on the outside to validate what they already believed, namely that this thing was possible." So McLeod and his Ballard colleagues found themselves playing the role of "third party in that whole selling process" within Daimler itself.

The negotiation of the Ballard-Daimler alliance was a watershed for Ballard, and it required taking some very tough decisions. The main thing Ballard brought to the partnership was its fuel cell stack technology, and under the deal Daimler got access to it and the right to license it. The main thing Daimler contributed, other than millions of dollars and its prestigious name, was its expertise in engineering the rest of the complex system needed to make a fuel cell power a car.

The toughest bullet for Ballard to bite was to abandon caution and take the risk of letting Daimler look inside the Ballard cell. In contrast to the arrangement with Dow, and contrary to the policy that prevailed regarding leasing the cell stacks as sealed black boxes, Daimler was to have full access to the inner workings of the specific models of Ballard stacks that were being jointly developed.[*]

---

[*] Ballard had other models of cell stacks, such as the one being developed with GM under a US government-funded program, that were kept from Daimler. And, of course, GM did not get to see the Daimler technology.

Keith Prater is frank about why Ballard had to let Daimler in on Ballard's proprietary secrets. "That was the strategic decision we made," he says. If Ballard wanted to induce a company with the reputation of Daimler to provide the money and "attach its name" to the fuel cell's development, there was no alternative. "They would not just send us money and hope we would deliver something at that level. And who can blame them? So we made the decision. We negotiated hard and got joint ownership of the jointly developed technology." The decision was not made lightly. But "under those circumstances, it was something we were able to convince the Ballard board of directors was the way to go. There *were* questions about whether one should do this. I think history has proven that it was probably a good deal. But they were the only organization at that point in time that we allowed to see the innards of the cell."

After drawn-out negotiations, in 1993 Daimler and Ballard agreed on a joint venture to which Daimler committed $35 million over four years. There were specified targets to reach or exceed by certain dates. Most concerned putting a series of prototype vehicles on the road by 1996-97, and all were achieved. It is precisely this kind of performance, from Ballard's side, that did so much to bolster investor confidence.

In exchange for funding the project, the resulting product, a complete fuel cell stack, would be jointly owned by Ballard and Daimler. Ballard would be free to sell these jointly developed stacks, or license their manufacture, to other automobile manufacturers. For its part, Daimler would also be free to manufacture fuel cells if it wished. Twenty-five million dollars of Daimler's $35 million contribution went directly to Ballard to fund a group that was working with Daimler on development of the new and improved Ballard stack. It was designed to be compact and flat to allow it to fit under the seats of later Daimler prototype vehicles. In addition, Daimler had its own group that worked on adapting the stack and integrating it into a complete vehicle.

It was when Daimler began seriously engineering the support systems for the Ballard stacks that some of the Ballard technical people became anxious about the nature of the relationship. In Canada, the Ballard bus transportation team under Paul Howard was simultaneously tackling some of the very same problems of integrating the fuel cell stacks with the rest of the systems needed to power a practical vehicle, the second Ballard bus. This was an intermediate vehicle that came between the first small bus and the transit buses for Chicago and Vancouver. Ideally, there should have been a high level of cooperation between these two efforts, but there was not, because the contract only provided for full sharing of information about the stack, not how it could be made to run a car or bus.

Far from being an equal relationship, says Howard, "It was a one-way street," with Daimler privy to a lot of what Ballard was doing but showing very few of the cards in its hand in return. Daimler's work on its fuel cell cars "was kept very secret from us," says Howard. Daimler did all its own work on integrating the fuel cell stacks into full vehicle systems. Meanwhile, "we were showing them our system technology, how our bus worked, and we were getting nothing in return in terms of how they were doing their systems for their cars." This caused considerable frustration at Ballard, he recalls. "Because we would have liked to learn. And we would debate this at the senior level. People said, 'Why are we showing them all our secrets, all of what we're doing? These guys can take what we're doing.'"

The inequality was built into the structure of the relationship. "They were only buying the stack from us," says Howard, telling Ballard what they wanted the stack to do. Even when Ballard people went over to Germany, says Howard, the results were meagre at best. "One fellow, our program manager for the stack, occasionally got to see the odd thing there, but he was about the only one. Our engineers kept saying, 'We'd like to go over and see what they're doing; we'd like to learn from them.' But that was not the agreement. They were buying stack development, and they were going to do their own engineering." Because of this situation, when after four years Daimler made the big decision to buy a large ownership share in Ballard and commit to joint manufacture of fuel cell engines, people like Howard and Prater breathed a lot easier. "We were relieved that the deal came together," says Howard, "because we had shown them a lot." Today, Ballard also participates in engine development with Daimler.

However frustrating it was for Ballard insiders, from the public standpoint it did not take long for the Ballard-Daimler partnership to bear fruit. The first visible success came in April 1994 when Daimler rolled out its first New Electric Car or NECAR (subsequently called NECAR I). This was a boxy three-and-one-half tonne cargo van that *Road & Track* magazine called "purely a rolling test lab and demonstration vehicle."[41]

In NECAR I, the fuel cells and equipment took up most of the space that normally would have gone to seating passengers. It ran on pure hydrogen and was powered by twelve stacks generating a bit over four kilowatts each, for a total of around fifty kilowatts. These were relatively low-powered, older model stacks similar to what went into the first Ballard bus. The compressed hydrogen was in large cylindrical tanks placed high up in the rear passenger area, where the passengers' heads would normally go. With only about sixty horsepower pushing such a heavy vehicle, it was a bit of a clunker, capable of a top speed of only ninety kilometres (fifty-five miles) an hour.

Still, Daimler's director of research and technology, Hartmut Weule, called it a "milestone on the road to ecological mobility" and proclaimed that the German company was ahead of such rivals as General Motors and Mazda in fuel cell technology and planned to stay ahead. He said that Daimler was "confident that the fundamental problems facing such a revolutionary drive system have been solved." He added, "We do not intend to wait until our Japanese or American competitors gain the upper hand in technology." Figuratively waving the company flag, he proclaimed: "We are at the very beginning of a new era of technology," one that is "comparable to the days when Gottlieb Daimler and Karl Benz were constructing the first vehicles powered by internal combustion engines."[42]

Ballard's management was more subdued. Of course, Ballard already had its own fuel cell bus on the road and so was less impressed by the achievement than some of the world's press. "We're stoic people around here," said Vice-President Mossadiq Umedaly. "We're taking it in stride. It's one notch of many still to go."[43] Still, having the first Daimler vehicle out on the road could not help but enhance Ballard's profile in the financial world. Just over a year later, Ballard common shares were admitted for trading in the US on NASDAQ. (They remained listed on the Toronto Stock Exchange as well.)

As the partnership with Daimler evolved, the speed of Ballard's advances and the quality of Ballard's engineering continued to impress their German counterparts. Some of the German engineers, says David McLeod, were openly envious of Ballard's creativity, lack of bureaucracy, and resulting ability to make rapid changes in design. "One guy came up to me in Dornier's corporate dining room and said, 'Mr. McLeod, I don't think you realize the impact that your company has had on my company.'" The Dornier people were impressed by what was possible if a company worked with a less complicated structure, and they told McLeod how at one time Dornier used to be as creative as Ballard. "It was quite a moment. Here was a guy from the ranks of the best engineers in the world, literally telling you that your company and your people are equal to or better than his own people."

The joint fuel cell stack development was being done mainly at Ballard Power. As one advance followed another, the Daimler people liked to come to Canada to visit the Ballard facilities and see the latest innovations that they would soon be able to incorporate into their own vehicles. Some may have had doubts at first about the commercial viability of a fuel cell car. The cell was not yet powerful enough, and the cost of the membrane and catalyst still seemed terribly high. Gradually, though, they became ever more convinced that the fuel cell vehicle was going to be much more than just another R & D project. "People wanted to believe it," says McLeod. "And they started to, because every time they came to our building there would be something new to see. I used to tell them that this is a movie, not a snapshot. That what you saw here today is not necessarily what you'll see here a month from now."

By October 1995 the extent of Ballard's progress was made public. Keith Prater flew to London to attend that year's International Grove Fuel Cell Conference, the big annual event in the fuel cell world. He proudly announced that Ballard's latest cell stack had topped the critical power density that the US government had estimated was required for use in an automobile. It generated over twenty-eight kilowatts per cubic foot (or 1,000 watts per litre and 700 watts per kilogram), which was more than five times better than the stacks used in the 1993 Ballard bus and Daimler's 1994 fuel cell van. "This achievement exceeds the power density targets for a practical fuel cell powered vehicle set by auto manufacturers and the US Department of Energy," said Prater.[44]

A half year later, this reduction in bulk and weight was incorporated into Daimler's new NECAR II, which was given a festive roll-out in May 1996 at Berlin's Brandenburg Gate. NECAR II was a smaller and lighter mini-van than NECAR I. Only two of the compact, new and jointly developed fuel cell stacks, each generating 25 kW, were required, and they fit neatly under the rear seat. The twin, cylindrical compressed hydrogen tanks were placed on the roof under a streamlined housing. This gave the van seating room for six and a range of 250 kilometres (155 miles) on a tank of hydrogen. With less weight to push, the van had a respectable top speed of 110 kilometres (70 miles) per hour. The world's media were almost universal in calling it the first practical fuel cell powered car. A *Fortune* magazine reporter who went for a ride in Germany swooned about its performance: "The only noticeable sound," he said, "comes from a compressor that varies the rate of gas flow into the stacks as the accelerator pedal is pressed or released. The power train responds briskly when the pedal is floored."[45]

Daimler executives were so ecstatic they promptly moved up their projections for the first commercial fuel cell vehicle. "Although we managed to solve the principal problems associated with the fuel cell drive a couple of years ago," said Research Director Hartmut Weule, "we reckoned it would be well after 2020 before these vehicles would be hitting the road. However, given the present state of the technology, it might now be as early as 2010, if not a lot sooner." CEO Helmut Werner was even more optimistic. He announced that a much smaller NECAR III was already in the works. Production of a fuel cell vehicle, he said, will be decided by the year 2000, and he was "fairly sure the decision will be positive."[46]

The roll-out and testing of the NECAR II, with its worldwide media splash, marked a sea of change in the profile of fuel cells for transportation. Whereas the NECAR I was an ungainly mobile laboratory, the NECAR II looked like a standard van and had room to carry passengers in quiet comfort. *The Times* of London called it a "breakthrough in pollution-free motoring."[47] Reuters called it a "giant step forward for Daimler and Ballard, which have reduced the cells to less than one-fifth of their original mass without sacrificing performance."[48] The specialized *Hydrogen & Fuel Cell Letter* pointed out that the US Energy Department's timetable did not call for a full-scale fuel cell power system until 1998, a concept vehicle until 2000, and a prototype before 2004. In the *Letter's* estimate, Daimler's announced timetable "puts Daimler-Benz ahead of US plans by at least four years."[49]

Geoffrey Ballard enjoyed the thrill of riding in the NECAR II a month after the roll-out when he flew to Germany to address a meeting of the World Hydrogen Conference. "Push, push, push," Ballard told his audience, imploring them to get industry and government moving to help fulfill his dream and "guarantee my grandchildren a better environment." That same year he also personally experienced what he felt was a rather sudden psychological breakthrough in industry attitudes towards fuel cells for transportation.

"Until 1996," he says, "there was a concerted effort by all of the automotive and oil industry to essentially put down or postpone the advent of the fuel cell to some distant time in the future. There was no perception of imminence." The change really started with Daimler putting a car on the road. "The Ballard bus was important, but it did not have the same commercial potential." All at once, though, "the evidence was just too powerful to ignore. There was a bus, then another bus. And Chicago stepped forward and ordered three for their fleet in The Loop. And then there was the Daimler-Benz car. It was no longer possible for everyone to just push it aside."

The Starting
PISTOL
Has Been FIRED

I n April 1997 a group of high-level Daimler-Benz executives flew to Vancouver. Joining Firoz Rasul and Ballard's other top executives on a decorated podium, the two groups regaled each other with speeches of extravagant praise and exchanged company flags, thereby becoming corporate blood brothers. The ceremony marked Ballard's biggest breakthrough on the business front and kicked off a determined race among auto makers to put a practical and commercially viable fuel cell car on the road.

What Ballard and Daimler were celebrating was a $508 million (Cdn.) deal under which Daimler acquired a twenty-five per cent stake in Ballard. (Daimler paid $198 million, or $35 a share, for the stock.) The two companies agreed to invest $310 million in a new company, DBB Fuel Cell Engines, which would be jointly owned— two-thirds by Daimler, one-third by Ballard. They would build a plant in Germany to manufacture the fuel cell engines, which integrate the fuel cell stacks with all of the fuel supply, cooling, electronic, and other equipment required. The fuel cell stacks themselves would be built by Ballard in British Columbia.

Daimler and Ballard also agreed to establish a separate company, called Ballard Automotive (owned fifty-fifty) that would market all Ballard fuel cells for vehicles and the fuel cell engines made by DBB, with Daimler enjoying priority in purchasing the company's output. Finally, Daimler gained the right to name two directors out of eight to Ballard Power Systems' board. The transaction formally closed in the fall of 1997.

The Daimler buy-in represented a quantum leap in commercialization plans for the Ballard fuel cell. "We are really convinced," enthused Daimler's senior vice-president and head of the fuel cell project group, Dr. Ferdinand Panik, "that from today's point of view, the fuel cell is the alternative drive system with the highest potential to compete, really compete, with the internal combustion engine."[50] Panik, whose long and slightly wild silvery hair contrasted with Firoz Rasul's trim, buttoned-down look, said that Daimler's aim was to go into quantity production of fuel cell engines within eight years.

Panik also gave the first hint of what quantity was being envisaged. "We are not aiming for a niche market. The objective is really to concentrate on mass production. We want to compete against the internal combustion engine, and the numbers will be high. We will start with a minimum of 100,000 units."[51] Once the Ballard-Daimler deal was formally approved, Panik took one of the Daimler seats on Ballard's board.

A Daimler press release laid out a rough timetable of events to come. "Over the next two years," it said, "every part of the fuel cell engine will be developed to the point where processes for mass production are established and engine performance and cost can be estimated with confidence." Meanwhile, the next fuel cell prototype, NECAR III, a compact four-to-five passenger car, would soon be unveiled. Unlike the Ballard buses and earlier Daimler vehicles, which ran on compressed hydrogen, this one would run on methanol. Daimler was also looking well beyond NECAR III, which would have some of its interior passenger space taken up by equipment. NECAR V, scheduled for late 1999, "will approach a production prototype configuration, with room for four persons and luggage." Like NECAR III, it would use the body of the very small A-Class vehicle that, powered by a conventional gasoline engine, Daimler was just beginning to market in Europe. In other words, NECAR V would likely be the last prototype before actual commercial production. And it, too, would run on methanol.

At the end of 1999, the Daimler announcement concluded, "a decision will be made whether to invest in manufacturing facilities for fuel cell engines." The decision to proceed would depend on "management confidence that fuel cell engines will be able to compete with conventional engines and vehicles on all points while being cleaner and more efficient." These conditions were not yet assured, but Daimler was "confident that DBB with its allies have the ability to engineer all aspects of fuel cell engine technology to the point of commercial viability when mass-produced." This meant "at least 100,000 engines and vehicles per year once full production is first established, and growing to perhaps 500,000 or more units per year eventually."

As for the financial commitments, "investments of more than $1 billion will be needed" before the manufacturing facilities are in place and operating. Even with a completely successful program, the cars would not be on sale before 2004-5. Daimler's commitment, however, was firm, particularly in view of looming emission requirements such as those in California. Daimler was "prepared to support the necessary investments" it said, because it believed that the fuel cell was likely the best alternative to the internal combustion engine "given the requirements for ever cleaner engines and the emerging pressures to reduce carbon dioxide emissions from automobiles."

Daimler conceded that costs would have to be reduced drastically by mass production. But Panik sounded quite confident on that score. "In the end," he said, "I believe the fuel cell can be done for the same price as the piston engine, or lower. And I believe it can let the owner travel fifty per cent farther for the fuel used, with an engine that will be truly maintenance-free."

Daimler may have been hedging its bets on cost, but Mike Brown reckons that they must be certain that costs can be brought into line. "What we have," he says, "is a group of absolutely fabulous development engineers" who know "how to make things in big volume, at low cost, that always work and deliver what they promise they'll deliver." The Daimler-Benz people "know that, for sure. And that *will* happen." He raps his hand on the table for emphasis.

For Ballard, the Daimler buy-in was a momentous occasion. Firoz Rasul called it nothing less than "the most significant event to occur to date in Ballard's history."[52] True to his personal style, though, Rasul also struck a note of caution, saying that the two companies would not be unduly hasty in putting fuel cell cars on the road. "A premature release of this technology would set us back."[53] And he reminded the assembled audience that "offering zero or low emissions levels will not be enough" to guarantee commercial success.[54] He reviewed the sobering history of an earlier Daimler effort to market a natural gas-powered automobile engine in Brazil. It produced sixty to eighty per cent lower emissions, Rasul noted, but it was a flop because it cost five to ten per cent more than competing products.

Meanwhile, Ballard sent a representative to Detroit to explain the Daimler deal to the Big Three US auto makers and assure them that the new alliance was not exclusionary. Both Ballard and Daimler, the pitch went, wanted fuel cell engines to be accepted by as many car companies, and put into as many vehicles, as possible. They looked forward to selling the new technologies to their auto industry rivals as well as putting them into Daimler-Benz cars themselves. And Ballard remained free to collaborate on separate fuel cell projects with other auto makers. Ballard remains "open for business," said Rasul.[55]

The Daimler buy-in raised the stakes in the entire fuel cell game and generated massive media attention. *Business Week* called it a "huge bet" by Daimler that "lights a fire under rivals."[56] The US magazine commented that "in one bold stroke, Daimler has accelerated the race to perfect fuel cells. Rival car makers must suddenly speed up their own fuel-cell research—or risk being left in the dust."[57] The *Financial Times* of London favourably quoted a business analyst who said that Ballard was "doing all the right things and they have the right partners. This gives them the muscle to get this technology to market and get costs down."[58]

The stock market responded to the news with enthusiasm. Ballard's share price surged $3.25 in one day to a new high of $39.25 and soon moved much higher. (Only a year and a half earlier, the stock had been trading at between $9 and $10.) And this performance came despite the fact that Ballard routinely posted annual losses, not profits. One financial reporter looked at the trend and concluded, "Despite continued progress, the research-driven company is not expected to break even until 1999 at the earliest. Nevertheless, the flow of red ink continues to sit well with its institutional investors."[59] This was possible because of "strong management and the company's continued ability to reach development goals."[60]

A Vancouver broker with a large position in Ballard stock called Ballard "the Bombardier of the West,"[61] referring to the highly successful Quebec-based company that pioneered the snowmobile and now manufactures everything from subway cars to small- and medium-size jet passenger aircraft. He looked beyond automobiles to the fuel cell's applications in power generation and submarines, and said "They have the lead. They've got more than 150 patents around the world. How can anyone compete without infringing on the company's patent protection?"[62]

During the rest of 1997, Ballard's share price continued to climb, breaking through $100 before year's end, when a second major buy-in took place, this time by Ford. Ballard stock had gained nearly 300 per cent in a single year. Then it surged even further, peaking at $188 within a few months. The shares were split three for one, to keep the price in an affordable range, but soon sank back to the pre-split equivalent of less than $100 as the Asian financial crisis and temporary bear market hit hard in mid-1998. Then it climbed right back up again. It was a wild roller-coaster ride for investors, but those who stuck it out ended 1998 with stock that was four times as valuable as it had been only two years earlier.

On the strength of this performance, Firoz Rasul was named top CEO in Canada for 1997 by Heidrick & Struggles, an international firm that specializes in recruiting CEOs and senior executives. Rasul headed a list of ten CEOs selected from companies on the Toronto Stock Exchange and based on total return for the year to share-holders (stock-price appreciation plus dividends). The next three companies behind Ballard on the list were also high-technology firms. And Ballard had enjoyed much more than a one-year surge. *BC Business* magazine pointed out that a $1,000 investment would have grown to more than $11,000 in the three years ending December 31, 1997.

A lot of people got rich very quickly, at least on paper, including the company's executives, founders, and members of the early fuel cell team, all of whom had large holdings of stock and options. Just how well some did was shown in May and June 1998 when, according to a *Vancouver Sun* article based on insider trading reports, Vice-President Mossadiq Umedaly cashed in many of the chips that he had accumulated since 1990. First he exercised options he had acquired under the company stock option plan. He bought stock at the much lower prices of earlier years, spending $ 2.2 million to do so. Then he sold most of his stock, grossing $21.1 million, and within the same time period announced his resignation from Ballard.[*]

The share price promptly plunged, and eyebrows were raised in Vancouver when the pattern of Umedaly's purchases and sales was revealed. The *Sun* reporter, David Baines, pointed out that "in previous disclosure documents, Ballard had advised that the company was 'dependent' on certain key staff members, and the loss of one or more of them 'could adversely affect Ballard.'"[63] Unloading so much of his stock and then resigning may not have made Umedaly very popular with other Ballard shareholders. But the Toronto Stock Exchange 300 Index also dipped quite sharply during the same period, so it was not only Ballard shares that took a temporary dive. And Umedaly probably was *forced* to sell at least some of his shares in order to acquire the several million in pre-tax dollars needed to pay for the options. Company rules were such that he had to exercise the options within thirty days of leaving Ballard or else lose them.[+]

Umedaly declined to be interviewed about his sudden departure. A company press release said, "As Ballard is making the transition to a manufacturing company and management roles evolve, he has chosen this time to resign." Umedaly said in the release that "the time is right for me to spend time with my family and consider other opportunities.... Building companies and creating value is, and will continue to be, a key part of my life." *The Economist* speculated that

---

[*] For comparison, *Maclean's* magazine reported that prior to the surge in Ballard's stock price in the first half of 1998, Firoz Rasul's 208,476 shares (before the three for one split) were worth more than $22 million. (At the share price prevailing in late Spring, 1999, these shares would be worth over $33 million.) Erik Heinrich, "A $600-million boost," *Maclean's* (Dec.29, 1997/Jan.5, 1998): 90.

[+] Umedaly was also paid just over $1 million under a "termination agreement" that provides for hefty compensation to any executive officer who leaves his employment with Ballard "as a consequence of action taken by the corporation that adversely affects his duties or compensation level after a change of control." The change of control was the buy-in by Daimler-Benz and Ford. *Notice of Annual Meeting and Management Proxy Circular 1999*, April 5, 1999, p. 17.

"The chief task ... is to turn Ballard from a research laboratory into a mass-production company.... Umedaly ... left ... because there was no role for him in the new structure.... The firm appointed a new chief operating officer, Layle Smith, who is a seasoned troubleshooter from Dow Chemical."[64]

As Ballard's share price climbed, Toronto's Bay Street saw it as an example of almost pure speculation, since it was difficult to put a realistic value on Ballard shares according to normal investment criteria. *The Globe and Mail* commented: "Since the company does not foresee profit until 2000 or later, analysts concede Ballard stock is tough to evaluate. In fact, it's more akin to a biotechnology stock with a potential pot at the end of the rainbow." As the Toronto daily noted, "Ballard stock has been fuelled by kudos from analysts. But they caution investors that this developmental-stage company has risks, including competitors who are working on similar technology."

Not all analysts were deterred by the threat of competition, though. Jason Zandberg of Pacific International Securities Inc. in Vancouver said he had confidence in Ballard because it had prestigious Daimler-Benz as a joint-venture partner and also because of the potential of the company's products. There was risk, he admitted, especially from Toyota, which was also developing a fuel cell car, but he thought Ballard had the edge. "Toyota has said it wants to bring theirs to market in ten years but Ballard and Daimler have said they will do it in eight years," said Zandberg. "They already have a two-year lead."[65]

Daimler wasted no time in throwing down the gauntlet and challenging the rival companies. Foremost among them was Toyota, which had recently unveiled a hybrid prototype vehicle with a combined battery and fuel cell drive system. "The starting pistol in the race to produce the first fuel cell vehicle" has been fired, said Juergen Hubbert, head of Daimler's passenger car division. "Whoever is first over the finishing line in this race—that is, whoever manages to produce a marketable vehicle—will be able to determine the rules of the game. We have set ourselves the task of occupying and retaining the leading position in fuel cell development. Our strategic aim is called 'first to market.'"[66]

Firoz Rasul, too, is a firm believer in the importance of being first to market. "If you get to market first," he says, "you get to set the rules by which the game will be played. And people who follow will have to play by those rules." There are "the regulations, the safety standards, the codes, the interfaces, the control systems. All these things. We get to set the rules. And that's what we're going to do."

As promised, a few months after the Daimler buy-in the German company unveiled its prototype NECAR III at an auto trade show in Frankfurt. Doing away with the bulky rooftop hydrogen tanks of the earlier NECARS (and the Ballard buses), it runs on liquid methanol that is converted to hydrogen by a device known as a reformer that is on board the vehicle. Its power comes from two compact twenty-five kilowatt Ballard fuel cell stacks, each consisting of 150 cells. These are shaped to lie flat and fit under the seats of the tiny but spiffy-looking three-and-one-half metre (twelve foot) long A-class sedan. With about sixty horsepower, the NECAR III has a range of about 400 kilometers (250 miles) on a full tank of around thirty-eight litres of methanol (eleven gallons), which is comparable to that of conventional vehicles.

Daimler saw the move to methanol as the key to commercial acceptance. "Dispensing with the hydrogen tanks not only reduces vehicle weight," the company said, "but it also greatly improves the everyday practicality of the new vehicle: the corner gas station can handle methanol, which doesn't require special safety measures, nearly as easily as gasoline or diesel."

Methanol *does* require an on-board reformer or fuel processing plant, though. Operating at around 280°C, the reformer vaporizes methanol and water to yield hydrogen, carbon dioxide, and carbon monoxide. Then the carbon monoxide is converted by catalytic oxidation to carbon dioxide, while the hydrogen is injected into the fuel cell. For the NECAR III the reformer had been reduced in size to "only" 47 centimetres (18 inches) in height, but Daimler admitted this still took up too much space at the rear of the tiny car, space that should be available for luggage. "Engineers at Daimler-Benz plan to drastically reduce the size of the components," a company brochure promised, "within the next few years."

Daimler was also proud of the NECAR III's fast response time. "Press the accelerator," a company handout gushed, "and an astonishing ninety per cent of the system's power is available in just two seconds. In terms of drive dynamics, this puts fuel cell vehicles using methanol on a par with conventional gasoline- or diesel-powered automobiles." With NECAR III on the road, Daimler announced that it was aiming decisively at the California market, with its requirement for zero-emission cars beginning in 2003.

Geoffrey Ballard is thrilled that Daimler is aiming from the start at the compact car, which, because of the size constraints, he calls the toughest automobile to do. "I don't want the fuel cell only in luxury automobiles. I want it out on the streets of America. I want it mass-produced for $18,000." Looking ahead, he hopes to get a little fuel cell car of his own, and as soon as possible, so he can drive it around and show it proudly to everyone he knows. "I told Firoz, 'When they bring out the first ones, put in an order for ten of the first fifty they produce. Mike Brown will take one. You'll take one. And I'll take one.'" He sits back and smiles at the prospect.

The Daimler buy-in was a giant step forward for Ballard. But 1997, Ballard Power's year of miracles, was not yet over. In December, after months of discreet negotiations, Ballard announced a second mega-deal—this one worth a total of $600 million—with the Ford Motor Company. Ford acquired a fifteen per cent stake in Ballard (thereby reducing Daimler-Benz's share to twenty per cent). The US company also committed itself to a three-way alliance to build fuel cell engines and produce electric drive trains for fuel cell powered vehicles. In this partnership, Ballard's role, as before, is to develop and manufacture the fuel cell stacks. DBB Fuel Cell Engines, still Daimler-dominated and based in Germany, will integrate the stacks with the fuel systems and other peripheral equipment. And a new Ford-dominated company, Ecostar (with minority ownership for Daimler and Ballard) will supply complete electric power trains, including electric motors and their electronic control systems.

The partnerships with Daimler and Ford put transportation firmly front and centre in Ballard's overall corporate strategy. But the company made strides in developing fuel cells for stationary power as well, and in gaining strategic partners interested in that side of the business. Under the partnership with Dow Chemical, Ballard had focused on developing a 250-kilowatt power generator to run on natural gas. After the Dow partnership ended, Ballard went looking for a new ally to help it fund and develop stationary plants. In 1996 it came to an agreement with GPU International, a subsidiary of New Jersey-based GPU, Inc. a company that provides power to thirteen million people in twelve countries.

Together they formed a new company, Ballard Generation Systems Inc. (BGS). BGS has its own separate facilities in Burnaby, BC, and a $94 million, three-year program to commercialize the 250-kilowatt power units. Under the agreement GPU invested $31.2 million (Cdn.) ($23.25 US) over two years in return for a minority (19.3 per cent) interest in BGS. As part of the development program, GPUI installed and tested two of the prototype stationary power generators.

Another financial boost to Ballard's stationary power program came in November 1996 when Prime Minister Jean Chrétien and federal Industry Minister John Manley attended the formal opening of Ballard Power's new corporate headquarters. They came bearing gifts in the form of a $30 million contribution to the BGS program, repayable on relatively easy terms out of future royalties on sales of the power units. The capacity and features of these units make them particularly suited for supplying power to customers using sensitive electronic equipment, where the fluctuations and occasional outages of the normal power grid are unacceptable. In addition, they are useful as back-up power for hospitals and for supplying power to remote villages and military installations that are far from centralized power grids.

In 1998 two more companies formed alliances with BGS. GEC Alsthom of France closed a $110 million deal under which it invested $56.5 million in BGS for a 21.4 per cent interest, part in cash and part in manufacturing technology and expertise. In addition, BGS and GEC Alsthom agreed to invest $54 million to form a European joint venture company called Alsthom BGS for the sale, distribution, and subsequent manufacture of fuel cell power plants in Europe. GEC Alsthom holds a fifty-one per cent interest and Ballard forty-nine per cent.

Around the same time, BGS signed a memorandum of understanding with a third stationary power strategic partner, the Japanese EBARA Corporation. This creates a joint venture company with exclusive rights to manufacture and sell power plants in the Japanese market. Under the $44 million deal, EBARA invested $21.5 million in cash for a 5.2 per cent interest in BGS and two units for field testing in Japan. In addition, BGS and EBARA jointly invested $22.9 million to form a new company in Japan to sell, distribute, and eventually manufacture PEM power plants.

Although not likely to become as big a market for Ballard as automobiles, the stationary PEM fuel cell is off to a good start, and one that can only enhance the clean, positive public image of fuel cells in general. Within months of first agreement, GEC Alsthom had its first order to purchase a unit, and in a location that was bound to grab attention. Berlin's municipal power company, Bewag, announced a $7.16 million (Cdn.) project to use a natural gas powered Ballard unit in an "environmentally friendly power and heat installation" (with surplus heat also being captured) in the Berlin district of Treptow. According to the daily *Berliner Morgenpost*, this is the first such fuel cell project of its kind in Europe. First test results for everyday utility are expected by the end of 1999. Bewag director Klaus Bechtold called it "a new form of energy supply."[67] Compared to existing systems it will have higher efficiency, will be largely free of emissions, and will be much quieter. In late 1998 GEC Alsthom announced plans to build Europe's first fuel cell technology plant in Dresden, Germany.

Besides transportation and stationary power, Ballard has developed marine fuel cells, which is fitting, since its very first unit went into a mini-submarine. In the mid-1990s it looked as though fuel cells for submarines could become a major part of Ballard's business. The company built a forty-kilowatt demonstration unit for the Canadian defence department, to run on methanol, and had a $9.3 million contract to develop hydrogen fuelled power plants for a German company, Howaldtswerke-Deutsche Werft AG in Kiel. But neither effort led to follow-up contracts. Marine power is somewhat on the back burner for now, although in late 1998 Ballard became part of a US Navy demonstration program that could lead to very large (2.5 megawatt) fuel cell power systems for ships.

In the late 1990s, Ballard also began to revisit the idea of building small, portable fuel cells for emergency power and other specialized applications. These would range up to one kilowatt in size. If this emerges as a significant area of business, it would bring the company full circle, back to the small units that had interest for the Canadian Department of National Defence. Geoffrey Ballard and his partners made the choice to aim fuel cell development away from small niche markets. But there is no reason why people should not have clean, reliable power for wheelchairs, electronic devices, or even for home back-up power when the normal electricity grid fails them. And so, before most of us actually own and drive a fuel cell car, there could well be a much smaller fuel cell in our lives.

—

The Intel
of the AUTO Industry

With Ford joining Daimler and Ballard, the race for the first commercial fuel cell car was really heating up. Soon another giant weighed in. In early 1998 General Motors, the world's largest automobile company, unveiled a hybrid fuel cell and battery engine (but not a prototype car) and announced that it, too, was in the running and would have its own fuel cell vehicle by 2004. GM would not cite figures, but claimed that it had a fuel cell program "at least as big" as its R & D program for hybrid and battery-powered cars. "We are totally serious," said Byron McCormick, GM's executive director for alternative propulsion systems. "The fuel cell is so compelling because of its enhanced efficiency and low pollution that we just have to go after this aggressively," McCormick said.[68] This was the same Byron McCormick who was head of the fuel cell program at Los Alamos National Laboratory when Ballard's David Watkins showed off the startling fourfold power increase in 1986.

A few months later, though, McCormick put a slightly different spin on GM's entry into the fuel cell auto market, and one that showed how unlikely it was that GM would have fuel cell cars on the road as early as the Daimler-Ballard ones. In an interview with the *Hydrogen & Fuel Cell Letter* he said that the year 2004 was the target for a "production-ready vehicle." This meant that "we will have the design done and the validation done, and have the business and market targeted. It is not a commitment to put it in the showroom on that date." There were many other "issues" that had to be sorted out first. "We have high confidence," he explained, "that you can build a reasonably well-performing fuel cell vehicle. The power densities are about where they need to be, the fuel processor is looking good, and we are moving forward." However, McCormick went on, "now we've got to get to the issues of matching all those things ... that customers have come to expect from the internal combustion engine: start-up issues, weather conditions, we have to worry about the availability of fuel that is out there, the quality of that fuel."[69]

Clearly GM was not going to forge ahead and put a fuel cell car into the showrooms regardless of whether the preconditions for success were right. (After all, its sporty electric car, the EV-1, had been pushed that way and turned out to be a terrible flop—with only a few hundred leased out in the first two years, 1996 and 1997.) McCormick wanted to be sure that any GM fuel cell car would have a "good market launch," that GM had "a product that the customer would be excited about." In short, they "want to be ready; we plan to be ready," but there are outstanding market and infrastructure issues and "all of that stuff has to equate."[70]

Nor did McCormick confirm that GM had attained the same level of power density in its fuel cells that Ballard had. He would not give exact numbers but said only that GM was in the same "ballpark" that Ballard had reached a couple of years earlier, namely around one kilowatt per litre. He added, though, "I want to be a little careful with that one because ... when you get into that ballpark ... the issue really becomes designing the system—cost effectiveness and everything. I think that even Ballard recently said we're not going to drive so much for power density, we're going to worry about cost. So I want to be very careful. I don't want to get into a power density race."[71]

With GM committed, all the Big Three US auto makers had their hats in the fuel cell ring. Ford was now part of the Ballard-Daimler alliance, but even earlier it had entered a program (funded in part by the Canadian government) to develop a fuel cell prototype car using Ballard fuel cells. Not to be left out was Chrysler. In 1998 Daimler and Chrysler merged, adding Chrysler's financial and market muscle to the Daimler-Ford-Ballard alliance. But as with Ford, even before this happened, Chrysler had been involved with Ballard and the US-based Arthur D. Little company in a fuel cell project under the aegis of the US government's Program for a New Generation of Vehicles. Chrysler's chosen niche was to develop a fuel cell system that can run on hydrogen derived not from methanol but from gasoline. The perceived advantage over methanol was that the infrastructure for gasoline already existed. Ballard's contribution to this project was to supply a thirty-kilowatt PEM cell stack.

But in January 1999 the Chrysler side of DaimlerChrysler largely gave up on gasoline in favour of methanol because of the difficulty of producing an efficient and compact gasoline reformer to turn the liquid fuel into useable hydrogen. "The technical challenges to turn gasoline into electricity have not been solved," said Chrysler Senior Vice-President Bernard Robertson. "We knew we were taking the most difficult path when we chose to pursue gasoline reformation.... Through that process, we're more certain that methanol will be the best fuel to power fuel cells when they are introduced into the market place around 2004.... We're not completely abandoning the research to reform gasoline into hydrogen, but it will take a back seat."[72]

With the Big Three firmly in the fuel cell race, people concerned about the environment were understandably gratified. That same month the *New York Times* published an editorial reviewing the history of the US auto industry and saying essentially that it was about time it finally got on side: "To anyone who has followed the big environmental struggles of the past quarter-century, Detroit's change of tune fit neatly into a familiar historical pattern." The *Times* argued that, "there has always been a big gap between industrial leaders who say they cannot do something and their engineers, who usually figure out a way to do it." The paper cited catalytic converters and much cleaner fuels, both of which were achieved without hurting auto industry profits. Then the editorial dealt with the issue of motivation. "As the record suggests, American industry is not known for spontaneous acts of environmental virtue. But it will respond to timely regulation and commercial realities. One such reality is that Japan is moving quickly to develop low-emission cars. The Japanese caught Detroit flat-footed with their small cars during the oil-price shock in the 1970s, and Detroit clearly does not wish to be left behind again."[73]

By the late 1990s, nearly every major auto company in the world had committed itself to a fuel cell program of one kind or another. A few were working on their own; others were basing their programs on buying the basic fuel cell stacks from Ballard or other manufacturers, and designing and building the rest of the power systems themselves. This would represent a major change in an industry in which each company has traditionally built its own engines. It could also give Ballard a future position in the automobile fuel cell business comparable to Intel in computers. As Japan's *Nikkei Business Magazine* commented: "If an industry-setting standard is reached in what is the core component of an automobile, the engine, then even a newcomer from outside the industry such as Ballard may be able to be the price leader. Such a company could enjoy the same position as Intel, which has a virtual monopoly in the central processing unit (CPU) of personal computers, and would be able to dominate the automobile manufacturers."[74]

But much will depend on just how far ahead Ballard is in the fuel cell race and how commanding its lead is. Given corporate secrecy, it is no small challenge to evaluate the companies and get a clear picture of how the competition stacks up. Every party involved has its own agendas and interests in either hyping their programs or keeping their cards close to their chests. Fortunately, there is one credible independent source of information, and it shows that the Ballard/Daimler alliance has a pretty solid lead in fuel cell engines.

In 1997 the California Air Resources Board (CARB, a state-wide agency, not to be confused with the regional South Coast Air Quality Management District) established a fuel cell technical advisory panel. The idea was to give the board "an independent assessment regarding the potential of fuel cell technology to become a viable option for zero or near-zero emission vehicles within the next five to ten years." The CARB Panel, consisting of prominent scientists headed by electrochemist Fritz Kalhammer of the Electric Power Research Institute of Palo Alto, collected information and travelled around the world to interview key management and engineering people. Although their main focus was the automobile and fuel cell makers, they also visited companies like Johnson Matthey and Dupont that only make certain components of the fuel cell package.

Not every company was equally open with the CARB panel. Some refused to let them see their fuel cell facilities at all. However, when they visited Ballard Power, they were particularly impressed by its willingness to show them around its facilities, explain in some detail what it was doing, and reveal its future plans. They felt they gained a pretty clear picture of the relative positions of the main companies, and they released their report in the summer of 1998.

One notable finding was that PEM was the only type of fuel cell suitable for automobiles. As for the phosphoric acid fuel cell, which had been backed by the US government until only a few years earlier, the panel concluded that it "has only modest power density, a deficit that translates into relatively large volume and weight as well as higher cost." In addition, phosphoric acid systems "cannot generate power at ambient temperature but must be preheated.... Meeting the automotive requirement for rapid start-up would, therefore, be very difficult."[75] They ruled out the alkaline cells used on the space shuttle, because although they have good power, even traces of carbon dioxide in the fuel "poisons" the catalyst, making only extremely pure hydrogen viable as a fuel. "In automotive applications," they said, "it will be impractical to remove carbon dioxide completely from the processed fuel, eliminating the alkaline fuel cell from consideration."[76]

Another important finding was that the development of a compact, affordable PEM stack was not the only severe hurdle facing major players in the quest to market a fuel cell car. Equally difficult was to develop the fuel processors, auxiliary equipment for pressurizing and humidifying the fuel cell gases, and the required sensors and controls. All these then have to be "integrated mechanically, thermally, chemically, and electrically into compact, fully functional, and potentially low cost fuel cell power plants." For Ballard Power, this is where the alliance with Daimler and Ford should really pay off. As the report noted, "Achieving this integration while preserving the potential of fuel cells for high efficiency and near-zero emissions is the ultimate challenge in the development of fuel cell electric engines for automobiles."[77]

Among the fourteen major companies in the world that were developing complete PEM fuel cells (and not merely certain components) the Ballard-Daimler alliance was clearly far ahead. In fact, the report's key findings section opens with a photo showing graphically the remarkable improvement in Ballard's power density. A 1991 stack capable of five kilowatts of peak power was shown next to a 1997 stack that can deliver fifty-four kilowatts from a slightly smaller volume, a boost of well over ten times the power in only six years. Only Ballard and Daimler had reached the stage where they were actively working on the techniques of stack manufacturing. Only they had a firm schedule to go into actual stack production, with a pilot production line planned to be up and running by 2002 and full production by 2004. "In order to meet this schedule," the report added, "the stack technology will have to be largely 'frozen' by the end of 1998."[78]

The report called Ballard the recognized "world leader in automotive PEM fuel cell technology," noting the overall size of its effort, with more than 200 people working on the automotive side of the fuel cell business. It also zeroed in on Ballard's great experience in stack fabrication ("more than 500 developmental stacks delivered to a wide variety of customers") and added that the joint ventures with Daimler and Ford, "provide Ballard with the resources and capabilities to pursue extensive programs of technology improvement and cost reduction." In parallel with its partners, Ballard would be able to "carry out engineering design and manufacturing development of cell and stack components, stack fabrication, and integration of stacks with fuel processors and other balance of power plant equipment."[79] In other words, Ballard, backed by Daimler and Ford, clearly had what was required to keep to its prescribed schedule and achieve commercialization circa 2004.

On the cost side, "all parts of Ballard's cell and stack technology are being designed for high-volume, low-cost manufacturability," the report noted. "Important unit operations such as catalyst screen printing, [membrane electrode assembly] bonding and sealing have been validated on the small-scale pilot level." With Daimler's help, "manufacturing processes are being standardized, documented, and computerized, and engineers at the Ballard plant site work closely with manufacturing groups at [Daimler-Benz] to convert these techniques into manufacturing methods." Once "mature production" at high rates is attained, "stack production cost is projected to decline to \$20-35" (US) per kilowatt,[80] which translates to between \$2,250 and \$3,750 for the seventy-five kilowatt stack that is slated to go into the first Daimler production cars. In short, Ballard and Daimler are on track to mass produce a competitive fuel cell engine.

As for the competition, only two other companies, General Motors and Toyota, had developed "full size" PEM stacks, that is stacks of twenty-five kilowatts or larger. All the rest of the contending firms had only mastered single-cell technology and combined these into "short" stacks of lower total power. (The challenge here is that heat and water management problems escalate as fuel cells are added together to form "full size" stacks of 150 to 200 cells.)

General Motors has generally been reluctant to show the cards in its fuel cell hand to journalists. GM was no different with the CARB panel. Its announced plans seemed to indicate a market launch of 2004, but "the current and planned commitments of GM to fuel cell electric engine and vehicle development were not revealed to the panel." GM told them that, "several hundred million dollars will be required over the relatively near term to establish a technology leadership position," and "GM intends to be among the leaders. The corporation appears fully committed to the development and commercialization of fuel cell electric vehicles 'if it can be done.'"[81]

General Motors, the report noted, had carried forward its fuel cell program "independently and with little publicity." It had designed, but apparently not yet built, a fifty-kilowatt stack. If the power performance of its single cells, as revealed to the panel, are anything to go by, though, it is behind Ballard by a factor of two or three. Probably because of this, GM has "left open the options whether and which PEM fuel cell components and subsystems will be manufactured by GM, or indeed whether GM will ultimately elect to purchase rather than manufacture stacks."[82]

The other significant competitor is Toyota, which, like GM, has experience designing and building electric vehicles. But Toyota's main fuel cell focus so far is on a hybrid vehicle that pairs up a smallish (twenty-five kilowatt) fuel cell stack with a modern nickel-metal hydride battery that is also capable of putting out twenty-five kilowatts. A mock-up of the system was displayed in 1997 at the Frankfurt International Automobile Exhibition. "According to Toyota," the CARB panel said, "a functionally integrated but still experimental vehicle is now being operated to demonstrate technical feasibility and to serve as a test bed for improving engine and vehicle operating characteristics. Toyota's plans are to follow this with a 'feasibility prototype' soon after the year 2000 and, assuming sufficient progress, with a production prototype."[83]

The Toyota fuel cell team was reluctant to give a timetable for these milestones. The report added diplomatically: "The Panel was unable to obtain estimates of the resources committed to Toyota's fuel cell and [fuel cell electric vehicle] development program and was not given the opportunity to see *any* of the facilities dedicated to the program" [author's italics]. "The best indication that these resources and facilities are likely to be extensive comes from staff comments to the Panel that 'Toyota wants to be first with fuel cell-powered electric cars' and from a recent statement by Toyota's President Hiroshi Okuda that, notwithstanding Daimler Benz' stated intent to put fuel cell vehicles into the market by 2004/5, 'our engineers have a strong feeling that we will be first to market.'"[84]

But according to data from Toyota in the CARB report, its fuel cell stacks are much bulkier relative to their power output than the Ballard ones, with a power density only about one-seventh the Ballard figure. How Toyota expects to be first to market, even with a hybrid fuel cell car, is therefore a mystery. In fact, Geoffrey Ballard is scathing in his dismissal of Toyota's prospects. "They're so far behind," he says, "it's embarrassing—to Toyota." At a Tokyo auto show that Ballard attended, Toyota displayed a dismantled fuel cell that he thought bore a remarkable similarity to the Ballard one.

The CARB report's summary chart and time line, allowing for some overlap and margin of error, shows Ballard-Daimler a year or two ahead of Toyota, which in turn is a year or so ahead of GM. Ford and Chrysler, using Ballard technology, are expected to have cars on the road around the same time as GM, or very slightly later. By late 1998, though, a German spokesman for GM's Opel subsidiary was sounding upbeat about the GM effort: "Technologically, we are already on the heels of the leaders Daimler and Toyota and will catch up in the near future."[85]

It was the Ballard fuel cell, however, that kept making headlines. In early 1999, DaimlerChrysler unveiled its latest Ballard-powered prototype, the liquid hydrogen-fuelled subcompact NECAR IV, at a ceremony in Washington, DC. According to the company, NECAR IV generates forty per cent more power from its fuel cell system than NECAR III, and it has a range of 450 kilometres (280 miles). "This is a real step forward," enthused Carol Browner, head of the US Environmental Protection Agency. "This car leaves a trail of water vapour, not clouds of carbon dioxide, nitrous oxide, and other pollutants."[86] The same week, Ferdinand Panik, head of the DaimlerChrysler fuel cell program, claimed his team was in the lead. "We're feeling we are out in front right now," he told *The Wall Street Journal*. "But it's a race."[87] His boss, DaimlerChrysler Chairman Juergen Schrempp, was less reluctant to tout his company's achievements. "Since 1994, DaimlerChrysler has presented five different non-hybrid driveable fuel cell vehicles [including a Daimler-Benz bus called NEBUS]. We have solved the most challenging technical problems. So let me say: Today we declare the race to demonstrate the technical viability of fuel cell vehicles over. Now, we begin the race to make them affordable."[88]

Then in April 1999 California Governor Gray Davis announced the California Fuel Cell Partnership in front of the state capitol in Sacramento. "Our long-term goal is very simple," he said. "Zero emissions in the air. Zero. Nada. Nothing. Zip."[89] The partnership involves cooperation between the DaimlerChrysler-Ford-Ballard alliance, three major oil companies, Atlantic Richfield (ARCO), Shell and Texaco, and the State of California. It will put a test fleet of about fifty vehicles powered by Ballard fuel cells (half cars and half buses) on the road between 2000 and 2003. The day of the announcement, Ford paraded its middle-size hydrogen-fuelled P2000 prototype sedan for the media. No price tag was put on the California program, but Firoz Rasul thought it would probably exceed $50 million.

The participation of the oil companies represented a dramatic new departure. "[They] will provide liquid hydrogen to fuel the demonstration fleet," wrote the *Vancouver Sun*. "'Following that they will be adding other fuels, methanol or petroleum-based products or others,' [said a Ballard spokesperson]. The oil companies are also expected to commit research money for the development of fuel infrastructure, one of the missing links in fuel-cell technology."[90] "We're going to be learning about how people will feel comfortable about fuelling these vehicles, how the mechanics feel about maintaining them, what sort of fuel infrastructure is needed," said Firoz Rasul. "It's a major step forward, getting the oil companies involved, prepared to work with us, prepared to provide their expertise, and also to provide financial support."[91]

Almost the same day, GM and Toyota announced a five-year program to team up on developing electric and fuel cell cars. "GM, the world's largest vehicle maker and Toyota … the world's third largest … have identified more than a dozen advanced vehicle and system projects for possible development," Reuters news agency commented. "GM and Toyota are on similar paths in many areas of research, so combining efforts makes sense."[92] This move did not seem to faze

Ballard Power executives. "It is a general recognition that fuel cells are ... something that the auto industry has to look at," said Vice-President for Corporate Development Paul Lancaster. "I think this GM-Toyota plan is a good thing for us. Having a broader number of companies involved ... can lead to better acceptance by the consuming public that fuel cells are a product they should consider."[93] Firoz Rasul also welcomed the competition from GM and Toyota. Together with Ford and DaimlerChrysler, he said in Sacramento, "you now have the four largest [car] companies in the world with probably more than 70 per cent of the world market between them making [a commitment to fuel cells]. That is a serious commitment and we're pleased to see it."[94] A month earlier, Rasul had pointed with satisfaction to the stepped-up pace of recent developments. "Auto companies who used to talk about 2025, then 2020, then 2015, are now talking about 2004. This is in the space of five years."[95]

With the first Daimler production cars expected to hit the roads in 2004, it is tempting to conclude that *this is it*, that the fuel cell is well and truly launched as the clean automotive technology of the near future. The Ballard Power team has accomplished a task of historic significance. Certainly that is Geoffrey Ballard's view. "Even if Ballard the company," is not successful in the long run, he told a California audience, "Ballard has changed the way the world thinks about power, and the world will not go back to where it was."[96]

But this is not the way Firoz Rasul looks at things, and the difference underscores the contrast between the goals and world-views of Rasul and Ballard. When asked whether, after taking a ride on the bus or in the Daimler car he gets the feeling that "this is finally 'it,'" Rasul is surprisingly reluctant to agree. "When we see the first car rolling off the production line. That for me will be 'it.' So far, it's been a journey. And each milestone is an important one to celebrate. But it's still a journey that we're moving on. And I don't want to belittle anything about the company. It's a great accomplishment. But I don't ever want to delude myself that we've arrived, because we haven't, until we make money and we can make products at a price that is competitive with the internal combustion engine car."

Not that Rasul lacks pride in his own achievements. When asked whether his three teenage daughters are proud of what he and his company has done, he beams. "Not to their dad's face," he laughs, but behind his back he knows that they have told their friends about their father's notoriety. "My daughter—the one in grade ten—told me a story the other day," he begins. "They had one of these classes in career planning and life skills. The teacher had brought in someone to explain budgeting and financing—how to take care of their money." The question arose, what should they do with their money once they started earning it? Where should they save and invest it. And this outside adviser told them, "You should put some in the bank, but you should also go out and buy some stock." At that point, one of the children in the class asked, "Well, which one would you recommend?" And the speaker mentioned that, along with several other stocks, "I would certainly recommend Ballard Power." At this point, nearly the entire class turned around to look at Rasul's daughter. "Everyone knew," that she was the daughter of the company president, Rasul chuckles. "But," she told him later at home, "I didn't have the heart to put up my hand and say, 'That's my dad's company.'"

But Ballard was also becoming a very different company. By the late 1990s, it was in the process of drastic growth and change. It was evolving from being a small regional company concerned mainly with research, development, and marketing, to being part of a huge partnership—in fact, several partnerships. Its focus was shifting towards manufacturing and production. In fact, it is hoping to become the central player—the Intel of fuel cell stacks—in what promises to be a very large new industry. Yet, however large it becomes, Ballard is now a corporation with so much of its equity in the hands of much larger partners that many key decisions are bound to be made elsewhere. Gone are the days when a few people like Ballard, Prater, and Howard decide things largely on the basis of what they think is right.

At the personnel level, too, the change has been dramatic. The main technical people from the early years—Watkins, Epp, Dircks, and Steck—are all still with the company. But between 1996 and 1998 nearly all the key people on the entrepreneurial side bowed out, either willingly or otherwise. The founders—Ballard, Prater, and Howard—are all gone now, with Geoffrey Ballard formally resigning his position as board chairman at the end of 1997 due to poor health. (All three of them have remained active, though, in hydrogen industry groups.) David McLeod is gone from the marketing side. (Of course, government funding, his speciality, plays a much smaller role now.) Mike Brown is also gone from the board of directors. (The share holdings of the Ventures West-led consortium are now dwarfed by those of other financial players.) Even Firoz Rasul's close associate Mossadiq Umedaly is gone as chief financial officer.

For just about all of them, the job is done. They took the PEM fuel cell to a new level of technical capability, marketed it and passed it on to the industrial giants of the world. So it was time to move on to other things in life. As Paul Howard described his own position, there was little reason to hang around. "With Daimler-Benz coming in, the company is now in an entirely new stage of its evolution. It was a convenient time for me to either leave or else jump in with both feet and put in more time, more hours, more travel. I don't need it, and it's not what I am good at. Ballard is becoming more a manufacturing and production company. But my interest is in prototypes, entrepreneurial start-ups, that kind of thing. And I'm fortunate that I don't need to work, from a financial point of view. I've done well."

Physically, the changes at Ballard are reflected in the size of the expanding facilities, their separation from each other, and the overall growth in the number of employees. By mid-1999 there were around 450. Besides the large corporate headquarters, there is now a separate facility for stationary power generation, and a new pilot manufacturing centre for stationary power plants is under construction. There is a facility in southern California devoted to bus engines that operate on methanol, and another small new one in Germany to handle Ballard's side of the Daimler alliance.

The separation of various Ballard projects from each other is apparent even when a visitor is taken through the main installation. On the ground floor hundreds of automated test stations tick away patiently, each with its own printer or computer monitor showing the results. But curtain walls isolate some sections of the floor from others. At one time the company was like a university. Everything was open, and everyone had access to all information. Not any more. Badges and a security system ensure that people working on one project do not necessarily get to see what is being done on others. "With so much top-secret information about future products flowing through Ballard's labs," *The Wall Street Journal* reports, "the company has to take extraordinary measures to ensure that information doesn't leak. Each auto maker's fuel-cell work is overseen by a different Ballard manager; technicians often aren't told what car company's contract they're working on at any given time. 'It's like a black program in the military,' says Alfred E. Steck, Ballard's vice-president for research and development."[97]

The company is also recruiting new people quite differently, especially at the highest levels. In the 1980s and early 1990s, Ballard management heard of likely employment prospects largely by word of mouth through the technological or financial grapevine. Most recruitment was done locally in the Vancouver area. For example, Paul Howard already knew Danny Epp from the submarine project. Ken Dircks was hired locally as well; like Epp, he had attended the BC Institute of Technology. Mike Brown knew Firoz Rasul personally, and Rasul was already based in BC. Rasul, in turn, brought in several other key people from his former company, MDI, and they were already based in BC.

By contrast, in 1998, when Ballard Power decided it needed a chief operating officer, it had a professional headhunting firm search among the heavy hitters of North American industry. They came up with Layle (Kip) Smith, the business vice-president at the specialty chemicals division of the Dow Chemical Company of Midland, Michigan. Smith was a corporate honcho who had responsibility for eighteen different business units with combined sales of more than $1.7 billion (US). (In May 1999, Smith also took on the post of president when Firoz Rasul became chairman of the board as well as CEO, replacing retiring interim chairman Dr. J. Fraser Mustard, who had served since Geoffrey Ballard's retirement at the end of 1997.)

Indeed, the very need for such an operating officer reflects the new reality of an expanded corporation. As president and CEO, Firoz Rasul had to direct most of his efforts outward, towards the market and the public. But there was also a need for someone to focus inwardly and look after the day-to-day business of the company. Rasul tried to do that as well, but he found himself stretched too thin. By the late 1990s the company was simply too big, and it had evolved into a more complex structure with too many divisions, separate teams, and projects for one person to look after. When Rasul was too busy—or when he was away from the office, which was often a good half of the time—Mossadiq Umedaly tried to fill the breach. But a full-time officer was needed.

Rasul says that Kip Smith was chosen as COO more for his experience "operating in competitive global manufacturing" than his background in the chemical industry. Smith's main roles are to look after product development and manufacturing operations. This involves helping Ballard develop a "strategic planning and operational vision," and then identify the capital assets and new people it needs to add to its team. "There are and will be different demands on Ballard during different eras in its corporate evolution," he says. Today, Ballard is becoming a manufacturing company, and Smith calls this a "good fit" for his talents and experience.[98]

Another example of reaching out far for top talent was the recruitment of Michael Graydon as vice-president and chief financial officer to replace Umedaly. Graydon had served as general manager of production control for Toyota Motor Manufacturing Canada. This involved running a plant with over 2,500 employees and a production capacity of 200,000 vehicles a year. Rasul saw Graydon's hiring as another example of strengthening the Ballard team, "as the company evolves from research and development to volume manufacturing."[99]

With rapid growth and the division of the company into more isolated sections and working groups, there are bound to be profound changes in the way things are done. Will the company continue to enjoy the small company personal commitment and ability to change direction quickly that characterized it in the past? The Ballard management is aware of the risk of losing this competitive edge and talks the talk about retaining it. "We are looking to create an industry," says Paul Lancaster, the long-time treasurer who, in late 1998 became vice-president for corporate development, "and we know we have to be fast, nimble, agile, and entrepreneurial to succeed."[100] But is this realistic, especially if, as the new operations officer Kip Smith foresees, Ballard grows to become "a major global manufacturer?" Can the management really stem the hardening of the corporate arteries?

Danny Epp, the technical whiz who did so much of the early cell building with his own hands, doesn't think so. In the late 1990s he had a key role in the marine division. He looks back with nostalgia at the early years and the way he could come up with his own design changes, then go into the machine shop himself and build something very quickly and try it out right away. "You could do that within a day or even within hours. That was our advantage." This held true even as late as the mid-1990s, he says, when, as we have seen, a Ballard engineer was able to blow away the visiting engineers of an American automobile company by conceiving, building, and testing a piece of equipment in a single day. "We were still a relatively small company and had those advantages compared to the biggies." But this has been changing rapidly.

There were "real personal issues" for Epp as the company grew. "I was used to a small company," with a high degree of personal control of purchasing, manufacturing, and development. In the much larger company that Ballard has already become, "control over all those functions now goes to other people and groups of other people." It has been difficult for someone like Epp, "to accept the bureaucracy and the inefficiency that comes with it." But he is resigned to this kind of change. "It's inevitable," he says, "and it's happening to a great extent already."

CHAPTER SIXTEEN

Dare
to be DIFFERENT

Howyer much Ballard Power Systems changes as a company in the coming years, the Ballard fuel cell itself represents a decisive step into a new age of hydrogen-based energy. But it is only the first step, and several other major ones will be required for the fuel cell to deliver the full environmental benefits it promises. So what will this hydrogen age look like in detail? Will it truly be the clean energy utopia that some enthusiasts imagine? And how big a role is Ballard Power likely to play in it?

There seem to be as many opinions on the future of hydrogen as there are people studying and thinking about it. Nature will not necessarily cooperate just because the world hopes for a particular breakthrough. Given this caveat, all forecasts relating to technological advances must be taken with a grain of salt. Most of the unknowns concern the fuel that will be used to power the cars, the energy source or sources used to produce it, the overall environmental impacts of these fuels and energy sources, and the speed with which they come on stream.

As Mike Brown, the venture capitalist, readily concedes, one of the most basic questions has not yet been answered. "What is the fuel that you put in your car going to be? Will it be gasoline, methanol, natural gas, or hydrogen? Whichever it is, we need some revolutions that have not happened yet." All sorts of fuel-related technologies are being developed, he says. "But before the fuel cell becomes ubiquitous—before you can go to Thailand and expect all of Bangkok to be driving fuel cell cars instead of two-cycle scooters—a whole fuel revolution has to take place on a world scale."

The Ballard buses that are currently plying the streets of Vancouver and Chicago run on compressed hydrogen gas. They are refuelled each day at depots that have special equipment for handling gas under high pressure. Compressed hydrogen is quite bulky, requiring a tank some five to ten times the size of the average gasoline or diesel tank for the equivalent range. The Ballard buses, therefore, carry their tanks on the roof. But centralized depots are not a practical way to supply fuel for the millions of personal passenger vehicles on the world's roads. And the bulkiness of compressed hydrogen is a potential handicap for its use in cars.

All of the automobile manufacturers that plan to put fuel cell cars on the market in the first decade of the twenty-first century expect at least the first generation of them to run on liquid fuels that will be converted to a hydrogen-rich gas by an auxiliary on-board device. The most likely fuel, and the one being focused on by the apparent leaders in the race, Daimler-Benz, Ford, Toyota, and General Motors, is methanol, sometimes called wood alcohol. Gasoline, as we have seen, was seriously considered for several years by Chrysler but is now on the back burner.

In principle—leaving aside for the moment where the hydrogen comes from and the environmental impact of producing it—fuel cells that run on pure hydrogen are virtually one hundred per cent environmentally benign. That is, they give off only water vapour and small amounts of heat. Methanol, though, does not bring with it quite the same benefits. On the one hand, if a large percentage of cars in a smog-plagued region like southern California were to run on such fuel cells, the levels of such "traditional" pollutants as carbon monoxide, nitrogen oxides, and airborne particulates would be greatly lowered. On the other hand, sizeable amounts of carbon dioxide would still be emitted. And carbon dioxide is a greenhouse gas that contributes to feared global warming.

So why is methanol the fuel of choice, at least for now? In part it is because so much of the air pollution caused by automobiles is concentrated in regions such as southern California, and methanol-powered cars *will* go a very long way towards reducing it. And in part it is because methanol is a convenient liquid fuel that can be dispensed at gas stations without radical changes in habits or technology. Moreover, using methanol in fuel cell cars will still make a very significant dent in greenhouse gas emissions.

Daimler-Benz has calculated that a methanol fuel cell system is likely to emit around thirty per cent less carbon dioxide than even the cleanest conventional internal combustion engine car.[*] Geoffrey Ballard thinks that with the high efficiency of fuel cells this could turn out to be closer to a fifty percent reduction.

There are other pluses for methanol. A modest methanol production infrastructure already exists, roughly the equivalent of six per cent of total US gasoline consumption. (The Methanex Corporation, which produces forty per cent of the world's methanol, is based in Vancouver and has supported Ballard Power's efforts.) California has thirty-eight gas stations already supplying methanol, and under state regulations, when new gas stations are built, or old ones have their tanks replaced, they are required to provide for methanol. Methanol is currently only slightly more expensive to produce than gasoline, when taxes are overlooked, so it is also a quite affordable fuel.

---

[*] This includes carbon dioxide emitted in the process of making the methanol from natural gas.

Even more significant from the environmental perspective is that methanol can be produced from natural gas, large quantities of which are currently burned off or simply released into the atmosphere at oil production sites. Methanol can also be produced from the biogas generated at landfill sites or from "digesters" using agricultural waste products. Its main disadvantage is that it is more corrosive than gasoline, but environmental engineers do not think this would prevent the establishment of a major distribution system. "Our estimates show that for about a $3 billion investment, methanol pumps could be added to one out of every three corner 'energy' stations in the country," says John Lynn, head of the American Methanol Institute. "This compares quite well with the $13 billion capital costs to produce the reformulated gasoline now sold in one-third of the nation."[101]

Methanol, therefore, is likely to be the first automobile fuel in the fuel cell era. But to believers in the hydrogen future, methanol is only an interim solution. David Scott, formerly chair of Mechanical Engineering at the University of Toronto and now at the University of Victoria, and vice-president (Americas) of the International Association for Hydrogen Energy, has long theorized about the future hydrogen economy. He sees methanol as at best a "bridging technology" for a period of perhaps a few decades. If fuel cells are to become the true magic bullet for a clean and sustainable transportation future, Scott thinks, they must run on hydrogen alone. And the hydrogen must be derived from a source that is sustainable, and produced in a way that does not emit carbon dioxide or otherwise contribute to environmental degradation. Even given an ideal hydrogen source, though, there are problems. *

---

* Some people point to safety problems involved in using hydrogen widely, but boosters of hydrogen think it has gotten a bad rap because of the explosion of the German airship Hindenburg in 1937. The gas is explosive, they point out, but so are the vapours from gasoline and so is propane. On the positive side, hydrogen is so light that it rises and dissipates quickly, unlike propane and gasoline fumes.

Compressed hydrogen is bulky. This may not matter much for the Ballard buses in Vancouver and Chicago. Daimler-Benz, too, has built its own fuel cell bus, which runs on compressed hydrogen. But the situation for cars is different. According to the CARB report, an efficient fuel cell car would require a 200 litre tank (about 75 US gallons) of compressed hydrogen to attain a range of about 560 kilometres (350 miles). The report's authors doubt that such a large rooftop tank would be acceptable for personal automobiles. But this may be overly pessimistic. Discounting the thickness of the tank, this volume of gas could fit into a tank one metre square (about three feet on a side) and only raise the car's height by twenty centimetres (about eight inches). This would increase wind resistance somewhat. But consumers buy increasing numbers of vans, including high-top campers, and many of the popular four by four sport utility vehicles also have relatively high profiles. The high pressure of compressed hydrogen requires very strong tanks, and this would add weight up top. But construction of such tanks from lightweight modern materials, such as spun carbon, could significantly reduce that handicap. Compressed hydrogen should not, therefore, be ruled out. The infrastructure for dispensing compressed hydrogen does not exist, but market entry could begin with fleets of taxis or delivery trucks that are refuelled at central depots like buses.

It certainly would make market entry and consumer acceptance easier, though, if hydrogen could be stored and carried around in a more compact form. The main alternatives to compressed hydrogen are liquefied hydrogen and hydrogen stored in the form of a metal alloy hydride. Both will require technological and cost breakthroughs before they are practical.

Probably a bigger problem than the storage and handling of liquid hydrogen is the cost of its production. Conventional liquefaction is a refrigeration process that consumes energy equal to roughly one-third of the energy content of the hydrogen itself. This reduces the overall energy efficiency of the entire fuel cycle, from production through distribution to consumption. A really plentiful and cheap energy source would mitigate this disadvantage. But there are also novel technologies on the horizon that could, in the future, liquefy hydrogen at much lower energy cost. Metal hydride storage might work, but it is expensive and would add considerable weight to the vehicle.

The ultimate questions to be faced on the road to the ideal hydrogen economy are the source of the hydrogen itself and the energy needed to produce it. "Free" gaseous hydrogen does not exist naturally on Earth, but it can be produced from many sources. About ninety five per cent of the hydrogen used in the US, for example, is produced by the steam reformation of methane or natural gas. Some of the possible "feedstocks" for methane are renewable biomass sources such as agricultural wastes. But the main source, natural gas from wells, is a non-renewable fossil fuel that will run out some day. Moreover, the production of hydrogen from natural gas generates nitrogen oxides as well as carbon dioxide, a greenhouse gas. Thus, while the use of hydrogen in fuel cells may be perfectly clean, the production of it may not be. Gaseous hydrogen, therefore, is not a freebie. It can only be produced either at some environmental cost, or by using energy from another source to split water into hydrogen and oxygen.

The true long-term answer has to take us back to something like David Scott's vision of the late 1970s and early 1980s. It must involve harnessing a clean, sustainable energy source, such as solar, wind, hydroelectric or tidal energy. Other exotic technologies that might serve include tapping geothermal energy (as is done in Iceland) or exploiting thermal gradients in the ocean (as is being tried experimentally in Hawaii). Nuclear energy is the other main contender—either fusion power, if it can be developed, or "conventional" fission, if it can be made safe enough and the problems of nuclear waste disposal can be solved. Today, with the fuel cell approaching commercial use, Geoffrey Ballard thinks that "the ultimate game will use nuclear energy," probably from fusion, to generate electricity.

The next step is to use that sustainable energy to produce gaseous hydrogen from water by electrolysis, which is a well-understood technology that has been around even longer than fuel cells themselves. The hydrogen would then be packaged (compressed or liquefied), distributed (by tanker trucks or pipelines) and used as a fuel in many ways. Among other applications, it could be burned to heat our homes and power jet aircraft. For ground transportation, of course, one of its main uses would be in fuel cells.

The hydrogen age will likely begin, therefore, using methanol and hydrogen derived from fossil fuels. The future challenge, though, is to develop a clean, affordable, renewable energy source, or more likely a combination of sources.

For the immediate future, there is another interesting question: Can a small company like Ballard Power Systems remain a significant player in this huge and rapidly evolving energy game? The short answer is yes—quite likely—but not, of course, alone. If everything goes as people at Ballard hope, it can continue to play a leading role in fuel cell development, but only as part of an alliance system dominated by DaimlerChrysler, Ford, and possibly other companies. And it will do so only by growing into a sizeable manufacturing company in its own right, which is already happening. Given a few breaks, Ballard might then play a role akin to Intel in the microchip industry, supplying a key component to many—perhaps even most—of the larger players who actually manufacture the cars.

Ballard's alliance system gives it the deep pockets needed to bring the fuel cell to the automobile market place. Within its alliance, Ballard's patents protect its position, while its partnership agreements give it the right to sell fuel cells even to companies outside its group. Or as Firoz Rasul said when the big Daimler deal was concluded, Ballard remains "open for business." Ballard's protected technology, combined with its allies' financial resources, appear to give the Ballard-DaimlerChrysler-Ford alliance the inside track. Other big players may well be tempted to buy the fuel cell technology from Ballard rather than to try and reinvent the wheel.

Whoever the ultimate "winner" in the fuel cell race turns out to be, there is no denying the magnitude of Ballard Power's accomplishment, which in the long run will make winners of us all. How and why did this tiny Canadian company succeed in bringing the world what promises to be the next great revolution in energy use? There is no single, simple answer. Instead, a number of favourable factors overlapped and reinforced each other. And the timing, too, happened to be impeccable: the world was crying out for a new energy technology. In short, taking the Ballard fuel cell to where it is today took inspiration, perspiration, and a heavy dose of serendipity.

First there was the character and vision of the company's leading founder, Geoffrey Ballard, who set the stage in the mid-1970s by recognizing the urgent need for a new and better form of portable energy conversion. It was Ballard's character and capability that inspired the key younger men, Keith Prater and Paul Howard, to join him in his venture. The three complemented each other, worked well as a team, and were willing in turn to pass along a fair share of the rewards to their employees. This created an unusually positive and creative company culture—agile, daring, and non-bureaucratic—with intense employee loyalty and commitment to hard work. Thus, by the early 1980s they had established a small but forward-looking high-tech battery and research company. It had superb skills and equipment in the field of electrochemistry, which left them ideally positioned to take the fuel cell project and run with it.

But Ballard Power did not invent the PEM fuel cell, General Electric did. So the second element of serendipity was some solid and well-targetted scientific thinking within the Canadian government. It took people like Chris Gardner and Martin Hammerli to recognize the untapped potential of the PEM cell. They realized that it had never been engineered with a view to lower cost and higher power. They saw that even a very small amount of government seed money could set the ball rolling. Finally, they had access to those funds and went fishing to find a company that could pick up that ball.

The third important element was the talented and dedicated technical team the Ballard founders recruited and encouraged: David Watkins, Danny Epp, and Ken Dircks, along with Fred Steck a bit later on the membrane side. They dove in, spared no effort, and did a magnificent job of hands-on engineering. Although they worked on a minimal budget, they were the first in the world to tackle many of the technical challenges, and they found ways to solve the most basic problems. This gave Ballard a strong patent position and a jump of many years over their nearest competition.

Even that technological edge, though, might have been for naught except for two additional factors. One was that the Ballard founders had the foresight to pump money of their own into the fuel cell project. This not only accelerated its progress, it also allowed them to hang onto shared ownership of the core technology, rather than letting it be taken over entirely by government or foreign industry. The second contributing factor was the hard-driving and flamboyant salesmanship of David McLeod, who believed so strongly in the fuel cell himself that his enthusiasm was contagious. Feeling his way through the corridors of power, McLeod roped in support and kept the needed cash flowing from government and the private sector.

As the money requirements escalated, Mike Brown of Ventures West stepped into a central role. He had the vision to see the nugget of gold in the embryonic fuel cell stack. Only someone with the savvy, credibility, and personal decency of Brown would have been trusted by the three Ballard partners when the time came to move on to the next stage. Brown was able to persuade them to give up their control of the company in the interest of "changing the world," which involved a major company expansion and infusion of capital that in turn required new and more experienced management.

In came Firoz Rasul and his colleague, Mossadiq Umedaly, who together with Brown orchestrated a sophisticated expansion program. Striking a delicate balance between fiscal caution and technological daring, they enlarged the company at a brisk but carefully controlled pace. When the time was right, they took Ballard public. Then they kept the institutional investors on side as they refined the technology, brought down costs, and successfully marketed the fuel cell to the giant corporations that have joined Ballard to take it into commercial production.

Finally, there was Daimler-Benz, the company with a difference. Daimler had a commitment to be the world leader in automobile technology, even if this meant investigating and investing in alternatives that would radically change the industry's status quo. Daimler was willing to take a multimillion dollar risk on the fuel cell at a time when the big North American car companies were dragging their heels and only seemed willing to fund fuel cell R & D when the US government stepped forward to pay the shot. With its prestige and deep pockets, Daimler took the Ballard fuel cell and put it on the road for all the world to see.

It is only fitting that the story of the Ballard fuel cell should end, as it began, with Geoffrey Ballard. Lionized today as a guru of fuel cells and the hydrogen future, he has received a number of honourary doctorates and has addressed many university audiences. He stresses the importance of teamwork in the success of Ballard Power's fuel cells. "These engines," he told students at Brock University in St. Catharines, Ontario, "did not come into being because one person had an idea." They are available, "because dozens of people chose to work together to make an idea come into existence." He went on to say that the Ballard fuel cell benefitted from excellent timing by coming to fruition just as the technological world was being driven by "an awakening environmental consciousness."

Cooperative effort and fortunate timing explain only part of Ballard Power's success, though. There remain the elements of character, vision, and a willingness to take risks. Geoffrey Ballard wrapped them up nicely in his advice to an audience of students who were graduating from the University of Victoria. "Do not be patient," he told them. "All things do not come to those who wait." Instead, his message was exactly the opposite, and it captures the way he has lived his own life. "Be impatient," he said. "Challenge the normal. Question conventional wisdom. Trust yourself and speak out what you believe. If what you believe is different, dare to be different. Dare to be in a hurry to change things for the better."

Endnotes

Preface

1. Tom Koppel, "Inventions With Good Intentions," *Financial Post Money-wise*, (June 1989): 46-47.

2. Tom Koppel, "It's Dr. Ballard's Fuel-Cell Car," *Reader's Digest* [Canada] (May 1998): 83-88.

Chapter 3

3. A.J. Appleby and F.R. Foulkes, *Fuel Cell Handbook* (New York: Van Nostrand Reinhold, 1989), 7.

4. Michael Collins, *Liftoff* (New York: Grove Press, 1988), 75.

5. *Ibid.*

6. *Ibid.*

7. *Ibid.*

8. *The New York Times* (Dec. 25, 1965): 16, col. 1.

Chapter 4

9. Russell McNeil, "Search for the Fuel of the Future: David Scott and the Dream of Hydrogen," *Canadian Geographic* (Dec. 1989/Jan.1990): 114.

10. Everett Banning,"Endless Energy!" *Winnipeg Free Press Magazine* (Sept. 27, 1980): 6-7.

11. *Ibid.*

12. Harland Manchester, "Potent New Power-Maker—The 'Fuel Cell'," *Reader's Digest* 77 (Aug. 1960): 187 [reprinted from *Quest* magazine].

13. C. Luciani, "Military Requirements for Portable Power," in *Proceedings, Third Canadian Fuel Cell Seminar, 13-14 Feb. 1969* (Ottawa: Defence Research Board, 1970), 19.

14. A.S. Gendron and E.E. Criddle, "Fuel Cells, State of the Art and Critical Problems," in *Proceedings, Third Canadian Fuel Cell Seminar, 13-14 Feb. 1969* (Ottawa: Defence Research Board, 1970), 1.

15. *Ibid.*, 4.

16. D.S. Scott, "Hydrogen, A Challenging Opportunity, The Role of Fuel Cells in Ontario's Hydrogen Future," *A Report Prepared for the Ontario Hydrogen Energy Task Force*, Vol. 8 (1981): 20.

Chapter 5

17. Ron Lowman, "Miniature Fuel Cell May Be Power Source for Tomorrow," *The Toronto Star* (Sept. 30, 1986): E4.

18. Tyrus Reiman, "The Twenty-Year Battery," *Canadian Research* 20, no. 5 (May 1987): 25.

Chapter 6

19. Peter Savage, "An Energy Surge from Fuel Cells," *Chemical Week* 140, no. 10 (March 18, 1987): 16.

20. Anne Fletcher, "Portable Energy Market Pursued," *The Vancouver Sun* (Nov. 5, 1986): E1.

Chapter 7

21. John H. Perry, Jr., *Never Say Impossible: The Life and Times of an American Entrepreneur* (Charlottesville, Virginia: Thomasson-Grant, 1996) 22.

22. *Ibid.*, 152.

23. *Ibid.*, 152.

24. *Ibid.*, 153.

25. David Cruise and Alison Griffiths, *Fleecing the Lamb: The Inside Story of the Vancouver Stock Exchange* (Vancouver: Douglas & McIntyre, 1987) viii.

26. William Annett, "The Odds Couple," *BC Business* 16, no. 12 (December 1988): 57.

Chapter 8

27. Jim Lyon, "The Art of the Deal," *PROFIT* 10, no. 1 (Jan./Feb. 1991): 8.

Chapter 9

28. David Leidl, "Powering Up," *BC Business* 19, no. 4 (April 1991): 52.

29. Geoffrey Cowley, "Ozone Breakaway," *Newsweek* (August 29, 1988): 49.

30. Marla Cone, "Firms Offer to Make Electric Cars in '96-'97," *The Los Angeles Times* (November 15, 1995): A3.

31. Marla Cone, "Air Resources Board to Ease State Mandate to Build Electric Cars," *The Los Angeles Times* (November 17, 1995): A3.

32. Marla Cone, "Firms Offer to Make Electric Cars in '96-'97," *The Los Angeles Times* (November 15, 1995): A3.

33. Associated Press (Detroit), "Toyota, GM to Make Fuel-Cell Cars," (April 19, 1999).

34. David Thomas, "New Fuel Cell a Source of Pollution-Free Energy," *The Financial Post* (November 11, 1995): Special Report p. 35.

35. "The Case for Charging Ahead with Electric Vehicles in Southern California," SCAQMD report (1995), from SCAQMD Internet Web site: www.aqmd.gov.monthly/while.html

36. "Importing Clean Air," *The Los Angeles Times* (October 19, 1988): 12.

Chapter 10

37. Alan Bayless, "Powering the Future with Hydrogen," by *Financial Times of Canada* (June 1, 1992) : 8.

38. John H. Perry, Jr., *Never Say Impossible: The Life and Times of an American Entrepreneur* (Charlottesville, Virginia: Thomasson-Grant, 1996) 192.

39. *Ibid.*, 195.

Chapter 11

40. Margot Hornblower, "Geoffrey Ballard: In a Hurry to Prove the 'Piston-heads' Wrong," *Time* [Canadian Edition] (February 1999): 51.

Chapter 13

41. Dennis Simanaitis, "Fuel Cells," *Road & Track* (December 1994): 162.

42. Andrew Fisher, "Milestone on the Road," *Financial Times* (April 15, 1994).

43. Robert Williamson, "High-Tech Fuel Cell Makes Debut in Mercedes," *The Globe and Mail* (April 14, 1994).

44. Roger Highfield, "Rocket Fuel Comes Clean Down to Earth," *The Daily Telegraph* [London] (October 25, 1995).

45. Stuart F. Brown, "The Automakers' Big-Time Bet on Fuel Cells," *Fortune* (March 30, 1998).

46. Steve Thompson, "Proton Power," *Autoweek* (May 27, 1996): www.pathfinder.com/fortune/1998/980330/IMT.HTML

47. Nick Nuttall, "Breathtaking...the Vehicle Powered by Air," *The Times* (May 15, 1996): 5.

48. "Daimler-Benz Drives Out Ballard Cell-Powered Van," *Vancouver Sun* (May 15, 1996): D1.

49. "Daimler-Benz to Unveil World's First Fuel Cell Passenger Car This Month," *Hydrogen & Fuel Cell Letter* XI, no. 5. (May 1996): www.ttcorp.com/nha/thl/may-96a.htm

Chapter 14

50. William Boei, "Mercedes, Ballard Team Up to Push Fuel-Cell Engines," *Vancouver Sun* (April 15, 1997).

51. Brandon Mitchener and Tamsin Carlisle, "Daimler, Ballard Team to Develop Fuel-Cell Engine," *The Wall Street Journal* (April 15, 1997).

52. Ann Gibbon, "Daimler Buys into Ballard," *The Globe and Mail* (April 15, 1997).

53. Mark Wilson, "Daimler Joins Ballard," *Vancouver Province* (April 15, 1997).

54. William Boei, "Mercedes, Ballard Team Up to Push Fuel-Cell Engines," *Vancouver Sun* (April 15, 1997).

55. *Ibid.*

56. David Woodruff and William C. Symonds, "The Hottest Thing in Green Wheels," *Business Week* (April 28, 1997).

57. *Ibid.*

58. Scott Morrison, "Clean-Air Technology, Blue-Sky Profits," *Financial Times* (June 3, 1997).

59. Keith Damsell, "Benz Backs Ballard in Electric Car Deal," *The Financial Post* (April 15, 1997): 2.

60. *Ibid.*

61. *Ibid.*

62. *Ibid.*

63. David Baines, "Shareholders are Jumping Off Ballard Power System's Stock Bandwagon," *Vancouver Sun* (August 28, 1998): F1.

64. "Intel on Wheels," *The Economist* (October 31, 1998).

65. Shirley Won, "Fuel Cell Hopes Power Ballard Shares," *The Globe and Mail* (April 14, 1997).

66. Daimler-Benz press release, Aug. 26, 1997.

67. "Berlin Startet Pilotprojekt mit Brennstoffzellen," *Berliner Morgenpost* (July 25, 1998) [author's translation]: www.berliner-morgenpost.de/bin/bm/search/suche archiv.cgi

Chapter 15

68. Stuart F. Brown, "The Automakers' Big-Time Bet on Fuel Cells," *Fortune* (March 30, 1998): www.pathfinder.com/fortune/1998/980330/imt.html

69. "GM Launches New Global PEM Fuel Cell Project with German Opel Subsidiary," *Hydrogen & Fuel Cell Letter* XIII, no. 3 (March 1998): www.ttcorp.com/nha/th1/mar 98.htm

70. *Ibid.*

71. *Ibid.*

72. "Jeep Commander Provides Status Report on Emerging Fuel Cell Technology," DaimlerChrysler press release: www.daimlerchrysler.de

73. "Detroit Turns a Corner," *New York Times* (January 11, 1998): http://beneton.dkrz.de:3688/homepages/georg/kimo/038.htm

74. "The Future of the Automobile," *Nikkei Business Magazine* (October 12, 1998) [translated and reprinted by Ballard Power Systems].

75. "Status and Prospects of Fuel Cells as Automobile Engines, A Report of the Fuel Cell Technical Advisory Panel," [Report of the California Air Resources Board, henceforth "CARB Report", July 22, 1998, from CARB Internet site.] p. II-5: www.arb.ca.gov/msprog/zevprog/fuecell/fue-cell.htm

76. *Ibid.*

77. CARB Report, p. II-3.

78. CARB Report, p. III-7.

79. CARB Report, p. III-6.

80. CARB Report, p. III-8.

81. CARB Report, III.3 Section C, n.p.

82. CARB Report, p. III-10.

83. CARB Report, III.3, Section C, n.p.

84. CARB Report, III.3 Section C, n.p.

85. "The Future of the Automobile," *Nikkei Business Magazine* (October 12, 1998) [translated by Ballard Power Systems].

86. Rob Ferguson, "Concept Car Powers Ballard Shares," *The Toronto Star* (March. 18, 1999): E12.

87. Jeffrey Ball, "Auto Makers Are Racing To Market 'Green' Cars Powered by Fuel Cells," *The Wall Street Journal* (March 15, 1999): A1.

88. "DaimlerChrysler Presents First Driveable Fuel Cell Technology Car in the US," DaimlerChrysler press release, Mar. 17, 1999.

89. "New Fuel Cell Cars to Hit the Road in California," Reuters, Apr. 20, 1999.

90. William Boei, "Ballard, Oil Giants Team Up," *Vancouver Sun* (April 21, 1999): www.vancouversun.com

91. William Boei, "California Steers to Ballard Road-Tests," *Vancouver Sun* (April 21, 1997): C1.

92. "GM, Toyota Form 5-Year Tech Pact," Reuters, Detroit, (April 19, 1999).

93. William Boei, "Ballard, Oil Giants Team Up," *Vancouver Sun* (April 21, 1999) [from Internet site]

94. William Boei, "California Steers to Ballard Road-Tests," *Vancouver Sun* (April 21, 1999): D10

95. Jeffrey Ball, "Auto Makers Are Racing To Market 'Green' Cars Powered by Fuel Cells," *The Wall Street Journal* (March 15, 1999): A1.

96. Speech to energy conference at Asilomar Center, Pacific Grove, California, Aug. 17, 1997.

97. Jeffrey Ball, "Auto Makers Are Racing To Market 'Green' Cars Powered by Fuel Cells," *The Wall Street Journal* (March 15, 1999): A8.

98. William Boei, "Ballard Recruits Dow Executive from US," *Vancouver Sun* (August 13, 1998): F2.

99. Ballard Power press release, Nov. 4, 1998.

100. Ballard Power press release, Aug. 10, 1998.

Chapter 16

101. Miguel Llanos, "First Compact 'Fuel-Cell' Car Unveiled," MSNBC [Microsoft-National Broadcasting Company] network, Mar. 17, 1999.

Index